W9-BNO-574

34.99

HTML5

Step by Step

Faithe Wempen

006.74
WEM

Published with the authorization of Microsoft Corporation by:
O'Reilly Media, Inc.
1005 Gravenstein Highway North
Sebastopol, California 95472

Copyright © 2011 Faithe Wempen

Complying with all applicable copyright laws is the responsibility of the user. All rights reserved. Without limiting the rights under copyright, no part of this document may be reproduced, stored in or introduced into a retrieval system, or transmitted in any form or by any means (electronic, mechanical, photocopying, recording, or otherwise), or for any purpose, without express written permission of O'Reilly Media, Inc.

Printed and bound in Canada.

1 2 3 4 5 6 7 8 9   TG   6 5 4 3 2 1

Microsoft Press titles may be purchased for educational, business or sales promotional use. Online editions are also available for most titles (http://my.safaribooksonline.com). For more information, contact our corporate/institutional sales department: (800) 998-9938 or corporate@oreilly.com. Visit our website at microsoftpress.oreilly.com. Send comments to mspinput@ microsoft.com.

Microsoft, Microsoft Press, ActiveX, Excel, FrontPage, Internet Explorer, PowerPoint, SharePoint, Webdings, Windows, and Windows 7 are either registered trademarks or trademarks of Microsoft Corporation in the United States and/or other countries. Other product and company names mentioned herein may be the trademarks of their respective owners.

Unless otherwise noted, the example companies, organizations, products, domain names, e-mail addresses, logos, people, places, and events depicted herein are fictitious, and no association with any real company, organization, product, domain name, e-mail address, logo, person, place, or event is intended or should be inferred.

This book expresses the author's views and opinions. The information contained in this book is provided without any express, statutory, or implied warranties. Neither the author, O'Reilly Media, Inc., Microsoft Corporation, nor their respective resellers or distributors, will be held liable for any damages caused or alleged to be caused either directly or indirectly by such information.

Acquisitions and Development Editors: Russell Jones and Kim Spilker
Production Editor: Kristen Borg
Production Services: Octal Publishing, Inc.
Technical Reviewer: Joydip Kanjilal
Indexing: Lucie Haskins
Cover: Karen Montgomery
Compositor: Octal Publishing, Inc.
Illustrator: Robert Romano

978-0-735-64526-4

To Margaret

Contents

What do you think of this book? We want to hear from you!

Microsoft is interested in hearing your feedback so we can continually improve our books and learning resources for you. To participate in a brief online survey, please visit:

> microsoft.com/learning/booksurvey

Part 2   Style Sheets and Graphics

Part 3   Page Layout and Navigation

Part 5   **Appendixes**

A   Designing for Usability   347

B   Designing for Accessibility   353

C   Tags Added and Removed in HTML5   363

Acknowledgments

Thank you to the wonderful editorial staff at O'Reilly Media for guiding this book smoothly through the editorial and production process. This is my first book for O'Reilly, and I certainly hope that it won't be the last. It was a pleasure working with you all.

Introduction

Hypertext Markup Language (HTML) is the underlying markup language of the World Wide Web. It's the common thread that ties together virtually every Web site, from large-scale corporate sites such as Microsoft's to single-page classroom projects at the local grade school.

Don't let the phrase "markup language" intimidate you. A markup language annotates or "marks up" plain text, letting a browser know how to format that text so it looks good on a Web page. It's easy to get started—in fact, you can create a simple Web page in just a few minutes. While full-featured What You See Is What You Get (WYSIWYG) tools exist that can help speed up the process of writing Web pages, all you really need is an ordinary text-editing program such as Microsoft Notepad. You don't need special software or extensive training.

In this introduction, you'll learn some basics about HTML. You'll find out how they turn plain text into attractive formatting, how they incorporate graphics and hyperlinks, and how anyone can create Web content in virtually any program that edits text. This introduction explains what cascading style sheets (CSS) are, and how they make formatting consistent across large Web sites. You'll also discover the differences between HTML4, XHTML, and HTML5, so you can make the important decision about which version of HTML you want your code to conform to. Finally, you'll learn about the conventions used in this book for pointing out special helps like notes, tips, cautions, and references to the data files.

How to Access Your Online Edition Hosted by Safari

The voucher bound in to the back of this book gives you access to an online edition of the book. (You can also download the online edition of the book to your own computer; see the next section.)

To access your online edition, do the following:

1. Locate your voucher inside the back cover, and scratch off the metallic foil to reveal your access code.

2. Go to *http://microsoftpress.oreilly.com/safarienabled*.

3. Enter your 24-character access code in the Coupon Code field under Step 1:

Step ❶

Coupon Code: 95QX-TEZQ-MHK2-F8QZ-N1SR   ⊕

CONFIRM COUPON

(Please note that the access code in this image is for illustration purposes only.)

4. Click the CONFIRM COUPON button.

   A message will appear to let you know that the code was entered correctly. If the code was not entered correctly, you will be prompted to re-enter the code.

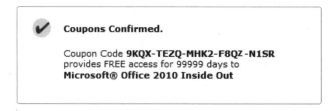

✔ **Coupons Confirmed.**

Coupon Code **9KQX-TEZQ-MHK2-F8QZ-N1SR** provides FREE access for 99999 days to **Microsoft® Office 2010 Inside Out**

5. In this step, you'll be asked whether you're a new or existing user of Safari Books Online. Proceed either with Step 5A or Step 5B.

   5A. If you already have a Safari account, click the EXISTING USER – SIGN IN button under Step 2.

Step ❷

EXISTING USER – SIGN IN

OR

NEW USER – FREE ACCOUNT

5B. If you are a new user, click the NEW USER – FREE ACCOUNT button under Step 2.

- You'll be taken to the "Register a New Account" page.

- This will require filling out a registration form and accepting an End User Agreement.

  - When complete, click the CONTINUE button.

6. On the Coupon Confirmation page, click the My Safari button.

7. On the My Safari page, look at the Bookshelf area and click the title of the book you want to access.

How to Download the Online Edition to Your Computer
=====

In addition to reading the online edition of this book, you can also download it to your computer. First, follow the steps in the preceding section. After Step 7, do the following:

1. On the page that appears after Step 7 in the previous section, click the Extras tab.

2. Find "Download the complete PDF of this book," and click the book title:

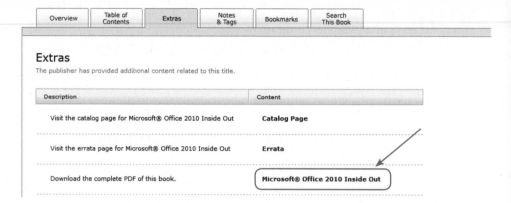

A new browser window or tab will open, followed by the File Download dialog box:

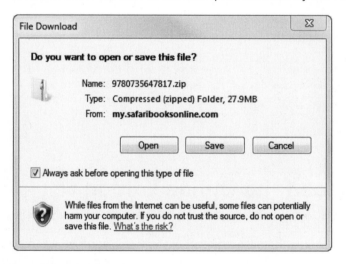

3. Click Save.

4. Choose Desktop and click Save.

5. Locate the .zip file on your desktop. Right-click the file, click Extract All, and then follow the instructions.

Note If you have a problem with your voucher or access code, please contact *mspbooksupport@oreilly.com*, or call 800-889-8969, where you'll reach O'Reilly Media, distributor of Microsoft Press books.

What Is HTML?

In simple terms, a *Web page* (or *HTML document*) is a plain text file that has been encoded using *Hypertext Markup Language (HTML)* so that it appears nicely formatted in a Web browser. Here's what HTML means, word-by-word:

- *Hypertext*   Text that you click to jump from document to document. This is a reference to the ability of Web pages to link to one another.

- *Markup*   Tags that apply layout and formatting conventions to plain text. Literally, the plain text is "marked up" with the tags.

- *Language*   A reference to the fact that HTML is considered a programming language.

Tip When people think of computer programming, they usually think of writing a compiled program. A compiled programming language runs the human-readable programming code through a utility that converts it to an executable file (usually with an .exe or .com extension), which is then distributed to users. In contrast, HTML is an interpreted programming language. That means the program is distributed in human-readable format to users, and the program in which it is opened takes care of running it. The HTML code for Web pages resides in files. Each time your Web browser opens a Web page, it processes the HTML code within the file.

Understanding HTML Tags

The code within an HTML file consists of text surrounded by *tags*. These tags indicate where the formatting should be applied, how the layout should appear, what pictures should be placed in certain locations, and more.

For example, suppose you wanted a certain word to be italicized, like this:

Everything is on sale.

In HTML, there's no Italics button to click, like there is in a word-processing program. Therefore, you have to "tag" the word that you want to be italicized. The code to turn on italics is *<i>*, and the code to turn italics off is *</i>*. Your HTML code would look something like this:

```
<i>Everything</i> is on sale.
```

That's an example of a *two-sided tag*, which encloses text between opening and closing tags, in this case *<i>* and *</i>*. Note the forward slash in the closing tag (*</i>*). That slash differentiates an opening tag from a closing tag. With a two-sided tag, there is always a corresponding closing tag for every opening tag.

To understand how this system of tagging came about, you need to know that back in the olden days of the Internet, nearly everyone connected to it by using a dial-up modem, at speeds ranging from 2400 bps to 28.8 Kbps. That's *really slow*. Text files transfer much faster than binary files, so for any type of information-sharing system to be popular, it had to be text-based. Otherwise, people would doze off while waiting for a page to load.

People designing Web pages also wanted their pages to be attractive. They couldn't just format pages in a word processor, though, because every word processor handled formatting differently, and it was impossible to know which one a visitor to a site might be using. Word processing files are also much larger than plain text files.

The Web's creators developed an elegant solution. Instead of sending the formatted pages over the Internet, they created an application—a Web browser—that could interpret plain-text code (HTML tags) as formatting instructions. The text could be sent quickly and efficiently in plain-text format, and then be processed and displayed attractively and graphically on the local PC.

HTML worked great all by itself for all kinds of text formatting, but some Web designers wanted to include graphics on their pages. To accommodate this, the *<img>* tag was created, which designers use to refer to a graphic stored on a server. When the Web browser gets to that tag, it requests that the image file be downloaded from the server and displayed on the page. (You'll learn how to insert images in Chapter 9, "Displaying Graphics.")

The *<img>* tag is different in several ways from the *<i>* tag. It is *one-sided*, meaning it does not have a closing tag, and it takes attributes. An *attribute* is text within the tag that contains information about how the tag should behave. For example, for an *<img>* tag, you have to specify a source, abbreviated *src*. Here's an example:

```
<img src="tree.gif">
```

This *<img>* tag uses the *src=* attribute, and specifies that the file *tree.gif* be displayed.

Many tags accept attributes, either optional or required. You'll see many examples throughout the exercises in this book.

With HTML, you can also create *hyperlinks* from one page to another. When a visitor to a Web site clicks a hyperlink, the Web browser loads the referenced page or jumps to a marked section (a "bookmark") within the same page. You will learn to create hyperlinks in Chapter 5, "Creating Hyperlinks and Anchors."

The tag for a hyperlink is *<a>*, a two-sided tag, but most people wouldn't recognize it without the attribute that specifies the file or location to which to jump. For example, to create a hyperlink with the words *Click Here* that jumps to the file *index.htm* when clicked, the coding would look like this:

```
<a href="index.htm">Click Here</a>
```

There's a lot more to HTML, of course, but that's basically how it works. Plain text is marked up with tags that indicate where elements such as formatting, hyperlinks, and graphics should be applied, and a Web browser interprets those tags and displays the page in its formatted state. The trick, of course, is to know which tags to use, and where they're appropriate, and what attributes they need. And that's the subject of this book.

Understanding Cascading Style Sheets

Web designers who worked with early versions of HTML to create large Web sites were often frustrated by the amount of repetition involved in their jobs. Suppose a Web site has 200 pages, all using the same basic layout and design. To make a design change to the entire site, a designer would have had to go in and manually edit each of those 200 pages.

Later versions of HTML have gotten around this by supporting *cascading style sheets*. Based on the same principle as style templates in a word-processing or page-layout program, Web designers use cascading style sheets to specify the formatting for a particular tag type—usually in a separate style sheet document—and then apply that style sheet to multiple pages. Need to make a change to the style? Simply make it in the style sheet, and the change is applied automatically to all pages.

Although you can still format documents by using older methods—and you'll learn how to do a little of that in this book—most Web designers rely almost exclusively on cascading style sheets for formatting these days, and XHTML all but demands that you do so. It might seem intimidating at first, but if you are creating a multi-page site, the extra trouble involved in setting up a cascading style sheet will pay for itself many times over.

Why Learn HTML in Notepad?

This book teaches beginner-level HTML coding, but it teaches it in a rather fundamentalist way: by creating plain text files in Notepad. There are so many good Web site creation programs on the market nowadays that you may be wondering why this book takes this approach.

Simply put, it's because doing your own coding is the best way to learn HTML. In this book you'll build a Web site from the ground up, writing every line of code yourself. It's slower and not as much fun as a fancy graphical program, but it's great training.

The last chapter of this book shows how to use Microsoft Expression Web to create Web content, and you may eventually choose to move to a program like that. However, you will be a much better Web designer—and understand what is going on in design programs much better—if you tough it out with Notepad in the beginning.

Choosing an HTML Version

Different versions of HTML use different tags for some types of content, although they more similar than different overall, especially at the beginner level covered in this book. Here's a quick comparison of the HTML versions you may encounter:

- *HTML4*   A very stable, universally accepted code set, which is also fairly forgiving of small coding errors. Using HTML4 codes is desirable when compatibility with all browsers is important.

- *XHTML*   A strict, standards-based implementation of HTML4 created with XML (eXtensible Markup Language). XHTML coding uses the same codes as HTML4, so it is compatible with the same browsers as HTML4. (See the sidebar about XML on the next page for more information.)

- *HTML5*   A revised code set that builds upon HTML4 to add new capabilities. HTML5 offers many dramatic improvements in the areas of application handling and multimedia, but a lot of those features are beyond the scope of this book. In terms of basic coding, which is what this book teaches, the biggest difference is that there are new specific codes for different types of content that were previously handled with more general codes. For example, HTML5 has *<audio>* and *<video>* tags for inserting multimedia content, whereas HTML4 inserts all types of multimedia content via a generic *<embed>* tag.

Since this is a book about HTML5, it might seem like an obvious decision to do your coding using HTML5 tags, but it is not quite as simple as that in real-world situations.

A good Web browser should ideally support every tag and every version of HTML it can, because the various HTML version differences should be completely invisible to the Web site visitor. However, HTML5 is so new that not all browsers have caught up to it yet, and people who use older computers may not have the latest version of a browser even if an HTML5 compatible version is available.

Tip Here's a site that lists what HTML5 features are supported by each version of each of the popular Web browsers: *http://caniuse.com*.

The code you will create as you work through the exercises in this book is based on HTML5, but I will also show you some workarounds in situations where HTML5 codes might cause problems in some browsers. You'll learn both ways of creating a certain effect, so that you can make the call of which codes to use in your real-life work as the situations arise.

What are XML and XHTML?

There is a language related to HTML called Extensible Markup Language (XML) that programmers use to create their own tags. It's widely used for Web databases, for example, because it can define tags for each data field. Because XML can be so completely customized, programmers can create almost any other markup language within it, just by re-creating all the officially accepted tags of that language. The W3C did just that: they re-created the entire HTML language in XML, and called it Extensible HTML (XHTML). Version 1.0 was released in 2001; the current version is XHTML 2.0, released in 2004.

XHTML, then, is HTML written within the larger language of XML. Because it is virtually identical to HTML in its functionality, the basic set of tags is the same, and you can learn both HTML and XHTML at the same time. You can also use XHTML to create new tags and extensions, which is a valuable feature for advanced Web developers.

There's just one thing about XHTML to watch out for: it's not tolerant of mistakes. For example, in HTML, technically you are supposed to begin each paragraph with *<p>* and end each paragraph with *</p>*. But in HTML you can leave out the closing *</p>* tag if you want (or if you forget it). That won't work in XHTML. There are lots of little ways that XHTML is picky like that.

At one point, it was thought that XHTML would eventually replace HTML4 as its successor, but due to interoperability problems, that has not happened; instead HTML5 is poised to succeed HTML4. This book doesn't explicitly cover XHTML, but most of what you will learn can be applied to XHTML coding.

Why Code in HTML5?

The short answer is: you should code in HTML5 because it's an investment in the future. Within a few years, it will be the standard on which nearly all Web sites are based.

A slightly longer answer is because it enables cleaner, easier-to-write code. Web page technology has grown by leaps and bounds, mostly due to the increase of the average person's Internet connection speed, but also because users, designers, and programmers increasingly demand more functionality from their Web pages, such as more precise control of fonts and layout, better rendering on devices that vary wildly in size from mobile phones to huge desktop monitors, better images, more interactivity, video, audio, animations, and better support for various image and file formats. Because most people have fast connections, they don't have to wait a long time for pages to load that contain large audio and video files, which means more and more sites are including audio and video content.

HTML was not originally designed for the rigors of multimedia content delivery, so more and more high-end professional sites have moved to other languages and technologies that piggyback on HTML to deliver that content, such as JavaScript, Java, and Active Server Pages (ASP).

HTML5 adds some important new tags to make audio, video, and application integration smoother and more reliable. You'll learn about many of these new tags in Chapters 15 and 16, including *<audio>*, *<video>*, and *<canvas>*.

HTML5 removes support for some of the older tags. For example, an old way (pre-HTML4) of specifying a font was the *<font>* tag. Today, most people use cascading style sheets to define fonts, so the *<font>* tag has not been used by many Web designers in a long time anyway. HTML5 formally removes it from the language.

One of the biggest things that HTML5 removes is the ability to create multi-framed Web sites with the *<frame>* and *<frameset>* commands. You can still create Web sites with multiple sections, but they're handled much more capably using tables or divisions. Chapter 11 covers divisions—the newer way, preferred by most professional Web designers. Chapters 12 and 13 cover tables, still an acceptable way, and preferred by many casual Web page designers who are familiar with tables from programs like Word.

Minimum System Requirements

There are no minimum system requirements for developing HTML; you can do it in any text editing program with any type of computer and any operating system. That's the beauty of HTML! This book uses Notepad as the text editor, but you can use any editor that you like.

For testing your work, you will need an HTML5-compliant Web browser application. The latest versions of Google Chrome and Firefox (both freely available online) will work fine for this, as will Internet Explorer 9 or higher.

Using the Practice Files

Each exercise in the lessons is preceded by a paragraph or paragraphs that list the files needed for that exercise and explain any file preparation you need to take care of before you start working through the exercise. The practice files are available for download from *http://oreilly.com/catalog/0790145302083/*. When you unzip them from the download file, separate folders will be created for each chapter, and separate folders within each of those for each exercise.

The following table lists the practice file folders for each chapter and the subfolders you'll find within them. The practice file folder for each chapter also includes a Solutions subfolder containing finished versions of the practice files used in that chapter.

Chapter	Folder	Subfolder
Chapter 1: HTML and XHTML Basics	01Editing	no subfolders
Chapter 2: Setting Up the Document Structure	02Structure	CreatingParagraphs PublishingFiles SpecifyingKeywords SpecifyingTitle
Chapter 3: Formatting Text by Using Tags	03Format	ApplyingBold ApplyingSuperscript ConfiguringSettings CreatingHeadings FormattingQuotes UsingMonospace
Chapter 4: Using Lists and Backgrounds	04Lists	ChoosingColors CreatingGlossary InsertingCharacters InsertingLines NestingLists SpecifyingImages
Chapter 5: Creating Hyperlinks and Anchors	05Links	CreatingAnchors CreatingHyperlinks LinkingEmail LinkingOther

Chapter	Folder	Subfolder
Chapter 6: Introduction to Style Sheets	06Styles	ConstructingRules CreatingClasses CreatingExternal CreatingNested StylingHyperlinks
Chapter 7: Formatting Text by Using Style Sheets	07Text	AdjustingSpacing ApplyingBold ApplyingStrike CreatingSpan SelectingFont SelectingSize
Chapter 8: Formatting Paragraphs Using Style Sheets	08Paragraphs	AddingBorders AdjustingHeight Indenting SettingAlignment
Chapter 9: Displaying Graphics	09Graphics	CaptioningFigures ClearingImages CreatingHyperlinks InsertingImages SizingImages UsingAlt UsingThumbnails
Chapter 10: Creating Navigational Aids	10Navigation	CreatingGraphicBar CreatingImageMap CreatingTextBar Redirecting
Chapter 11: Creating Division-Based Layouts	11Divisions	CreatingDivisions FormattingDivisions PositioningDivisions UsingSemantic
Chapter 12: Creating Tables	12Tables	CreatingTable SettingWidth SpanningCells SpecifyingSize UsingTables

Chapter	Folder	Subfolder
Chapter 13: Formatting Tables	13FmtTables	ApplyingBackground ApplyingBorders ChangingPadding
Chapter 14: Creating User Forms	14Forms	CreatingButtons CreatingForms CreatingLists
Chapter 15: Incorporating Sound and Video	15AudioVideo	
Chapter 16: Including JavaScript and External Content	16Canvas	
Chapter 17: HTML and Microsoft Expression Web	17Expression	ViewingPage

Getting Help

Every effort has been made to ensure the accuracy of this book. If you do run into problems, please contact the sources listed in the following topics.

Getting Help with This Book

If your question or issue concerns the content of this book or its practice files, please first consult the book's errata page, which can be accessed at:

http://oreilly.com/catalog/0790145302083/

This page provides information about known errors and corrections to the book. If you do not find your answer on the errata page, send your question or comment to O'Reilly Media Customer Service at:

mspbooksupport@oreilly.com

Conventions and Features in This Book

You can save time when you use this book by understanding how the *Step by Step* series shows special instructions, keys to press, buttons to click, and so on.

Convention	Meaning
➡ SET UP	These words are found at the beginning of paragraphs preceding step-by-step exercises. They point out items you should check or actions you should carry out before beginning an exercise.
Use Open	These words are found within the SET UP paragraphs that pre-cede step-by-step exercises. They draw your attention to practice files that you'll need to use in the exercise.
✖ CLEAN UP	These words are found at the beginning of paragraphs following step-by-step exercises. They give instructions for closing open files or programs before moving on to another topic.
1.	Numbered steps guide you through hands-on exercises in each topic.
●	A round bullet indicates an exercise that has only one step.
Troubleshooting	These paragraphs show you how to fix a common problem that might prevent you from continuing with the exercise.
Tip	These paragraphs provide a helpful hint or shortcut that makes working through a task easier.
Important	These paragraphs point out information that you need to know to complete a procedure.
Note	These paragraphs provide supplementary or related information.
Compatibility	These paragraphs explain alternate coding you can use for greater backward compatibility
Ctrl+C	A plus sign (+) between two key names means that you must hold down the first key while you press the second key. For exam-ple, "press **Ctrl+C**" means "hold down the **Ctrl** key while you press the **c** key."
user interface elements	In exercises, the names of program elements such as buttons, commands, and dialog boxes.
user input	Anything you are supposed to type.
glossary terms	Terms explained in the glossary at the end of the book.

What Next?

To get started, turn the page to Chapter 1 and start reading and working through the exercises. The lessons are designed to be tackled in the order they appear in the book, but feel free to skip around if you just need to fill in some holes in your HTML knowledge.

Part 1

Getting Started with HTML

Chapter at a Glance

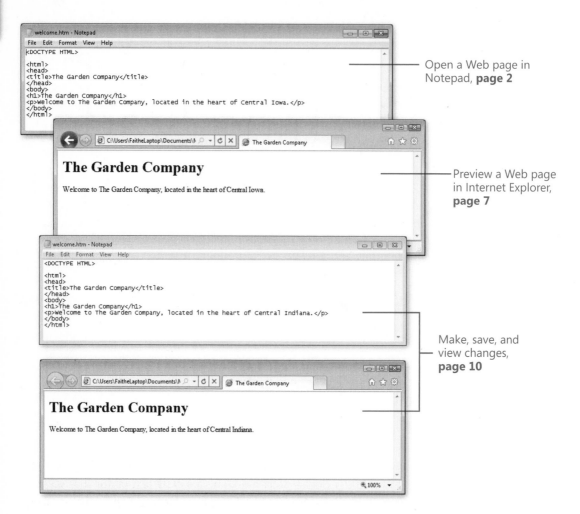

Open a Web page in Notepad, **page 2**

Preview a Web page in Internet Explorer, **page 7**

Make, save, and view changes, **page 10**

1 Editing and Viewing HTML Files

In this chapter, you will learn how to

- ✔ Open a Web page in Notepad.
- ✔ Preview a Web page in Internet Explorer.
- ✔ Make, save, and view changes.

As you work through this book's exercises, you'll learn HTML by creating and editing text files in Notepad, and then viewing them in a Web browser to check your work. This chapter teaches the important basic skills you need to work in these programs.

See Also Do you need only a quick refresher on the topics in this chapter? See the Key Points section at the end of this chapter.

> **Practice Files** Before you can use the practice files provided for this chapter, you need to download and install them from the book's companion content location. See "Using the Practice Files" at the beginning of this book for more information.

Opening a Web Page in Notepad

Notepad is included with all versions of Windows, and you'll find it in the All Programs (or Programs)/Accessories folder on the Start menu. It's a simple text editor that saves only in plain text format. That's ideal for HTML editing because you don't need to worry about any extra word processing formatting being included in the file.

Note You are welcome to use a different text editor application to complete the exercises in this book. Notepad is just a suggestion.

When saving or opening files in Notepad, the default file extension is .txt. The Save and Open dialog boxes are set by default to filter file listings so only those files with .txt extensions appear. That means each time you browse for a file, you need to change the file type to All Files so you can browse for Web pages (which have .htm or .html extensions).

Note You may run into various extensions on Web page files on the Internet, such as .php, .asp, and .jsp. Those are all special formats designed for use with specific server technologies. This book only covers developing the basic type of Web page: the type with an .htm or .html extension.

In this exercise, you will open a Web page in Notepad and examine its text and tags.

 SET UP Use the *welcome* file in the practice file folder for this topic. This practice file is located in the Documents\Microsoft Press\HTML5 SBS\01Editing folder.

1. From the **Start** menu, select **All Programs | Accessories | Notepad**.

2. In the untitled Notepad window, select **File | Open**.

3. Navigate to the folder containing the practice files for this chapter.

   On the Places bar, click Documents (or My Documents if you are using Windows XP). In the Open dialog box, double-click Microsoft Press, HTML5 SBS, and then 01Editing.

   Note You won't see any files in the list at this point. The only thing that you should see is just a _Solutions folder. (That folder contains the solution files for the lesson, but you don't need those now.)

4. Click the **Files Of Type** down arrow, and then click **All Files**.

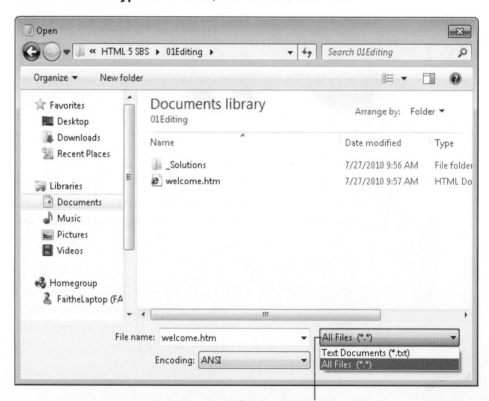

Click here to open Files of Type list

5. In the **Open** dialog box, click *welcome.htm*, and then click **Open**.

The welcome.htm file opens in Notepad.

Note The .htm extension might not appear on the welcome file in the Open dialog box. By default, file extensions for known file types are turned off in Windows. To turn them on, open Computer (or My Computer), and on the Tools menu (press the Alt key for the menu bar if you don't see it), click Folder Options. On the View tab of the Folder Options dialog box, clear the Hide Extensions For Known File Types check box, and then click OK.

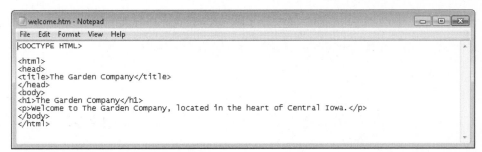

6. Locate the *<html>* and *</html>* tags.

These tags signify the beginning and end of the HTML code.

7. Locate the *<body>* and *</body>* tags.

These tags signify the beginning and end of the visible portion of the Web page when viewed in a browser.

8. Locate the *<p>* and *</p>* tags.

These tags signify the beginning and end of a paragraph.

 CLEAN UP Leave the page open in Notepad for later use.

Adding the Data File Location to the Favorites List

In the course of working through this book, you will open many files in Notepad. To save yourself the trouble of navigating to the data file folder each time (HTML5 SBS), you might want to add that folder to your Favorites bar in the Open dialog box for easy access to the data files.

In this exercise, you will add to the Favorites bar a shortcut that brings you directly to the HTML5 SBS folder.

SET UP Open Notepad.

1. Select **File | Open**.

2. Navigate to the folder containing the practice files for this chapter.

   On the Places bar, click Documents (or My Documents if you are using Windows XP). In the Open dialog box, double-click Microsoft Press. The HTML5 SBS folder appears as an icon.

3. Drag the **HTML5 SBS** icon to the Favorites list on the left side of the window.

   A shortcut for it appears on the Favorites list.

Drag the folder here to create a shortcut

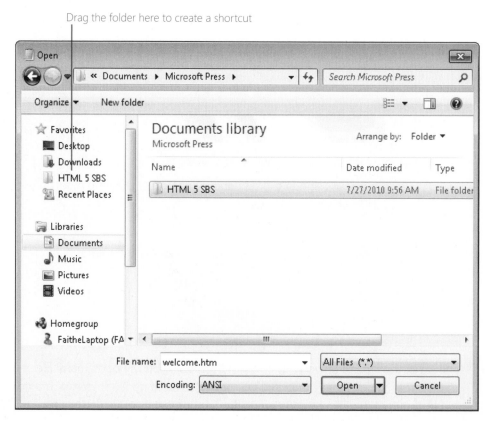

CLEAN UP Close the Windows Explorer window

Now, the next time you want to open a file in the Open dialog box, you can double-click that shortcut, and then double-click the folder for the chapter you are working on, which is much more convenient!

Opening a File from Windows Explorer

A quick way to open most file types in their default applications is to double-click them from any Windows Explorer window. However, the problem with doing that for HTML files is that the default application is your Web browser, not Notepad; thus, instead of the file opening in Notepad, it opens in your Web browser. One way to get around this is to right-click a file in Windows Explorer, choose Open With from the contextual menu, and then click Notepad. This opens Notepad and loads the file.

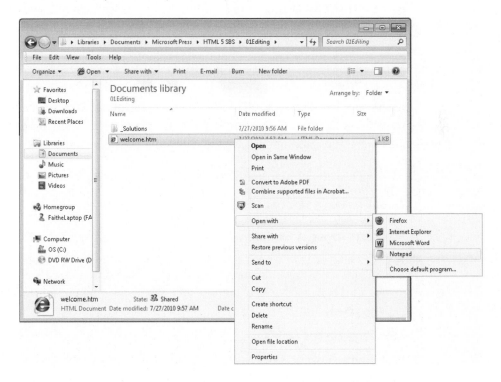

Previewing a Web Page in a Web Browser

Because Notepad is not a WYSIWYG ("What You See Is What You Get") program, you won't be able to immediately see how the tags you type will affect the finished product. To work around this, most Web page designers keep a browser window open next to Notepad.

You can preview your work in any browser; you do not need to use Internet Explorer 9 (although that's what I use in this book's examples). In fact, as you progress with your Web development skills, you will probably want to acquire several different browsers to test your pages because each browser might display page elements a little differently.

For beginners, though, Internet Explorer is a good choice because it's the most popular browser—the one your target audience is most likely to be using. Other popular browsers include Google Chrome, Firefox, Safari, and Opera.

Caution Versions of Internet Explorer prior to version 9 do not support some of the HTML5 features. You will probably want to test your Web pages in an earlier version to make sure that people who use them will be able to view your page. But don't use an earlier version of Internet Explorer as you work through this book's examples; you won't get the full effect of the new HTML5 features.

Tip If the video card in your computer has two monitor connectors on it, or if you have an additional video card that you could install in your system, you might want to set up two monitors side-by-side. That way you could work on your HTML code in Notepad on one monitor and display the page full-screen in Internet Explorer in the other. All recent versions of Windows support at least two monitors, and some versions support even more.

In this exercise, you will display an HTML file in Internet Explorer. To see the displayed file and the underlying code at the same time, open the practice files from this exercise and the previous exercise in separate windows and arrange them so both are visible.

SET UP Use the *welcome* file from the previous exercise, or use the one in the practice file folder for this topic. The practice file is located in the Documents\ Microsoft Press\HTML5 SBS\01Editing folder.

1. Select **Start | Internet Explorer**.

   Note Depending on your system and your default browser, Internet Explorer might not be pinned to the top of your Start menu. If it is not, click Start | All Programs | Internet Explorer.

2. Select **File | Open**.

   The Open dialog box appears.

   Note If the menu bar does not appear in Internet Explorer, press the **Alt** key to display it.

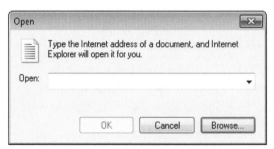

3. Click the **Browse** button, and then browse to Documents\Microsoft Press\HTML5 SBS\01Editing.

   Tip If you created the shortcut in the Favorites bar earlier in the chapter, you can use it to save a few clicks when browsing for the location.

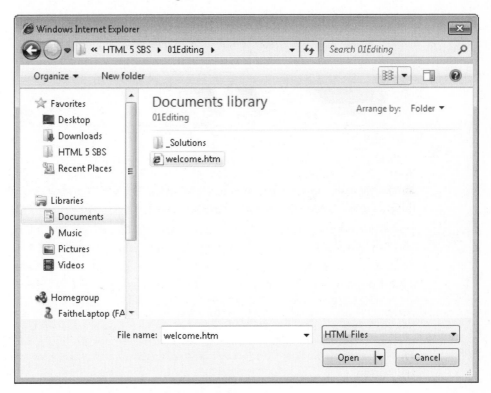

4. Click **welcome.htm**, and then click **Open**.

   The path to the file appears in the Open dialog box.

5. Click **OK**.

The file opens in Internet Explorer.

 CLEAN UP Leave Internet Explorer open for the next exercise.

The method you just learned works especially well when you already have your Web browser open, in which case you can skip step 1. An alternate method is to browse to the storage location by using Windows Explorer, and double-click the file. Remember that you can't just double-click a Web page to edit it; you must right-click it. By default, the double-click operation is reserved for opening the page in your Web browser. What was a hardship only a few pages ago is now a convenience!

Tip Not all Web browser software displays pages exactly the same way. For example, one browser's idea of what text should look like might be different from another. It's a good idea to check your pages in multiple Web browsers, such as Firefox, Netscape, and Opera. These are available as free downloads from *www.firefox.com*, *www.netscape.com*, and *www.opera.com*, respectively.

Making, Saving, and Viewing Changes

After you've made a change to a Web page, you will probably want to preview the result of that change. If you set up your Internet Explorer and Notepad windows side by side in the preceding two exercises, it's easy to view those changes. Simply save your work in Notepad, and then refresh the display in Internet Explorer.

In this exercise, you will change "Iowa" to "Indiana" in the welcome.htm file, and then preview that change in Internet Explorer. This exercise builds on the previous two, so make sure you have completed them. You can use this procedure throughout the rest of the book to preview your work from each exercise.

 SET UP Be sure to have the *welcome* file open in Notepad and in Internet Explorer before beginning this exercise. Use the *welcome* file from the previous exercise, or use the one in the practice file folder for this topic. The practice file is located in the Documents\Microsoft Press\HTML5 SBS\01Editing folder.

1. In Notepad, locate the word *Iowa*, and change it to **Indiana**, as shown in bold text in the following code:

   <p>Welcome to the Garden Company, located in the heart of Central **Indiana.** *</p>*

2. Save your work (**File | Save**).

3. On the Internet Explorer toolbar, click the **Refresh** button.

   Notice that the Web page shown in Internet Explorer now reads "Indiana," too.

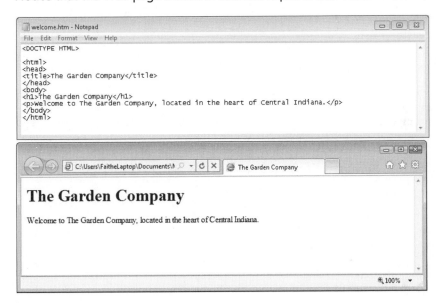

✖ **CLEAN UP** Close the *welcome* file, and then exit Notepad and Internet Explorer.

Key Points

- Any plain text editor, including Notepad, can be an HTML editor.

- Most Web pages have an .htm or .html extension. You can open them in Notepad, but first you need to change the Files Of Type setting in the Open dialog box to All Files. You must change this setting each time you use the Open dialog box.

- An alternative way to open a Web page in Notepad is to right-click it in Windows Explorer, select Open With from the contextual menu, and then click Notepad.

- To preview a page in a Web browser, select File | Open from the browser's menu.

- You can double-click an .htm or .html file in Windows Explorer to open it automatically in your default Web browser.

- To see changes you make in Notepad reflected in your Web browser, save your work in Notepad, and then click Refresh in the browser window.

Chapter at a Glance

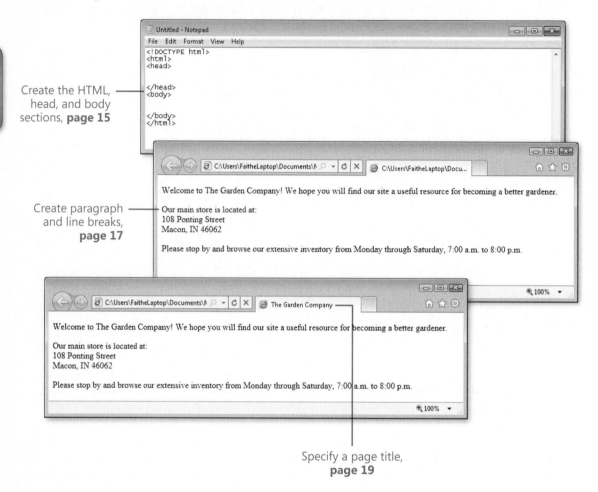

Create the HTML, head, and body sections, **page 15**

Create paragraph and line breaks, **page 17**

Specify a page title, **page 19**

2 Setting Up the Document Structure

In this chapter, you will learn how to

✔ Specify the document type.

✔ Create the HTML, Head, and Body sections.

✔ Create paragraphs and line breaks.

✔ Specify a page title and keywords.

✔ Publish a file to a server.

Every society needs an infrastructure with certain rules that everyone agrees to for the general public good. For example, we have all agreed that a red light means "stop" and a green light means "go." Everyone who wants to participate in the transportation system must play by those rules, or chaos ensues.

HTML is the same way. You can get creative with your Web content, but there must be an underlying structure in place for Web browsers to read and render your Web pages properly. That means the document must contain certain tags that delineate its major sections and indicate to the browser what type of coding the document uses.

In this chapter, you'll learn how to structure a document with the correct underlying tags. You'll learn how to specify the type of HTML you are writing and how to create Head and Body sections. You'll also learn how to create paragraph and line breaks, specify a page title, enter hidden keywords by which your page can be found in search engines, and publish a test page to a Web server.

See Also Do you need only a quick refresher on the topics in this chapter? See the Key Points section at the end of this chapter.

> **Practice Files** Before you can use the practice files provided for this chapter, you need to download and install them from the book's companion content location. See "Using the Practice Files" at the beginning of this book for more information.

Specifying the Document Type

When creating an HTML5 document, the first line of the document should be this tag:

```
<!DOCTYPE html>
```

The *DOCTYPE* tag always begins with an exclamation point and is always placed at the beginning of the document, before any other tag. Most HTML tags are not case-sensitive, but the word *DOCTYPE* should always be uppercase.

Using the *DOCTYPE* tag is like signing a contract. It is an optional tag, but when you use it, you are promising that your coding will conform to certain standards. When a Web browser encounters a *DOCTYPE* tag, it processes the page in *standards mode*. When it doesn't encounter the *DOCTYPE* tag, it assumes that there is something quirky about the page, and processes the page in *quirks mode*. When the browser sees the tag *<!DOC-TYPE html>*, it assumes you are using HTML5.

The distinction between standards mode and quirks mode came about in earlier days, when there were problems with standardization between Web browsers. In some browsers, to display pages properly, you needed to get a little creative with the HTML code. Modern HTML coding does not allow that, but some older pages still include these obsolete workarounds. By using the *DOCTYPE* tag, you are making a promise to the Web browser that there is nothing but pure HTML code in the page.

Earlier versions of HTML used more complex *DOCTYPE* tags. If you're using HTML Version 4.01, the syntax for the tag is:

```
<!DOCTYPE HTML PUBLIC "-//W3C/DTD HTML 4.01 Transitional//EN"
    "http://www.w3.org/TR/html4/loose.dtd">
```

If you're using XHTML, the syntax for the tag is:

```
<!DOCTYPE HTML PUBLIC "-//W3C/DTD XHTML 1.0 Transitional//EN"
    "http://www.w3.org/TR/xhtml1/DTD/xhtml1-transitional.dtd">
```

Note If you are writing XHTML code, the *DOCTYPE* tag is required.

Creating the HTML, Head, and Body Sections

All of your HTML coding—except the *DOCTYPE* tag—should be placed within the two-sided *<html>* tag. Recall from the Introduction that when a tag is two-sided, it requires a corresponding closing tag that is identical to the opening tag but contains a slash: *</html>*. The tags *<html>* and *</html>* serve as a "wrapper" around all the other tags in the document.

In addition, your document should have two sections: a Head and a Body. The *Head* section is defined by the two-sided tag *<head>*. The Head section contains the *page title*, which is the text that will appear in the title bar of the Web browser and on the Microsoft Windows taskbar button. It also includes information about the document that is not displayed, such as its *<meta>* tags (which you'll learn about on page 19). You can also include lines of code that run scripts, like Javascript.

The *Body* section is defined by the two-sided tag *<body>*, and it contains all the information that appears in the Web browser when you view the page.

Note The *<html>*, *<head>*, and *<body>* tags are all optional in HTML—but you should still use them because it's a good design practice. They are required in XHTML. In addition, in XHTML you must add an argument to the *<html>* tag that declares its XML namespace, a reference to the fact that XHTML is created within XML (as you learned in Chapter 1, "Editing and Viewing HTML Files"). Here's how the opening *<html>* tag should look in an XHTML document: *<html xlmns="http://www.w3.org/1999/xhtml">*.

In this exercise, you will create an HTML5 template file that you can reuse later for your own work.

 SET UP Start Microsoft Notepad before beginning this exercise.

1. In Notepad, open the **Format** menu. **Word Wrap** should have a check mark next to it. If it does not, click it to enable the Word Wrap feature.

   Tip Using Word Wrap makes it easier to see long lines of HTML coding without scrolling.

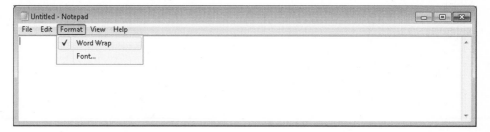

2. In the Notepad window, type the following:

```
<!DOCTYPE html>
```

3. Press **Enter**, and then type:

```
<html>
<head>
```

4. Press **Enter** two or three times to add some blank lines, and then type:

```
</head>
<body>
```

5. Press **Enter** two or three times to add some blank lines, and then type:

```
</body>
</html>
```

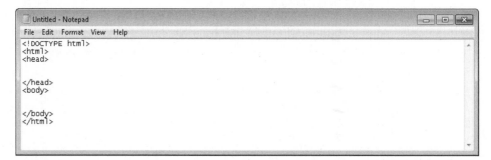

6. Save the file as **HTML5.htm** on your Windows desktop (or to any other location that is convenient for you).

Note Most of the files you work with in this book will be stored elsewhere, but you might find it helpful to keep the templates created in this exercise handy for reuse. The desktop is a convenient place to store them, or you can store them anywhere you like.

 CLEAN UP Close the Notepad window.

You now have a template for creating any HTML documents you like. You can reopen this template file and save it under different names, which will save time re-creating these basic tags.

Tip If you want to avoid accidentally editing the template in the future, make it read-only. To do so, in Windows Explorer, right-click the file, and then select Properties from the contextual menu. In the Properties dialog box, select the Read-Only check box. When you try to save changes to a read-only file, an error message appears and a Save As dialog box prompts you to save a copy of it with a new name.

Creating Paragraphs and Line Breaks

Within the *<body>* section of the document, you type the text that will appear on the Web page. Each paragraph of text should be enclosed in a two-sided tag that indicates its type.

The most basic paragraph type is the body paragraph, indicated by the *<p>* tag. It is a two-sided tag, so the paragraph text is placed between a *<p>* and a *</p>*.

Note In HTML, the code will still work even if the *</p>* is omitted; in XHTML, it won't. However, even if you never plan on coding in XHTML, it is a good practice to include the *</p>* tag. This way, you won't fall into any sloppy habits.

When a browser displays a Web page, it inserts vertical white space between paragraphs:

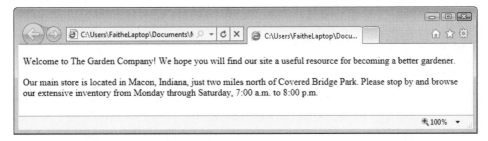

That spacing is usually convenient, but it can be a problem when the extra space between lines is unwanted, such as with an address.

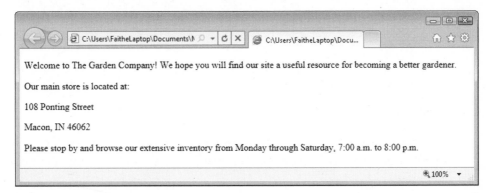

To create a line break without officially starting a new paragraph (and thereby adding that extra white space), use the *
* tag. This is a one-sided tag placed within a paragraph, at the end of each line, like this:

```
<p>David Jaffe<br>
317-555-8882</p>
```

Note In XHTML, the line break tag is *
*. The end slash (and the space) is necessary to indicate that it's a self-closing tag. Notice that the slash is placed *after* the letters, not before, as with the closing end of a two-sided tag. In XHTML, one-sided tags must end with a slash to indicate that they are self-closing. The space between the text and the final slash is also required so the tag will be recognized in HTML.

In this exercise, you will add text to an HTML file template, and then preview it in Microsoft Internet Explorer.

SET UP Use the *HTML5.htm* file from the previous exercise or in the practice file folder for this topic. This practice file is located in the Documents\Microsoft Press\ HTML5 SBS\02Structure\CreatingParagraphs folder. Open the *HTML5* file in Notepad.

1. Save the *HTML5* file in the Documents\Microsoft Press\HTML5 SBS folder as **index.htm**.

   Note It is customary to name the opening page of a Web site index.htm, index.html, default.htm, or default.html. When users type a URL in their Web browsers but omit the file name (for example, typing *www.microsoft.com* rather than *www.microsoft.com/ filename.htm*), most servers will automatically respond with the index or default page if one exists.

2. Open the *index* file in Internet Explorer and arrange the Notepad and Internet Explorer windows so that both are visible.

   The index file displayed in Internet Explorer is currently blank.

3. In the Notepad window, type the following between the *<body>* and *</body>* tags:

   ```
   <p>Welcome to The Garden Company! We hope you will find our site a useful
   resource for becoming a better gardener.<p>
   <p>Our main store is located at:<br>
   108 Ponting Street<br>
   Macon, IN 46062</p>
   <p>Please stop by and browse our extensive inventory from Monday through
   Saturday, 7:00 a.m. to 8:00 p.m.</p>
   ```

4. Save your work, and then press **F5** or click the **Refresh** button at the right side of the Address bar to refresh the display in Internet Explorer to see the result of the changes. Leave both windows open for the next exercise.

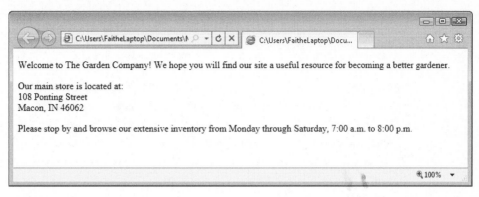

Note Your screen might look slightly different, depending on the settings you have configured in your browser.

 CLEAN UP Close the Notepad and Internet Explorer windows.

Specifying a Page Title and Metatags

Perhaps you noticed in the preceding exercise that the complete path to the file appeared in the title bar of Internet Explorer. Usually when you view a Web page, a friendly, descriptive title appears in that spot instead. That text is specified by a *<title>* tag that is placed in the *<head>* section (also called the *header*). Here's an example:

```
<head>
<title>The Garden Company</title>
</head>
```

Troubleshooting Make sure you place the *<title>* tag in the *<head>* section, and not in the *<body>* section.

Another element you can place in the header is the *<meta>* tag. The *<meta>* tag has several purposes. One of these is to identify keywords related to your page. Placing appropriate keywords on your page can make it easier for people to find your page when they are searching the Web using a search engine such as MSN. When some search engines index your page, they rely not only on the full text of the page, but also on any keywords they find in the *<meta>* tag area.

Note Not all search engines refer to *<meta>* tags. Google does not, for example; it indexes only the text contained in the *<body>* area. Because of the potential for abuse of the system, such as Web developers packing their pages with unrelated keywords, fewer and fewer search engines these days are using them.

For example, suppose The Garden Company's Web site would be useful to people who are searching for information about all types of gardening problems, such as pests, weeds, and fungus, and about growing flowers and vegetables. Perhaps all these topics are not mentioned on the main page, but you want people who search for those words to be directed to the main page anyway. You could place the following in the *<head>* section:

```
<meta name="keywords" content="pests, weeds, fungus, plants, flowers,
vegetables">
```

Notice that the *<meta>* tag in the above code is a single-sided tag that contains two attributes: *name* and *content*. The values for each of those arguments follow the equals sign and are contained in double quotation marks.

Note If you are coding in XHTML, you would add a space and a slash (/) at the end of a *<meta>* tag because it is a one-sided (self-closing) tag. This is not necessary in HTML.

The *<meta>* tag can also be used to redirect visitors to another page. For example, suppose you told everyone the address of your Web site, and then you needed to move it to another URL. You could place a "We've Moved" page at the original address and use the *<meta>* tag to redirect users to the new address after five seconds, like this:

```
<meta http-equiv="refresh" content="5; url=http://www.contoso.com/newpage.htm">
```

Here's yet another common use: the *<meta>* tag can specify a character encoding scheme. This is not a big issue if you are coding only in English (or in a language like English that uses a Roman character set), but it is considered a tidy coding practice to include anyway. If you want, you can add *<meta charset="utf-8">* to the *<head>* section of your document to explicitly spell out that your page is in English.

In this exercise, you will add a page title and some keywords to the index.htm page you created in the preceding exercise.

SET UP Use the *index.htm* file from the previous exercise or in the practice file folder for this topic. This practice file is located in the Documents\Microsoft Press\HTML5 SBS\02Structure\SpecifyingTitle folder. Open the *index* file in Notepad.

1. Between the *<head>* and *</head>* tags, type the following to create the page title:

   `<title>The Garden Company</title>`

2. After the title, type the following *<meta>* tag:

   `<meta name="keywords" content="pests, weeds, fungus, plants, flowers, vegetables">`

3. Press **Enter** to start a new line, and type the following *<meta>* tag:

   `<meta encoding="utf-8">`

4. Save your work, and then view the file in Internet Explorer.

   The tab displays the site name, but notice that the inclusion of the *<meta>* tags caused no apparent difference in the displayed text of the page. This is because the keywords and encoding specification do not appear on the Web page itself.

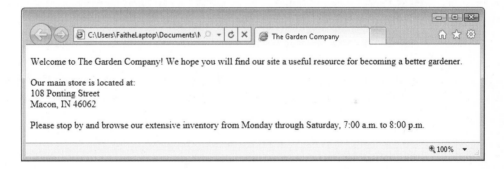

 CLEAN UP Close the Notepad and Internet Explorer windows.

Publishing a File to a Server

Throughout most of this book's exercises, you will save pages to your own hard drive. That way they don't get into the public's hands before they are completed. When a page is finalized, however, you will want to transfer it to a publicly accessible Web server (that is, to publish it) so that others can view it.

There are several ways to transfer files to a server. The company or individual in charge of the server should be able to advise you about your options. Here are some of the possibilities that might be available:

- **Uploading through an FTP connection by using Internet Explorer.**   You do this by entering the address of an FTP server (which will start with *ftp://*) in the Address bar of Internet Explorer. A dialog box prompts you for your user name and password for that server. If you enter those correctly, a Windows Explorer-like file-management window appears, just as though you were browsing any folder on your hard disk. You can then transfer the files by dragging them into that window, or copying them and pasting them into the FTP window.

- **Uploading through an FTP connection by using FTP software.**   There are many third-party FTP applications available that make it simple to transfer files. These utilities have some advantages over the Internet Explorer transfer method, such as the ability to restart uploads that are interrupted due to communication errors. Some examples include FileZilla (*www.filezilla-project.org*) and BulletProof FTP (*www.bpftp.com*).

- **Saving directly to a Web folder.**   Most Web development tools, such as Microsoft Expression Web, let you to save directly to a Web server by typing the URL of the site into the Save As dialog box. That's very convenient! Unfortunately, you can't do that in Notepad,.

This book doesn't include an exercise for practicing transferring files to a server because the process details differ depending on many factors, including the site you are saving to, the availability of FTP software, and the version of Windows you are using. If you have questions about how to upload your files, ask the network administrator or tech support staff for advice.

Key Points

- To specify HTML5 as the document type, add *<!DOCTYPE html>* at the beginning of the file.

- All the HTML coding in a document (except the *DOCTYPE*) is enclosed within a two-sided *<html>* tag.

- The *<html>* and *</html>* tags enclose the *<head>* and *<body>* sections.

- The *<head>* area contains the page title (*<title>*) and any *<meta>* tags. The *<body>* area contains all the displayable text for the page.

- Enclose each paragraph in a two-sided *<p>* tag. Most browsers add space between paragraphs when displaying the page.

- To create a line break without starting a new paragraph, use the one-sided *
* tag.

- When coding for XHTML, end one-sided tags with a space and a slash (/). The space is required for recognition in HTML, and the slash is necessary for recognition in XHTML.

- Use *<meta>* tags in the *<head>* section to indicate keywords and the document encoding language.

- Use the *<title>* and *</title>* tags to enclose the text that should appear in the browser's title bar. Place these in the *<head>* section of the file.

- To publish pages directly to a server, you can use an FTP utility or the FTP capability built into Windows, or (with some tools) you can save files directly to a server. However, Notepad does not offer this capability.

Chapter at a Glance

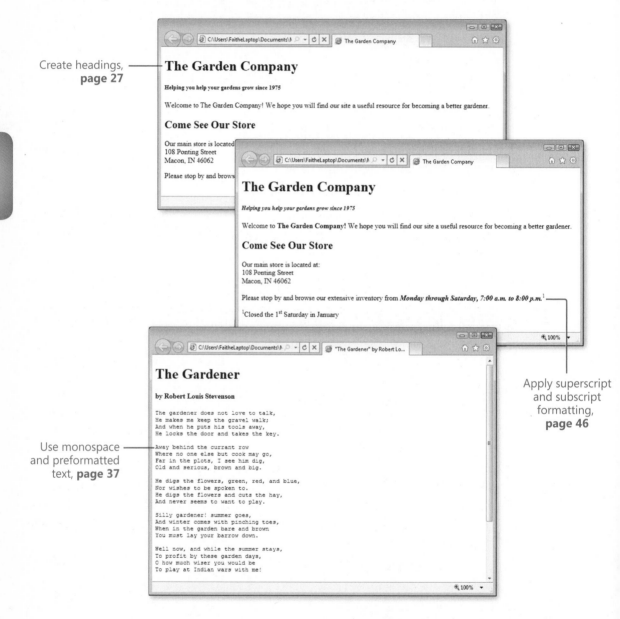

Create headings,
page 27

Use monospace
and preformatted
text, **page 37**

Apply superscript
and subscript
formatting,
page 46

3 Formatting Text by Using Tags

In this chapter, you will learn how to

- ✔ Create headings.
- ✔ Apply bold and italic formatting.
- ✔ Apply superscript and subscript formatting.
- ✔ Use monospaced and preformatted text.
- ✔ Format a block quotation.
- ✔ Configure Internet Explorer view settings.

Creating Web pages is not word processing. It's important to keep that in mind as you learn HTML, because I'm going to ask you to be patient for a few chapters as you learn HTML the *right* way—that is, the standards-compliant way.

When most people think of formatting text, the first thing that pops into their minds is choosing a font—a typeface, size, and color. That's easy to do in a word-processing document, but in HTML it's more complicated. Early versions of HTML used a *<font>* tag to specify a particular typeface, size, and color. If it were ten years ago, I would be happy to teach you that tag in this chapter, but the *<font>* tag has been removed from HTML5. Even though most browsers still recognize the *<font>* tag, you shouldn't use it: it's obsolete. Therefore, rather than teach you bad habits with old tags, I'm going to teach you how to apply typefaces, sizes, and colors to text with *styles*—but not in this chapter. Although using styles is a superior way of applying fonts to text, it is a little more advanced than you're ready for just yet. You'll learn all about using fonts in HTML code in Part 2, "Style Sheets and Graphics."

This chapter introduces several important tags that format text according to its purpose. In Chapter 2, "Setting Up the Document Structure," you learned about the *<p>* tag for regular paragraphs, but there are many other tags that are used for headings, programming code, quotations, and more. Most of the tags discussed in this chapter are *semantic tags*; they describe the *function* of the text, rather than provide directions for formatting. For example, the *<h1>* heading tag specifies that the text within it should be formatted as a major heading, but it provides no specifics as to what that formatting should be.

The formatting specifics for semantic tags can come from a variety of sources:

- **Styles**   As you will learn in Part 2 of this book, you can specify the font families and sizes to use throughout your entire Web site. For example, you can select a font family that will be suggested to the browser whenever a certain tag is applied.

- **The Web browser in use**   Each Web browser has defaults for the standard HTML tags. For example, in Internet Explorer (and most other browsers), <h1> is left-aligned, 18-point Times New Roman. Most browsers use the same defaults for the very basic tags, but non-standard browsers, such as those on phones, often display text differently.

- **Individual user customization**   A user can customize his Web browser to suit his preferences. Later in this chapter, you'll get to play with these settings in Internet Explorer so you'll know what your potential audience might be doing.

Keep in mind as you practice using tags that their formatting is not fixed. The results you see when previewing the exercise pages in Internet Explorer represent the default settings for your version of Internet Explorer (or whatever browser you are using to preview them); the style is not intrinsic to those tags themselves. That will become important in Part 2 of the book, when you learn how to define more specific formatting for tags.

See Also **Do you need only a quick refresher on the topics in this chapter?** See the Key Points section at the end of this chapter.

> **Practice Files**   Before you can use the practice files provided for this chapter, you need to download and install them from the book's companion content location. See "Using the Practice Files" at the beginning of this book for more information.

Creating Headings

Headings in Web pages function the same way as they do in printed documents—they separate text into sections. The HTML standard defines six levels of headings, *<h1>* through *<h6>*, each one progressively smaller in font size.

As noted earlier, there are no *specific* sizes or fonts assigned to the heading tags—their appearance can vary depending on the browser and its settings. But the heading levels connote *relative* sizes; the higher the heading number, the smaller the size in which it will render on the screen. In Internet Explorer 9, for example, using the default settings will make these six heading levels look as shown in the following graphic.

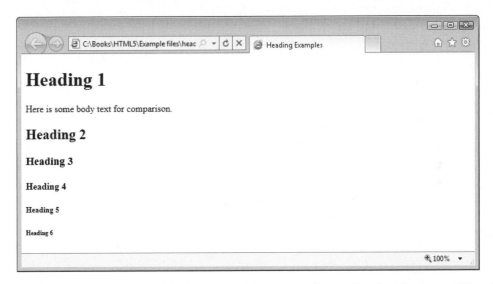

Perhaps you noticed that headings 5 and 6 are actually smaller than body text. Keep in mind, though, that these are just the default settings; you can redefine these headings to appear any way you want.

Many screen reader programs use the heading codes *<h1>* through *<h6>* to help visually-impaired users navigate a document, and some page structures rely on headings for outlining, too. (HTML5 has a new way of outlining documents, but that's beyond the scope of this book.) In some cases, though, you might have a stack of headings that collectively should take up only one spot in an outline, like this:

```
<h1>Dog Agility Club of Indiana</h1>

<h2>Training for canine athletes and their humans</h2>
```

HTML5 introduces a new tag to deal with this situation, called *<hgroup>*. When you enclose a stack of headings within *<hgroup>*, only the first heading in the stack will appear in an outline; the others will be ignored by screen readers and other outlining tools.

```
<hgroup>
```

```
<h1>Dog Agility Club of Indiana</h1>

<h2>Training for canine athletes and their humans</h2>

</hgroup>
```

Browsers that do not support this tag simply ignore it, so there is no harm in using it when appropriate.

In this exercise, you will create some headings for the opening page of The Garden Company's Web site.

SET UP In both Internet Explorer and Notepad, open the *index.htm* file that you created in Chapter 2, or use the *index.htm* file in the practice file folder for this topic. This practice file is located in the Documents\Microsoft Press\HTML5 SBS\03Format\ CreatingHeadings folder.

1. Immediately below the *<body>* tag, type the following:

   <hgroup>

   <h1>The Garden Company</h1>

   <h5>Helping you help your gardens grow since 1975</h5>

   </hgroup>

   Note Some coding purists will tell you that you should use an *<h2>* heading instead of *<h5>* for the subtitle above, and then apply a style to make the text look the way you want, but because it is a few chapters yet until you will learn about styles, I'm taking a shortcut. For now, the default appearance of the *<h5>* heading is much closer to the desired look we want for this exercise.

2. Immediately above the line containing the text *Our Main Store is Located At*, type the following:

   <h2>Come See Our Store</h2>

3. Save the file, and then refresh the Internet Explorer display to check your work.

   The new heading appears in the body of the page.

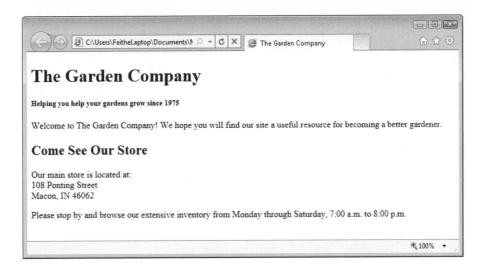

 CLEAN UP Close the Notepad and Internet Explorer windows.

Applying Bold and Italic Formatting

Applying bold and italic styles are two ways of making text stand out and attract attention. You generally use these styles in paragraphs rather than in headings, but it's perfectly acceptable to use them anywhere.

For simple **boldface** and *italics*, use the ** and *<i>* tags, respectively. These are two-sided tags that enclose the text to be formatted. For example:

```
<p>I had a <i>great</i> time at the party.</p>
<p>The reception will be held at <b>The Arbor Arch</b> in Plainfield.</p>
```

If you want to apply both bold and italic formatting, you can nest one tag inside the other. Don't mix up their order, though. When nesting tags, the rule is: *first in, last out*. So this is correct:

```
<p>The next book we will read is <b><i>The Catcher in the Rye</i></b></p>
```

In contrast, the following example is wrong, because the order of the ending ** and *</i>* tags are reversed:

```
<p>The next book we will read is <b><i>The Catcher in the Rye</b></i></p>
```

Even though the tags in the preceding example are improperly nested, most browsers will still display them correctly, provided you are using HTML as the document type. In an XHTML document, however, this type of tag reversal is not accepted.

Note HTML also allows the *<strong>* tag as a substitute for *<b>*, and the *<em>* tag (emphasis) as a substitute for *<i>*. For example, Expression Web (covered in Chapter 17, "HTML and Microsoft Expression Web") uses *<em>* and *<strong>* when you apply italics and boldface from its toolbar. You will probably never use those, but you should know what they are in case you come across them. You can also define bold and italic attributes for styles, as you will learn in Part 2.

In this exercise, you will make text bold and italic.

SET UP In both Internet Explorer and Notepad, open the *index.htm* file from the previous exercise, or use the *index.htm* file in the practice file folder for this topic. This practice file is located in the Documents\Microsoft Press\HTML5 SBS\03Format\ ApplyingBold folder.

1. In the *index* file, locate the *<h5>* heading near the top of the document, and then enclose it in an *<i>* tag:

   `<i><h5>Helping you help your gardens grow since 1975</h5></i>`

2. In the first body paragraph, enclose *The Garden Company* in a *<b>* tag.

   `<p>Welcome to <b>The Garden Company!</b> We hope you will find our site a useful resource for becoming a better gardener.</p>`

3. Enclose the store hours in *<b>* and *<i>* tags.

   `<p>Please stop by and browse our extensive inventory from <b><i>Monday through Saturday, 7:00 a.m. to 8:00 p.m.</i></b></p>`

   Note Remember the "first in, last out" rule. If you begin with *<b><i>*, end with */i></b>*.

4. Save the file, and then refresh the Internet Explorer display to view the results.

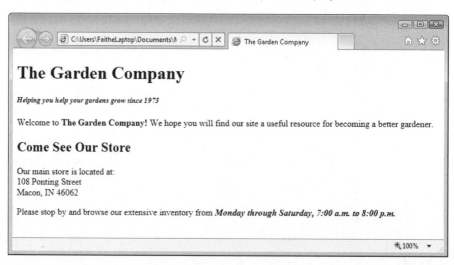

CLEAN UP Close the Notepad and Internet Explorer windows.

Applying Superscript and Subscript Formatting

Superscript formatting makes text smaller and raises it off the *baseline*. You'd typically use superscript to format exponents in math equations (for example, $X^2 + 1$) and for footnote numbers and symbols (like this*). You can also use superscript to format ordinal numbers such as 1st, 2nd, and 3rd to make your page look more polished.

Subscript makes text smaller and lowers it below the baseline. The most common use for subscripts is in chemical formulas (for example, H_2SO_4).

Note How much the text shifts up or down, and how much smaller the font size becomes, depends on the browser.

In this exercise, you will apply superscript formatting to create a footnote and an ordinal.

 SET UP In both Internet Explorer and Notepad, open the *index.htm* file from the previous exercise, or use the *index.htm* file in the practice file folder for this topic. This practice file is located in the Documents\Microsoft Press\HTML5 SBS\03Format\ ApplyingSuperscript folder.

1. At the end of the last line of text, between the *</b>* and the *</p>* tags, insert a code for a 1 in superscript, as shown in the following:

   ```
   <p>Please stop by and browse our extensive inventory from <b><i>Monday
   through Saturday, 7:00 a.m. to 8:00 p.m.</i></b><sup>1</sup></p>
   ```

   This creates a superscript number for a footnote.

2. Immediately before the *</body>* tag, type the following:

   ```
   <p><sup>1</sup>Closed the 1<sup>st</sup> Saturday in January</p>
   ```

   This creates the footnote itself.

3. Save the file, and then refresh the page in Internet Explorer to view the results.

 CLEAN UP Close the Notepad and Internet Explorer windows.

Using Monospace and Preformatted Text

Most of the text in this book is set in a *proportional font*. This means that individual characters take up varying amounts of space horizontally, depending on the size of the individual character. For example, the letter *M* takes up more space than the letter *I*, so a string of Ms occupies more space than a string of Is. As a demonstration, let's take a look at 10 of each character to see the difference:

MMMMMMMMMM

IIIIIIIIII

Most Web pages that we're accustomed to viewing use proportional fonts; they are attractive, professional-looking, and easier to read.

In contrast, a *monospace font* is one whose characters occupy exactly the same amount of horizontal space, regardless of the actual size and shape of the individual character. Back in the days of the typewriter, all type was monospaced because of the way the typewriter worked: the carriage moved exactly the same amount of space to the right as you typed, no matter which letter was keyed. Here are those same 10 Ms and Is in a monospace font:

MMMMMMMMMM

IIIIIIIIII

Some common uses for monospaced text include:

- Lines of programming code (like the HTML lines in this book)
- Text that you are instructing a user to type
- ASCII art (artwork created by using text characters)

It is uncommon to use monospaced text on a Web site, but for special situations it's nice to have that capability. To apply monospace style, you can use any of the tags outlined in the following table. Most browsers do not make a formatting distinction between these tags by default, but you can define them differently in your styles if you like.

Tag	Description
<kbd>	(Keyboard) The tag used for monospaced text to indicate something a user should type on a keyboard
<code>	(Code) The tag used for monospaced text applied to programming code
<samp>	(Sample) The tag used for sample text, which is largely the same thing as *<code>*

Note The *<tt>* tag was widely used for monospace text in a document in earlier HTML versions, but it is not supported in HTML5.

Note There are many different monospace fonts. Most browsers use Courier (or a variant) unless you specify otherwise. On page 40, you will learn how to specify a plain text font in Internet Explorer by changing the setting in the browser that controls the font used for monospace.

These tags work nicely if you just want to make certain that characters appear in a monospaced font, but they don't change the fact that HTML omits extra spacing and line breaks that the text might include. When formatting something that requires the verbatim inclusion of white space such as spaces or line breaks, you must use the *<pre>* tag, which stands for "preformatted." The *<pre>* tag not only displays the text in monospace, but also preserves all the spaces and line breaks that the Web browser would usually ignore, so the text will look very similar to the original.

The *<pre>* tag can also come in handy when text that you copied and pasted from another source contains a lot of line and paragraph breaks. You could manually enter a *
* for every line break and a *<p>* for every paragraph break, but that is pretty labor intensive for a large file with a lot of breaks. Using the *<pre>* tag is a shortcut. One common use for the *<pre>* tag is in poetry archives, for example, where line breaks and spacing add meaning to the poems.

In this exercise, you will add monospaced text to an existing page, and you will create a new page consisting of a poem and an ASCII graphic.

SET UP Use the *instructions.htm*, *poem.htm*, and *poemtext.txt* files in the practice file folder for this topic. (These practice files are located in the Documents\Microsoft Press\HTML5 SBS\03Format\UsingMonospace folder.) Open the *instructions* file in Notepad and Internet Explorer.

1. In Notepad, enclose the words *premium* in step 2 and *customer* in step 4 in *<kbd>* tags.

   ```
   <p>1. Click in the Login box<br>
   2. Type <kbd>premium</kbd><br>
   3. Click in the Password box<br>
   4. Type <kbd>customer</kbd></p>
   ```

2. Save the file, and then refresh the Internet Explorer display.

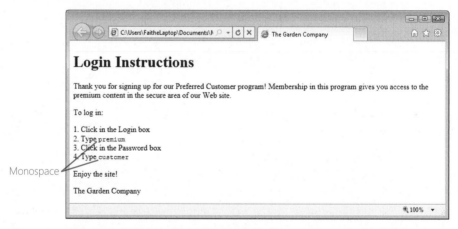

The text is now monospace, but it doesn't stand out very well. Let's make it more noticeable by formatting it as bold, as well.

3. Enclose the two monospace words in *<b>* tags (inside the *<kbd>* tags).

```
<p>1. Click in the Login box<br>
2. Type <kbd><b>premium</b></kbd><br>
3. Click in the Password box<br>
4. Type <kbd><b>customer</b></kbd></p>
```

Note You can place the *<b>* tags either inside or outside the *<kbd>* tags, as long as you remember the "first-in, last-out" rule consistently. For example, you could either write *<b><kbd>customer</kbd></b>* or *<kbd><b>customer</b></kbd>*, but you should not mix up the tag order like this: *<b><kbd>customer</b></kbd>*. Improperly nested codes often render properly in HTML, but not in XHTML.

4. Save your work, and then refresh Internet Explorer to see the changes.

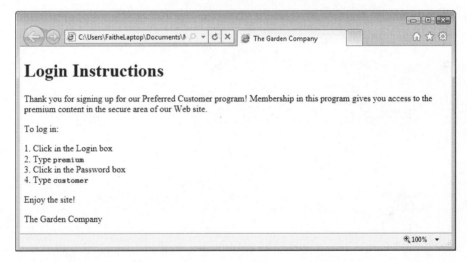

5. Close the *instructions* file and the Internet Explorer window.

6. Open the *poem* file in Notepad and Internet Explorer.

7. In Notepad, in the *<head>* section, create the following title:

```
<title>"The Gardener" by Robert Louis Stevenson</title>
```

8. In another copy of Notepad, open the *poemtext* file.

9. Select the poem title, attribution, and text (but not the biography note at the bottom of the file), and then press **Ctrl**+**C** to copy it to the Clipboard.

10. Close the *poemtext* file.

11. In the *poem* file, click below the *<body>* tag and press **Ctrl+V** to paste the copied text between the *<body>* and *</body>* tags.

12. Apply the *<h1>* tag to the poem title within the *<body>* section.

    <h1>The Gardener**</h1>**

13. Apply the *<h4>* tag to the attribution.

    <h4>by Robert Louis Stevenson**</h4>**

    Note Because this Web page is so simple, the *<hgroup>* tag you learned about earlier in the chapter would be superfluous here. Avoid using tags for their own sake; this makes your code needlessly bloated.

14. Apply the *<pre>* tag to the rest of the poem.

```
<pre>The gardener does not love to talk,
He makes me keep the gravel walk;
And when he puts his tools away,
He locks the door and takes the key.
...
Well now, and while the summer stays,
To profit by these garden days,
O how much wiser you would be
To play at Indian wars with me!</pre>
```

15. Save the file, and then refresh the Internet Explorer display to check your work.

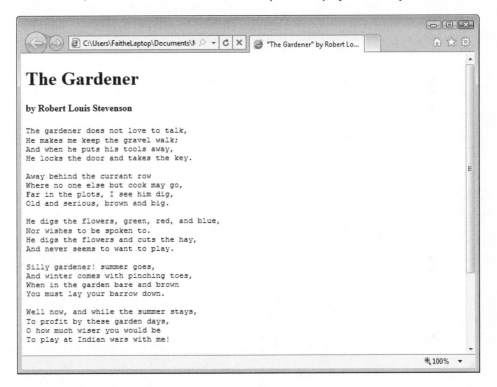

 **CLEAN UP** Close the Notepad and Internet Explorer windows.

Formatting a Block Quotation

When quoting blocks from other sources, it is customary—both on Web pages and in print—to indent those blocks from the main body of the text. The *<blockquote>* tag does exactly that. And don't feel constrained about using it; you can use *<blockquote>* for any text that you want to indent, not just quotations.

The *<blockquote>* tag has a *cite="URL"* attribute, but most browsers don't do anything with it. If you happen to know the URL for the source you are citing, it is good practice to include it in the tag for browsers that do support the attribute, and as an aid to anyone who might be viewing or editing your raw HTML code later.

Note There is also a *<q>* tag, which is used for formatting inline quotations. Its only functionality is to place quotation marks around the text that it encloses. Most people don't use this tag because it is much easier to simply type the quotation marks.

In this exercise, you will add a block quotation to a Web page.

SET UP Open the *poem* and *poemtext* files from the previous exercise (or in the practice file folder for this topic) in separate instances of Notepad. These practice files are located in the Documents\Microsoft Press\HTML5 SBS\03Format\ FormattingQuotes folder.

1. In the *poemtext* file, select only the text below the poem (the heading and the biographical note), and then press **Ctrl+C** to copy it to the Clipboard.

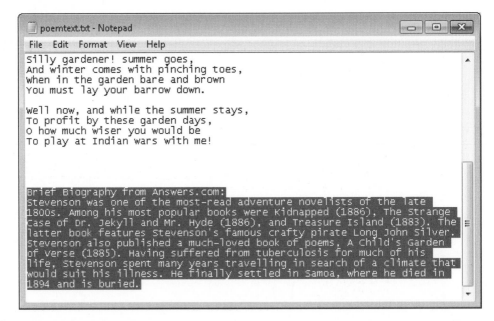

2. In the *poem* file, click above the *</body>* tag, and then press **Ctrl+V** to paste the copied text after the poem.

3. Enclose the text *Brief Biography from Answers.com:* in an *<h4>* tag.

```
<h4>Brief Biography from Answers.com:</h4>
```

4. Enclose the biographical note in a *<p>* tag:

<p>Stevenson was one of the most-read adventure novelists of the late 1800s. Among his most popular books were Kidnapped (1886), The Strange Case of Dr. Jekyll and Mr. Hyde (1886), and Treasure Island (1883). The latter book features Stevenson's famous crafty pirate Long John Silver. Stevenson also published a much-loved book of poems, A Child's Garden of Verse (1885). Having suffered from tuberculosis for much of his life, Stevenson spent many years travelling in search of a climate that would suit his illness. He finally settled in Samoa, where he died in 1894 and is buried.**</p>**

5. Immediately before the opening *<p>* tag in the previous example, enter this opening *<blockquote>* tag:

<blockquote cite="http://www.answers.com/topic/robert-louis-stevenson">

Note Don't remove the *<p>* tags for the quoted paragraphs; place the *<blockquote>* tags around the outside of them.

6. At the end of the paragraph, after the *</p>* tag, enter the closing *</blockquote>* tag.

</blockquote>

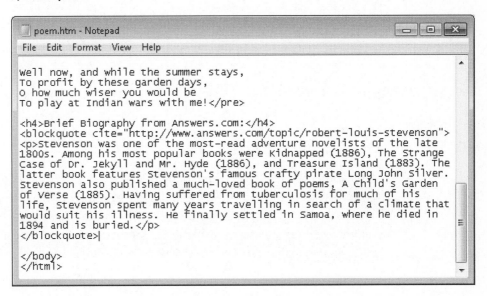

7. Save the *poem* file, and then display it in Internet Explorer to check your work.

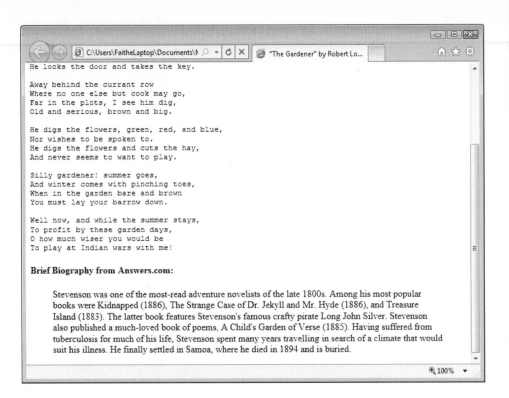

CLEAN UP Close the Notepad and Internet Explorer windows.

Configuring View Settings in Internet Explorer

At the beginning of the chapter, I mentioned that users can customize how certain tags are displayed on their own systems by setting the viewing preferences in their browsers. To understand what people might be doing with your pages, take a few moments to examine the settings in Internet Explorer 9. The customization capabilities in other browsers, including earlier versions of Internet Explorer, are similar.

In this exercise, you will view HTML pages in Internet Explorer 9 and specify a variety of settings.

SET UP Use the *poem.htm* and *index.htm* files from the previous exercises, or use those in the practice file folder for this topic. These practice files are located in the Documents\Microsoft Press\HTML5 SBS\03Format\ConfiguringSettings folder. Open the *index* file in Internet Explorer.

1. If the menu bar doesn't appear in Internet Explorer, press **Alt** to make it visible.

2. Choose **View | Text Size | Largest**.

   All the text on the page increases in size.

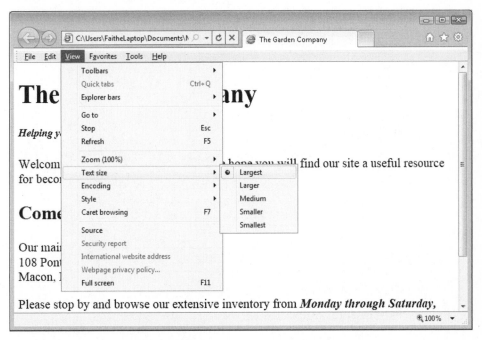

3. Choose **View | Text Size | Smallest**.

   All the text on the page decreases in size.

4. Choose **View | Text Size | Medium**.

   The text returns to its default size.

5. Choose **Tools | Internet Options**.

   The Internet Options dialog box appears.

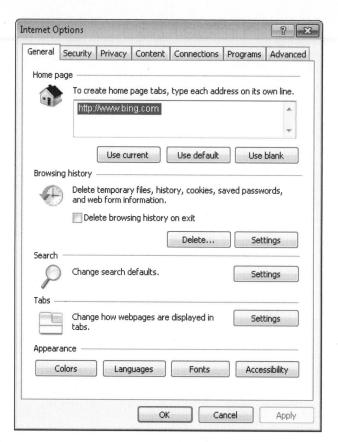

6. On the **General** tab, click the **Fonts** button.

   The Fonts dialog box appears.

7. In the **Webpage font** list, click **Arial**.

8. In the **Plain text font** list, click **Lucida Console** (if you have it; otherwise, select another font).

   Your choices are immediately reflected in the sample text below the font lists.

   Note Windows comes with a basic set of fonts, and you get more fonts when you install some applications, such as Microsoft Office. Arial comes with Windows, but Lucida Console does not; it comes with Office.

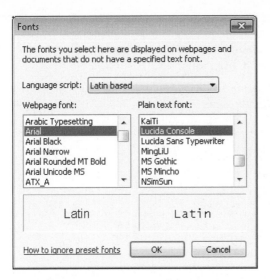

9. Click **OK** to close the **Fonts** dialog box.

10. Click **OK** to close the **Internet Options** dialog box.

The page now appears in Arial font. Your font choices are now overriding Internet Explorer's defaults.

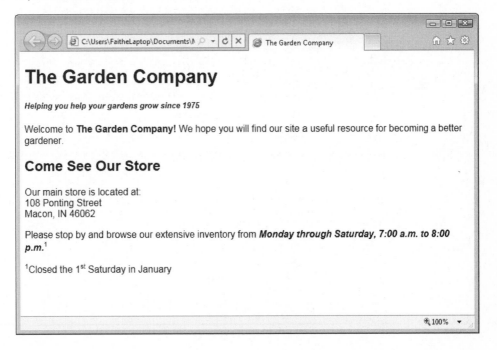

11. Open the *poem* file in Internet Explorer.

Notice that the plain text font you chose in step 8 is applied to the poem; the remaining text appears in Arial font.

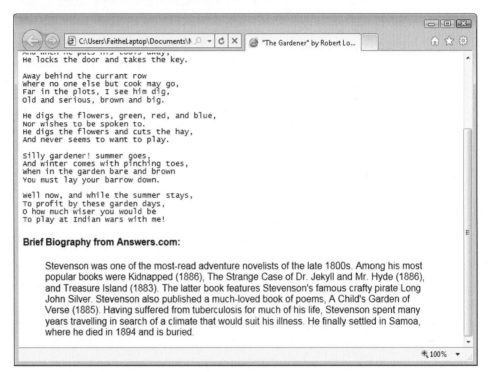

12. Repeat steps 5 through 10, changing the Web page font back to Times New Roman and the plain text font back to Courier New.

Note You do not need to perform step 12 if you prefer the new font choices, but it is generally a good idea to preview your Web pages in the same font that most people will be using to view them.

 **CLEAN UP** Close the Internet Explorer window.

Key Points

- Most tags are based on function, not formatting. They specify that text has a certain function, such as a heading or quotation, rather than specifying a certain way it should appear.

- The exact formatting (the appearance) applied to tagged text is controlled by the default settings of the browser, by individual user customization, or by styles.

- Define headings by using the tags *<h1>* through *<h6>* (largest to smallest).

- When one heading immediately follows another as a subheading, you might want to group them with *<hgroup>* so that screen readers and outlines show them as a single unit.

- To make text bold, use the *<b>* tag; to italicize it, use the *<i>* tag.

- The tag for superscript is *<sup>*; the tag for subscript is *<sub>*.

- Monospaced text uses a font whose characters all occupy the same amount of horizontal space, no matter the specific character; its opposite is proportional text.

- By default, most Web text appears in a proportional font. To specify a monospaced font, use the *<kbd>*, *<code>*, or *<samp>* tag. HTML5 no longer supports the obsolete *<tt>* code for monospaced text.

- By default, a Web browser strips out any extra spaces and ignores paragraph breaks (except for those created when using the *<p>* tag). To force the browser to render spaces and line breaks in text, enclose that text in a *<pre>* tag.

- To set off a block quotation, use the *<blockquote>* tag. The tag can take a *cite="URL"* attribute, but most browsers do not make use of it.

- In Internet Explorer, you can choose a default text size from the View menu. This affects only your copy of Internet Explorer, not the page itself.

- In Internet Explorer, you can choose a default text font by opening the Internet Options dialog box, clicking Fonts, and specifying the fonts to use for various purposes.

Chapter at a Glance

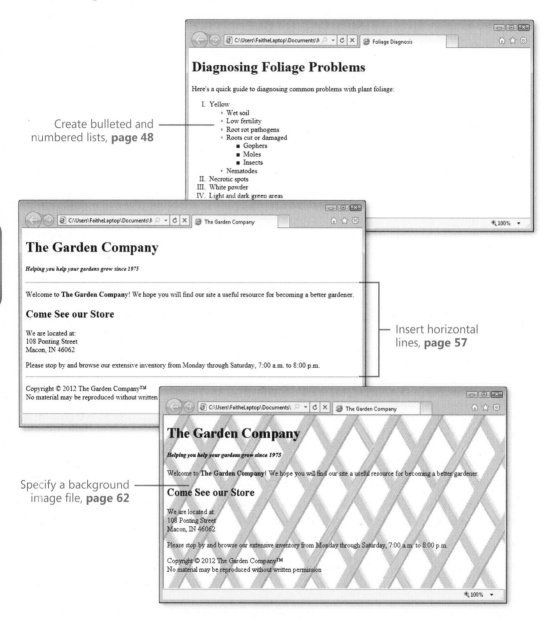

Create bulleted and numbered lists, **page 48**

Insert horizontal lines, **page 57**

Specify a background image file, **page 62**

4 Using Lists and Backgrounds

In this chapter, you will learn how to

✔ Create bulleted and numbered lists.

✔ Create definition lists.

✔ Insert special characters.

✔ Insert horizontal lines.

✔ Choose background and foreground colors.

✔ Specify a background image file.

Suppose you're studying for an important test or gathering information for a big project at work. There's a lot of data and very little time in which to digest it. Which would you rather browse through: a long report on the topic, or a list of the important points?

If you're like most people, you would probably prefer a list. Lists make text easier to skim. English teachers might wring their hands over this (and I can say this because I *was* an English teacher), but we've become a society of skimmers and browsers. People don't like to read paragraph after paragraph of plain text. They like their information divided up into easily digestible chunks.

In this chapter, you'll learn to create several types of lists by using HTML, including bulleted lists, numbered lists, and definition lists. You'll learn how to create nested lists within lists, how to use styles to specify the bullet character or numbering style, and how to create horizontal lines (which in HTML-speak are called *rules*) that further help divide a page.

You'll also learn about entity codes that make it possible to insert special characters or symbols that are not on your keyboard, including symbols such as greater than (>) and less than (<) that would ordinarily be interpreted as HTML tag markers.

Finally, this chapter takes a quick look at Web page backgrounds, both solid color and graphics. Most professional Web designers do not use background colors or background graphics, but many hobbyists find them fun. In addition, when you learn about using divisions in Chapter 11, "Creating Division-Based Layouts," you'll see how understanding backgrounds can come in handy for creating a navigation bar that contrasts with the main page.

See Also **Do you need only a quick refresher on the topics in this chapter?** See the Key Points section at the end of this chapter.

Practice Files Before you can use the practice files provided for this chapter, you need to download and install them from the book's companion content location. See "Using the Practice Files" at the beginning of this book for more information.

Creating Bulleted and Numbered Lists

In Chapter 2, "Setting Up the Document Structure," you worked with a file that contained a numbered list, but it was set up as a regular *<p>* paragraph with *
* breaks for each line, such as the following:

```
<p>1. Click in the Login box<br>
2. Type <b>premium</b>><br>
3. Click in the Password box<br>
4. Type <b>customer</b></p>
```

Tagging the list this way worked in this instance because the lines were short and simple, but HTML has tags designed specifically for creating lists, and it's better to use those tags when possible. They accept attributes that you can use to control formatting, and they create hanging bullets and numbers (that is, bullets and numbers that extend, or "hang," off the left margin of the paragraph).

The tag for a numbered list is *<ol>*, which stands for ordered list. For a bulleted list, the tag is *<ul>*, which stands for unordered list. Each numbered or bulleted item within the list is tagged *<li>*, for list item. You start the list with the opening *<ol>* or *<ul>* tag, enclose each list item with *<li>* and *</li>* tags, and then end the list with the closing *</ol>* or *</ul>* tag. Here's the numbered list from the previous example, this time using the proper tags:

```
<ol>
    <li>Click in the Login box</li>
    <li>Type <b>premium</b></li>
    <li>Click in the Password box</li>
    <li>Type <b>customer</b></li>
</ol>
```

Note The indentation is added to make the text easier for you to read, but the browser ignores extra spaces, as you learned in Chapter 2. In fact, if the *<ol>* tag had been placed on the same line as the first *<li>* item, it would not have made any difference.

You've probably noticed that what's missing here is the numbers themselves. That's because when creating an ordered list in HTML, you don't assign the numbers to the items yourself. You let HTML handle that for you as well as the paragraph alignment. The result is a standard, recognizable numbered list.

1. Click in the Login box
2. Type **premium**
3. Click in the Password box
4. Type **customer**

A bulleted list works the same way, except you use *<ul>* tags. Here's an example:

```
<ul>
    <li>Bring in the mail</li>
    <li>Take out the trash</li>
    <li>Feed the dogs</li>
    <li>Stop the newspaper delivery</li>
</ul>
```

This produces a basic bullet list on a Web page.

- Bring in the mail
- Take out the trash
- Feed the dogs
- Stop the newspaper delivery

Nesting Lists

You can nest lists within one another. In the following example, we have a bulleted list embedded within a numbered list. Notice how this nested list was constructed. The bulleted sublist (the *<ul>* tag) is placed within one of the *<li>* tags within the numbered *<ol>* list.

```
<ol>
    <li>Thursday: Do Algebra homework</li>
    <li>Friday: Housesit for neighbors:
        <ul><li>Bring in the mail</li>
        <li>Take out the trash</li>
        <li>Feed the dogs</li>
        <li>Stop the newspaper delivery</li></ul></li>
    <li>Saturday: Wash car</li>
</ol>
```

On a Web page, it would look like this.

1. Thursday: Do Algebra homework
2. Friday: Housesit for neighbors:
    ◦ Bring in the mail
    ◦ Take out the trash
    ◦ Feed the dogs
    ◦ Stop the newspaper delivery
3. Saturday: Wash car

Changing the Bullet or Number Character

Bulleted and numbered lists can be styled by using a *list-style-type: type* attribute. This is a type of style-based attribute that you will be seeing a lot more of later in this book, but for now we're using it as a standalone technique for changing the bullet character or numbering style. You can use the values shown in Table 4-1 for the *list-style-type* attribute. (This isn't a comprehensive list, but it covers all the values you are likely to use.)

TABLE 4-1 Common List Style Type Attribute Values

List Style	Value	Result
Bulleted	disc	Filled circle (the default)
	circle	Unfilled circle
	square	Filled square
Numbered	decimal	1, 2, 3, 4 (the default)
	decimal-leading-zero	01, 02, 03, 04
	lower-roman	i, ii, iii, iv
	upper-roman	I, II, III, IV
	lower-alpha	a, b, c, d
	upper-alpha	A, B, C, D
	none	(nothing)

To apply the attribute, place it in the opening *<ul>* or *<ol>* tag. For example, to create a bulleted list that uses the square bullet character, start the list off this way:

```
<ul style="list-style-type: square">
```

To create a numbered list that uses uppercase Roman numerals, start the list this way:

```
<ol style="list-style-type: upper-roman">
```

Note Another way of specifying the bullet or number type is use a cascading style sheet (CSS); you will learn about CSS later in the book.

Specifying the Start of a Numbered List

To start a numbered list at a number other than 1, you use the *start="n"* attribute with the *<ol>* tag, where *n* is the starting number. For example:

```
<ol start="3">
```

Note that you always specify the starting number as an Arabic numeral, even if you have chosen a Roman numeral or letter style for the list.

You can use the *value="n"* attribute for an individual list item *<li>* if you want to change the numbering for one item only.

For example, to force a particular list item to be numbered with a 5 (or in a list with Roman numerals, a V), insert the *value="n"* attribute, as shown here:

```
<li value="5">
```

Note The *start=* and *value=* attributes are both deprecated, but they still work in HTML5.

In this exercise, you will create and nest ordered and unordered lists.

SET UP Use the *foliage.htm* file in the practice file folder for this topic. This practice file is located in the Documents\Microsoft Press\HTML5 SBS\04Lists\NestingLists folder. Open the *foliage* file in Notepad and in Internet Explorer.

1. Create the following numbered list above the *</body>* tag:

   ```
   <ol>
   <li>Yellow</li>
   <li>Necrotic spots</li>
   <li>White powder</li>
   <li>Light and dark green areas</li>
   <li>Holes or chewed areas</li>
   </ol>
   ```

2. Save the file, and then refresh the Internet Explorer display to view your work.

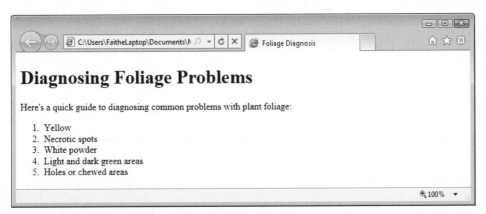

3. After the first item in the list, create a nested list, as shown in the following, and then save and check your work.

```
<ol>
<li>Yellow
    <ul><li>Wet soil</li>
    <li>Low fertility</li>
    <li>Root rot pathogens</li>
    <li>Roots cut or damaged</li>
    <li>Nematodes</li></ul></li>
```

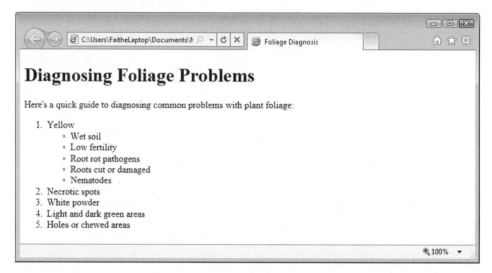

Tip The indentation of the lines in the nested list is optional. It makes no difference in the browser, but it does help you to see your code more easily. You can indent using either the Tab key or the space bar.

4. Within the nested bulleted list, create another layer of nesting, as shown in the following, and then save and check your work.

```
<li>Yellow
<ul><li>Wet soil</li>
    <li>Low fertility</li>
    <li>Root rot pathogens</li>
    <li>Roots cut or damaged<ul>
        <li>Gophers</li>
        <li>Moles</li>
        <li>Insects</li></ul></li>
    <li>Nematodes</li></ul></li>
```

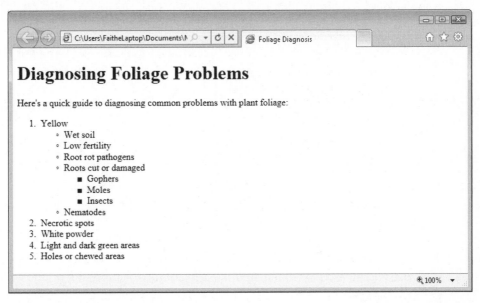

5. Change the opening tag of the top-level numbered list so that it uses uppercase Roman numerals.

```
<ol style="list-style-type: upper-roman">
```

6. Save and check your work.

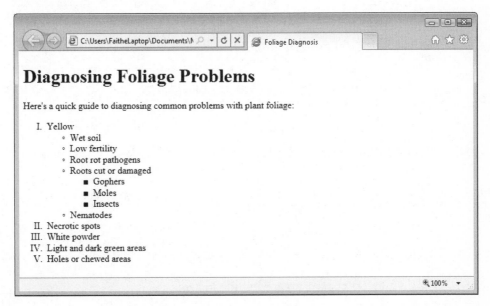

✖ CLEAN UP Close the Notepad and Internet Explorer windows.

Creating Definition Lists

A definition list is just what it sounds like: a list that presents terms with their definitions, such as you would see in a glossary. The word being defined serves as a heading, and the definition paragraph is indented under it.

Fungus
    A primitive, non-vascular, non-photosynthetic form of plant life. Examples include mildews, molds, and mushrooms.
Nematode
    A microscopic roundworm that lives in the soil. There are both harmful and beneficial nematodes. Harmful ones take their toll on the roots of the plant.

The complete list (headings and definition paragraphs) is contained within the *<dl>* and *</dl>* tags, which stands for *definition list*. Each word to be defined is contained in a *<dt>* (*definition term*) tag, and the definition paragraphs are in *<dd>* (*definition description-tion*) tags. Here's the code for the example just shown:

```
<dl>
<dt>Fungus</dt>
<dd>A primitive, non-vascular, non-photosynthetic form of plant life. Examples
include mildews, molds, and mushrooms.</dd>
<dt>Nematode</dt>
<dd>A microscopic roundworm that lives in the soil. There are both harmful and
beneficial nematodes. Harmful ones take their toll on the roots of the plant.
</dd>
</dl>
```

This example shows a one-to-one relationship between words and definitions (one definition for each word), but that's not a requirement. You can have multiple consecutive entries of either type. You might do this to accommodate situations in which a single word has two meanings or two words have the same definition.

Note HTML permits you to omit the closing *</dt>* and *</dd>* tags, but you should get into the habit of using them anyway. XHTML requires them.

In this exercise, you will create a glossary of terms on a Web page.

 SET UP Use the *glossary.htm* file in the practice file folder for this topic. This practice file is located in the Documents\Microsoft Press\HTML5 SBS\04Lists\CreatingGlossary folder. Open the *glossary* file in Notepad and in Internet Explorer.

1. In the *<body>* area, enter the following:

    ```
    <h1>Gardening Terms</h1>
    <p>Here are some useful gardening terms:</p>
    ```

2. After the text you just entered, create the following definition list:

```
<dl>
<dt>Acid Soil</dt>
<dd>Soil that is lower than 7.0 pH. Acidity is measured by the amount of
calcium in the soil. The opposite of acidic soil is alkaline soil.</dd>
<dt>Deciduous</dt>
<dd>A tree or plant that loses its leaves at the end of the growing season,
such as a maple tree.</dd>
<dt>Fungus</dt>
<dd>A primitive, non-vascular, non-photosynthetic form of plant life.
Examples include mildews, molds, and mushrooms.</dd>
<dt>Nematode</dt>
<dd>A microscopic roundworm that lives in the soil. There are both harmful
and beneficial nematodes. Harmful ones take their toll on the roots of the
plant.</dd>
</dl>
```

3. Save the file, and then refresh the Internet Explorer display to view your work.

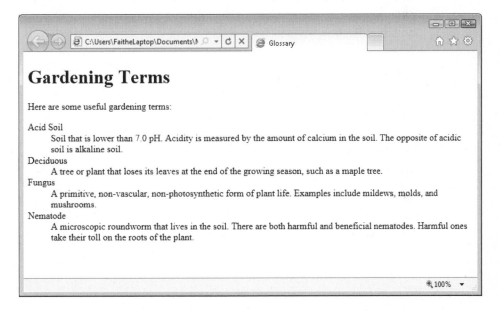

 CLEAN UP Close the Notepad and Internet Explorer windows.

Inserting Special Characters

Special characters are characters that are not included on a standard English keyboard. Examples include letters with accent marks over them such as in résumé, or an ownership symbol like © or ™. In HTML, these special characters are referred to as *entities*, and you create them by using codes beginning with an ampersand (&), followed by an entity name or an entity number, and ending with a semicolon. The entity names and entity numbers both represent the same thing; you can use either one. For example * * or * * both render as a non-breaking space.

In addition to the non-keyboard symbols, certain other symbols must be created as entities in HTML because they have a specific meaning in HTML. The most common are the ampersand (&), the greater than sign (>), and the less than sign (<). You can't just type those symbols in HTML code because a browser would interpret them as tags or entities rather than characters to display.

The following table lists the most common entities. For a more complete list, refer to the file *entities.htm* included with the data files for this book.

Symbol	Entity Name	Entity Number
& (ampersand)	&amp;	&#38;
< (less than)	&lt;	&#60;
> (greater than)	&gt;	&#62;
(nonbreaking space)		
¢ (cent)	&cent;	&#162;
£ (pound)	&pound;	&#163;
¥ (yen)	&yen;	&#165;
© (copyright)	&copy;	&#169;
® (registered trademark)	&reg;	&#174;
° (degree)	&deg;	&#176;
± (plus or minus)	&plusmn;	&#177;
† (dagger)	&dagger;	&#8224;
™ (trademark)	&trade;	&#8482;

Note The nonbreaking space entity * * is very popular for creating spaces, and in fact, many WYSIWYG Web site creation programs like Microsoft Expression Web and Adobe Dreamweaver insert them for you when you press the spacebar. Don't use nonbreaking spaces instead of good layout techniques, though. For example, if something needs to be indented a certain amount, use the correct HTML tags and styles to create the indent, don't just "space over" with a half-dozen * * codes.

In this exercise, you will add copyright and trademark symbols to a Web page.

SET UP Use the *index.htm* file in the practice file folder for this topic. This practice file is located in the Documents\Microsoft Press\HTML5 SBS\04Lists\ InsertingCharacters folder. Open the *index* file in Notepad and in Internet Explorer.

1. Add copyright and trademark symbols to the copyright notice at the bottom of the file.

   ```
   <p>Copyright &copy; 2012 The Garden Company&trade;<br>
   No material may be reproduced without written permission</p>
   ```

2. Save the file, and then refresh the Internet Explorer display to check your work.

 CLEAN UP Close the Notepad and Internet Explorer windows.

Inserting Horizontal Lines

Horizontal lines can be useful as dividers between sections of text in a Web page. For example, in the preceding exercise, you created a copyright notice that blends in perhaps a little too well with the rest of the text on the page; it would stand out more if it were separated from the rest of the document by a horizontal line. You might also want to add another horizontal line between the first two headings and the rest of the document.

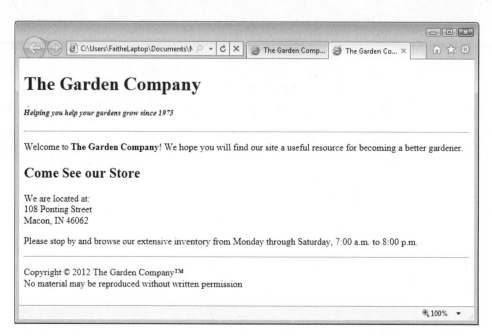

To add a horizontal line, simply add the following one-sided tag where you want the line to appear:

<hr>

Note In XHTML, you must add a space and closing slash, like this: *<hr />*. HTML5 also recognizes that syntax as an optional alternative. The slash is required for XHTML compatibility, while the space preceding the slash enables older browsers to read the tag correctly.

By default, the line runs the entire width of the browser window, is two pixels in height, and is black with a chiseled effect. You can change these characteristics by applying attributes within the tag.

Most of the original attributes for the *<hr>* tag were deprecated in HTML Version 4.01; attributes such as *align*, *color*, *size*, and *width* are not supported at all in HTML5. You now set the rendering characteristics for a horizontal line using styles, as you will learn in Chapter 6, "Introduction to Style Sheets." It's best to specify a uniform appearance for all lines with a cascading style sheet, as you'll learn to do in Chapter 6, but you can also add styling directly to the *<hr>* tag by simply including the *style="attributes"* attribute. The attributes you can set are *color*, *background-color*, *width*, and *height*. For example, to create a green line that is 3 pixels thick and spans 50% of the window's width, you would write:

<hr style="color: green; background-color: green; height: 3; width: 50%">

Some browsers use *color* to assign a color to the line, others use *background-color*; therefore, you should include both tags and assign the same color for both.

HTML recognizes these 16 basic color names:

- Aqua
- Black
- Blue
- Fuchsia

- Gray
- Green
- Lime
- Maroon

- Navy
- Olive
- Purple
- Red

- Silver
- Teal
- White
- Yellow

Note To see full-color samples of these, refer to Documents\Microsoft Press\HTML5 SBS\Reference\colors.htm.

In this exercise, you will add two horizontal rules to a Web page.

 SET UP Use the *index.htm* file from the previous exercise, or use the one in the practice file folder for this topic. The practice file is located in the Documents\Microsoft Press\HTML5 SBS\04Lists\InsertingLines folder. Open the *index* file in Notepad and in Internet Explorer.

1. Immediately above the copyright notice, add this tag:

   ```
   <hr style="color: green; background-color: green; height: 3">
   ```

2. Copy and paste that same tag immediately below the *<h5>* heading near the top.

3. Save the file, and then refresh the Internet Explorer display to check your work.

 CLEAN UP Close the Notepad and Internet Explorer windows.

Choosing Background and Foreground Colors

Many Web design experts caution against dark or patterned backgrounds on Web pages, because they can make it difficult to read the text. Some designers go so far as to say that you should not use *any* background color at all; they prefer that black text on a white background be the norm. A quick look at a few major commercial Web sites will confirm the near-universality of this opinion. Check out high-traffic sites like *www. msn.com*, *news.google.com*, and *www.microsoft.com*, and you'll find that the body text is almost exclusively black (or another dark color) on a white (or other pale) background.

Rules are made to be broken, however, and you might find situations in which a colored or patterned background is perfect for a certain page (or set of pages). For example, you might assign a background color to a Web page that you want to differentiate from other pages of a Web site.

Specifying Colors

The 16 basic colors presented earlier in the section, "Inserting Horizontal Lines," are the best colors to use on Web pages because they are universally accepted. Every browser interprets these colors the same way. However, you will probably find many situations in which none of those 16 colors is appropriate. For example, you might find that they are all too dark or too vivid to make an attractive page background. Therefore, you will sometimes need to rely on other ways of specifying colors.

One way to specify a color is by its RGB (red-green-blue) value. Using this method, you can describe a color using a series of three numbers, from 0 to 255. Each number represents the component of red, green, or blue that makes up the color. For example, pure red is *255, 0 ,0*; that is, maximum red (255), no green (0), and no blue (0). You can create a large range of colors using these three values. For example, *255, 153, 0* represents a particular shade of orange—full red, a little more than half green, and no blue.

Another way to express color values in HTML is by using a hexadecimal value. The hexadecimal values represent the RGB values converted to the base-16 numbering system. For example, the value 255 converts to FF, so the RGB value *255, 255, 0* can also be expressed as the hexadecimal value *#FFFF00*.

The problem with defining colors by using RGB or hexadecimal values is that not every display supports that many colors. Any unsupported colors appear as *dithered* (that is, formed with a cross-hatch pattern of two colors blended together). Therefore, most Web designers try to stick with what are called web-safe colors. A web-safe color is one that exactly matches one of the colors in a standard 8-bit color display. Web-safe colors use only the following numeric values for red, green, and blue: 0, 51, 102, 153, 204, and 255. To see full-color samples of all the web-safe colors, refer to Documents\Microsoft Press\ HTML5 SBS\Reference\websafe.htm.

Yet another way to express color values is by using extended names. These are similar to the basic color names, but there are a lot more of them. Officially, they are supported only by Internet Explorer, but in reality, most modern browsers recognize them. To see full-color samples of all the extended colors, refer to Documents\Microsoft Press\ HTML5 SBS\Reference\extended.htm.

Note Not all named colors in the extended set are web-safe; in fact, most of them aren't. Colors from the extended set are convenient because they are named, but web-safe colors are often a better choice.

Applying a Background Color

To specify a background color for an entire page, insert the *style="background-color: color"* attribute into the opening *<body>* tag. For example, to make the background of an entire page yellow, use the following:

```
<body style="background-color: yellow">
```

You can use the color name, the RGB value, or the hexadecimal value. Therefore, the following are equivalent to the code just shown:

```
<body style="background-color: #FFFF00">
<body style="background-color: rgb(255,255,0)">
```

Applying a Foreground Color

The foreground color is the default text color for the page. You can set the foreground color by using the *style="color: color"* attribute. It can be combined with the attribute for the background color in a single *style=* statement. For example, to set yellow text on a navy blue background, use the following:

```
<body style="background-color: navy; color: yellow">
```

When you combine two attributes in a single *style=* statement, you separate them with a semicolon, as shown in the preceding example.

Note This method of applying background and foreground colors uses styles, which you will learn more about in Chapter 6. HTML5 does not support the older method of applying colors within the *<body>* tag.

In this exercise, you will change the foreground and background colors of a Web page.

SET UP Use the *foliage.htm* file in the practice file folder for this topic. This practice file is located in the Documents\Microsoft Press\HTML5 SBS\04Lists\ChoosingColors folder. Open the foliage file in Notepad and in Internet Explorer.

1. Add the following style attribute to the *<body>* tag:

   ```
   <body style="color: green; background-color: beige">
   ```

2. Save the file, and then refresh the Internet Explorer display to check your work.

   The Web page text should now be green, and the page background should be beige.

✖ **CLEAN UP** Close the Notepad and Internet Explorer windows.

Specifying a Background Image File

A background image appears behind the text on a page. By default, the image is tiled to fill the page and scrolls with the page.

Unfortunately, there are plenty of examples of ineffective or distracting backgrounds on the Web. Here are some tips for making yours better than those:

Choose images that are designed to be tiled so that each copy blends smoothly into the next. When the image's edges blend well, it will look like a single, large image. In the following figure, the edges do not blend well:

On the other hand, the edges of the tiled copies of the following image blend together well in both directions.

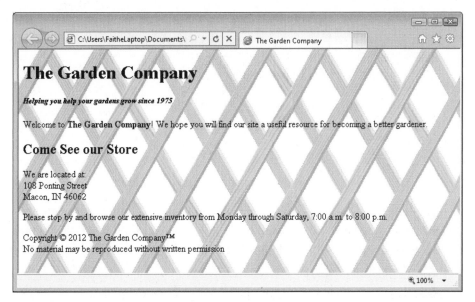

Use subtle patterns that don't distract from the text. The preceding examples fail that test; they impede readability. Here's a better one:

If you specify a background image, you should also specify a background color. The color will not be visible unless the image fails to display for some reason, or unless the image has transparent areas in it. The background color is especially important if you use a dark background image and a light foreground color; if the image does not appear, the text still must appear on a dark background to be readable.

To use a background image file, use a *style="background-image: url(image)"* attribute in the opening *<body>* tag, as you did for foreground and background colors in the preceding section. For example, to use the background image file called *granite.gif* that is located in the same folder as the HTML file, you would write:

```
<body style="background-image: url(granite.gif)">
```

Notice that you must enclose the image file name in parentheses following the *url*.

The *<body>* tag can hold many style specifications in a single *style=* attribute. Separate them with semicolons, as you did earlier with the foreground and background colors. For example, to combine the background image, background color, and foreground color in a single attribute, do the following:

```
<body style="background-image: url(granite.gif); color: green; background-color:
beige">
```

By default, the background image is repeated both horizontally and vertically to fill the window. You can force it not to repeat by adding the *background-repeat=* attribute to the *<body>* tag and specifying *repeat-x* (repeat horizontally only), *repeat-y* (repeat vertically only), or *no-repeat*. For example, to prevent any repeating, use the following:

```
<body style="background-image: url(granite.gif); background-color: beige; back-
ground-repeat: no-repeat">
```

By default, the background image scrolls with the text when the user scrolls down the page. To force the image to stay fixed, add the *background-attachment=fixed* attribute to the *<body>* tag, as follows:

```
<body style="background-image: url(granite.gif); background-color: beige;
background-attachment=fixed">
```

In this exercise, you will display an image as a Web page background.

 SET UP Use the *foliage.htm* and *stucco.jpg* files in the practice file folder for this topic. These practice files are located in the Documents\Microsoft Press\HTML5 SBS\04Lists\SpecifyingImages folder. Open the *foliage* file in Notepad and in Internet Explorer.

1. Replace the existing opening *<body>* tag with this one:

   ```
   <body style="background-image: url(stucco.jpg); background-color: beige">
   ```

   Note To avoid having to specify a path to the image file, place the image file and the HTML file in the same folder.

2. Save the file, and then refresh the Internet Explorer display to check your work.

✖ **CLEAN UP** Close the Notepad and Internet Explorer windows.

Key Points

- To create a numbered (ordered) list, use the *<ol>* tags. For a bulleted (unordered) list, use the *<ul>* tags.

- Within the *<ol>* or *<ul>* tags, use *<li>* tags for each list item. These tags are all two-sided. HTML does not require the closing *</li>*, but XHTML does.

- Ordered and unordered lists can be nested. Enclose the second-level *<ul>* or *<ol>* list within a *<li></li>* tag inside the main list.

- To use a different bullet character or numbering style, use the *style="list-style-type: type"* attribute in the *<ul>* or *<ol>* opening tag.

- To create a definition list, use the *<dl></dl>* tags. Within the *<dl>* tags, enclose each term in a *<dt></dt>* tag, and enclose each definition in a *<dd></dd>* tag.

- You can display special characters on a Web page by using HTML character entity references.

- To insert a horizontal line, use the *<hr>* tag. This is a one-sided tag. Put any specifications for the line within it, such as color, height, and width.

- You can specify colors by using basic or extended names, RGB values, or hexadecimal values.

- To assign a background color to a page, insert a *style="background-color: color"* attribute into the *<body>* opening tag. For a foreground color, use *style="color: color"*. These attributes can be combined into a single statement with a semicolon separator, like this: *style="background-color: red; color: white"*.

- To assign a background image to a page, insert a *style="background-image: image"* attribute into the *<body>* opening tag.

Chapter at a Glance

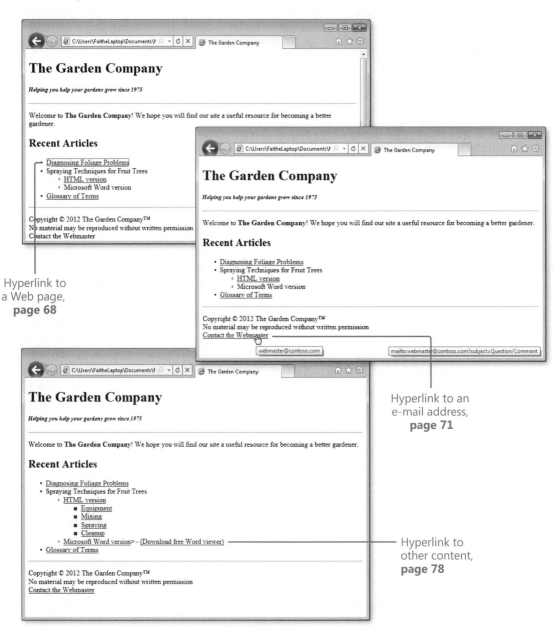

Hyperlink to
a Web page,
page 68

Hyperlink to an
e-mail address,
page 71

Hyperlink to
other content,
page 78

5 Creating Hyperlinks and Anchors

In this chapter, you will learn how to

✔ Hyperlink to a Web page.

✔ Hyperlink to an e-mail address.

✔ Create and hyperlink to anchors.

✔ Hyperlink to other content.

The Web is based on hyperlinks. Each Web page contains active links to other pages, which in turn link to even more pages, until presumably the entire Web (or at least a great chunk of it) is bound together. In fact, that's where the name "web" comes from. Hyperlinks can connect to other places on a Web page, to other pages within your Web site, to pages outside your site, and to many types of Web and non-Web content.

You activate a *hyperlink* by clicking a designated bit of text or a graphic that, depending on the link, takes you to a different location on the page, opens a different Web page, starts an e-mail message, downloads a file, lets you view a movie or listen to a sound clip, starts a Web-based program, and so on. You have probably clicked thousands of hyperlinks, perhaps without thinking much about the coding behind them. After this chapter, you'll understand *how* they work, and you'll be able to create your own.

In this chapter, you'll learn about the *<a>* tag, which is used to create various types of hyperlinks. You'll find out how to create hyperlinks to Web pages and e-mail addresses, how to create anchor points within a document, and how to hyperlink directly to an anchor point. I'll also show you how to hyperlink to non-Web content, like a Microsoft Word document or Microsoft Excel spreadsheet.

See Also Do you need only a quick refresher on the topics in this chapter? See the Key Points section at the end of this chapter.

> **Practice Files** Before you can use the practice files provided for this chapter, you need to download and install them from the book's companion content location. See "Using the Practice Files" at the beginning of this book for more information.

Hyperlinking to a Web Page

No matter what type of hyperlink you want to create, the basic syntax is the same. It starts with the *<a>* tag, and then uses an *href=* attribute which provides the URL or the path to the destination. For example, an opening tag might look like this:

```
<a href="http://www.microsoft.com">
```

This is followed by the text that will appear underlined as the link text that you click, or by a reference to the image that will serve as a hyperlink. (You'll learn more about images in Chapter 9, "Displaying Graphics.") After that text is the closing *</a>* tag. Here's a complete example:

```
Visit <a href="http://www.microsoft.com">Microsoft.com</a> for the latest
information.
```

When viewed in a browser, this produces a text-based hyperlink similar to that shown in the following image:

Visit Microsoft.com for the latest information.

Hyperlinks are underlined by default. You can specify alternative formatting for hyperlinks by using styles, as explained in Chapter 6, "Introduction to Style Sheets."

Using Partial Paths and Filenames

In some cases, you do not need to provide a file name or a complete path to the destination in a hyperlink. It depends on the context and the file's name.

If you do not link to a specific page, the server that hosts the Web site responds by displaying the default page for that site (if one is available). If a browser does not request a specific page when accessing a server, most servers will send the default page, which is usually named either *index* or *default*. Perhaps you wondered why the main page of The Garden Company's Web site is called *index.htm*—now you know.

In Internet Explorer, type the following URL in the Address bar:

http://www.microsoft.com/en/us

The opening page of the US version of the Microsoft Web site opens. Now type this URL instead:

http://www.microsoft.com/en/us/default.aspx

The same page loads. The first time, when you omitted the file name, the Web server responded by sending the default file, which is named *default.aspx*.

Note The URL in this example points to a page named *default.aspx*. *ASP* stands for Active Server Pages, which is an advanced technology used for commercial Web development. Pages created with ASP typically have .asp or .aspx extensions. For your own pages, you should continue to use the .htm extension.

If you want to link to a specific page, you must specify the complete file name. For example, if you wanted to provide a direct link to the page where users can download Windows Media Player, you would use this tag:

```
<a href=
"http://www.microsoft.com/windows/windowsmedia/player/download/download.aspx">
Download Windows Media Player</a>
```

Using Relative and Absolute Paths

Paths that contain a complete address that anyone can use to get to that page are called *absolute paths*. Absolute paths are very reliable, but they are also long and awkward to type. For example:

```
<a href="http://www.contoso.com/gardener/images/foliage.htm">Diagnosing Foliage
Problems</a>
```

When you are linking to files in the same Web site as the link itself, you do not need to include the complete path to the file; you can simply provide its name. When the file is in the same folder, you need only supply the file name. For example, if the *index.htm* and *foliage.htm* pages of The Garden Company Web site were in the same folder, in the *index.htm* file, you could refer to *foliage.htm* like this:

```
<a href="foliage.htm">Diagnosing Foliage Problems</a>
```

This is called a *relative path*, because the destination file is relative to the current file's location. Relative paths make it easier to develop and test your Web site in a different file location than the one where it will eventually be stored. For example, in this book, you'll be doing most of your development in the Documents\Microsoft Press\HTML5 SBS folder, which would typically not be the final destination for a site you are developing. By making as many relative references as possible, you avoid the need to re-code every URL when your site is moved to its final destination.

When creating a link to a file that's stored in a subfolder of the current one, you can point to that subfolder but otherwise leave the path relative. For example, suppose that *index.htm* is stored in a folder called c:\main, and *foliage.htm* is stored in c:\main\articles, which would be considered a subfolder (or *child folder*) of it. To refer to *foliage.htm* from within *index.htm*, you would use a tag like this:

```
<a href="articles/foliage.htm">Diagnosing Foliage Problems</a>
```

You can also create a link to a file that is up one level (a *parent folder*) with a relative reference. For example, suppose you wanted to refer to *index.htm* from within *foliage.htm* (both in the same locations as before). You would precede the reference with *../* to indicate that the file is one level up:

```
<a href="../index.htm">Home</a>
```

Setting a Target Window

By default, a hyperlink opens the referenced page in the same browser window. That means the new page replaces the previous page in your browser. Usually this is fine, but in some cases you might want the hyperlink to open in a new window. For example, perhaps you want to recommend that visitors check out a page on another site, but you don't want them to leave your site.

To direct the hyperlink to open a page in a new window, add the attribute *target="_blank"* to the *<a>* tag. For example, to open the *foliage.htm* file in a new window, the tag would be structured like this:

```
<a href="foliage.htm" target="_blank">Diagnosing Foliage Problems</a>
```

Note The *target=* attribute is not allowed in XHTML. W3C suggests that you use JavaScript for such situations.

In this exercise, you will create hyperlinks to other files.

Note Use the practice file provided for this exercise rather than a file created in a previous exercise.

 SET UP Use the *index.htm* file in the practice file folder for this topic. This file is located in the Documents\Microsoft Press\HTML5 SBS\05Links\CreatingHyperlinks folder. Open the *index* file in Notepad and in Internet Explorer.

1. Locate the text *Diagnosing Foliage Problems* and enclose it with an *<a>* tag that refers to *foliage.htm*.

   ```
   <li><a href="foliage.htm">Diagnosing Foliage Problems</a></li>
   ```

2. Locate the text *HTML version* and enclose it with an *<a>* tag that refers to *spray.htm*.

   `<li><a href="spray.htm">HTML version</a></li>`

3. Locate the text *Glossary of Terms* and enclose it with an *<a>* tag that refers to *glossary.htm* and opens the glossary in a new window.

   `<li><a href="glossary.htm" target="_blank">Glossary of Terms</a></li>`

4. Save the file, and then refresh the Internet Explorer display.

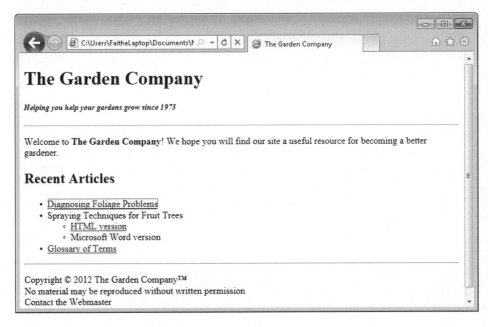

✖ **CLEAN UP** Close the Notepad and Internet Explorer windows.

Hyperlinking to an E-Mail Address

Hyperlinks can point to anything, not just to Web pages. You can create e-mail hyperlinks, for example, that start the user's default e-mail program, create a new message, and enter the recipient's address. (You can also set it to fill in the message subject, if you like.)

E-mail hyperlinks are useful when you want to direct someone to send a message to a particular person. For example, it is common to include a link to e-mail a site's webmaster. To create a hyperlink to an e-mail address, use the same *href=* attribute as you did previously, but instead of a Web address, type *mailto:* followed by the e-mail address, like this:

```
<a href="mailto:support@adatum.com">Contact Us</a>
```

Note Not everyone who has Web access also has an appropriate e-mail program set up to take advantage of a mailto: hyperlink. You might prefer to set up a Web-based contact form, which you will learn about in Chapter 14, "Creating User Forms."

Not all browsers support live e-mail hyperlinks. It's a good idea to also include the actual e-mail address in text form on the page, in case someone cannot use your hyperlink. In such a case, the text would mirror the address as follows:

```
Contact <a href="mailto:support@adatum.com">support@adatum.com</a>
```

Caution Including an e-mail address on a publicly accessible Web page is bound to generate a certain amount of incoming junk mail, or *spam*. For this reason, do not put your main e-mail address on a public page. If you have your own domain, or if your ISP or hosting company allows you to have multiple e-mail addresses, create a special account to be used for public contact (or ask your IT specialist to create one for you). That way, if you get too much junk mail, you can delete that address and start over with a new one without disrupting your main e-mail account. If you don't have access to multiple e-mail accounts, consider a free Web-based account.

To add a default subject line to the e-mail, add a *?subject=* attribute after the e-mail address, like this:

```
<a href="mailto:support@adatum.com?subject=Comment">Contact Us</a>
```

The person using the hyperlink to contact you can change the subject line in her e-mail program before sending the message.

Tip Even if all e-mail from the site is directed to the same person, you might still create multiple e-mail hyperlinks, each one with different default subject lines.

Another option, *title=*, specifies a ScreenTip for the hyperlink. This attribute displays a message when the user hovers the mouse pointer over the hyperlink. By default, the ScreenTip for a hyperlink shows the address of the link, but you can make it display anything you like.

In the following example, because the text is the same as the hyperlink, it would be a waste for the ScreenTip to repeat the same hyperlink yet again:

```
Contact <a href="mailto:support@adatum.com">support@adatum.com</a>
```

To display the message *Please contact us with questions or comments*, add the following to the code:

```
<a href="mailto:support@adatum.com" title="Please contact us with questions or
comments">support@adatum.com</a>
```

You can also use the *title=* attribute to omit extraneous portions of the complete hyperlink so visitors do not see them in the ScreenTip. For example, creating a title that contains only the e-mail address, and not the subject or title parts of the tag, makes it easier to read.

In this exercise, you will create a mailto: hyperlink.

Note Use the practice file provided specifically for this exercise rather than a file created in a previous exercise.

 SET UP Use the *index.htm* file in the practice file folder for this topic. This file is located in the Documents\Microsoft Press\HTML5 SBS\05Links\LinkingEmail folder. Open the *index* file in Notepad and in Internet Explorer.

1. Locate the text *Contact the Webmaster* at the bottom of the document and enclose it in a hyperlink that sends e-mail to *webmaster@contoso.com*.

   ```
   <a href="mailto:webmaster@contoso.com">Contact the Webmaster</a></p>
   ```

2. Add a subject line of *Question/Comment* to the hyperlink.

   ```
   <a href="mailto:webmaster@contoso.com?subject=Question/Comment">Contact the
   Webmaster</a></p>
   ```

3. Add a title to the hyperlink that will display *webmaster@contoso.com* as a ScreenTip.

   ```
   <a href="mailto:webmaster@contoso.com?subject=Question/Comment" title=
   "webmaster@contoso.com">Contact the Webmaster</a></p>
   ```

4. Save the file, and then refresh the Internet Explorer display.

5. In Internet Explorer, point to the **Contact the Webmaster** hyperlink at the bottom of the page.

   The ScreenTip appears.

Note The full text of the hyperlink is visible either in the status bar or in a separate pop-up ScreenTip, depending on the browser and whether the status bar is displayed. In Internet Explorer, it appears as shown in the image that follows because the status bar is hidden. To toggle the status bar on/off in Internet Explorer 9, choose View | Toolbars | Status Bar.

ScreenTip

If the browser window has a status bar, the URL appears there instead of in a ScreenTip

6. Click the **Contact the Webmaster** hyperlink.

Your default e-mail program starts if it was not already running, and a new e-mail message opens with the specified information in the To: and Subject: lines. (Microsoft Outlook 2010 is shown here.)

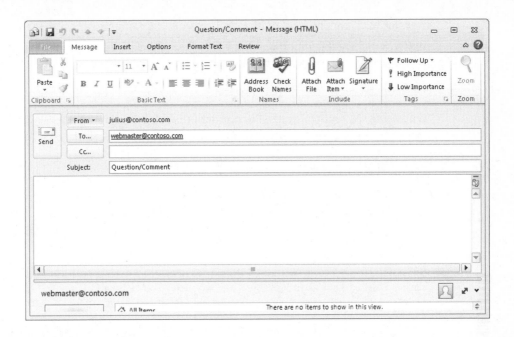

![X] **CLEAN UP** Close the e-mail message window without sending the message, and then close the Notepad and Internet Explorer windows.

Creating and Hyperlinking to Anchors

An *anchor* is a marker within an HTML document, roughly analogous to a bookmark in a Word document. You define a specific location in the document with an anchor name, and then you can hyperlink directly to that anchor.

Anchors are most valuable in long documents with multiple sections. They provide a means for users to jump directly to whatever section they want rather than having to read or scroll through the entire document. You can do this internally by creating a list of hyperlinks at the top of the document, or you can do this externally by including an anchor name in a hyperlink to another document. There are two parts to the process: you mark the anchor location, and then you create a hyperlink that refers to it.

To define an anchor, create an *<a>* tag around the destination text and include a *name=* attribute. For example, suppose you have a heading that reads *Conclusion*, and you want to create an anchor point with that same name:

```
<a name="conclusion">Conclusion</a>
```

To refer to the anchor point, include its name in the *href=* attribute. Precede the anchor name with a pound sign (#). If the anchor point is in the same document as the hyperlink, you can use a relative reference like this:

```
<a href="#conclusion">View the Conclusion</a>
```

Otherwise, you must include the name of the file in which the anchor is located. For example, if the anchor were in a file called *report.htm*, it would look like this:

```
<a href="report.htm#conclusion">View the Conclusion</a>
```

The same rules apply to the file name as they do with regular hyperlinks. If the document is not in the same folder, you must refer to the folder either absolutely or relatively.

In this exercise, you will create and link to anchor points in an HTML document.

SET UP Use the *spray.htm* and *index.htm* files in the practice file folder for this topic. These files are located in the Documents\Microsoft Press\HTML5 SBS\05Links\ CreatingAnchors folder. Open the *spray* file in Notepad and in Internet Explorer.

1. Locate the *Equipment* heading (not the list item), enclose it with an anchor tag, and include *equipment* with the *name=* attribute.

   ```
   <a name="equipment"><h2>Equipment</h2></a>
   ```

   Note You can nest the *<a>* tags within the *<h2>* tags or vice versa, but be consistent at both ends.

2. Repeat step 1 for the other *<h2>* level headings in the document, using the lower-case title of each one as the anchor name.

   ```
   <a name="mixing"><h2>Mixing</h2></a>
   ...
   <a name="spraying"><h2>Spraying</h2></a>
   ...
   <a name="cleanup"><h2>Cleanup</h2></a>
   ```

3. In the bulleted list at the top of the document, create a hyperlink from the *Equipment* list item to the corresponding heading.

   ```
   <a href="#equipment"><li>Equipment</li></a>
   ```

4. Repeat step 3 for each of the other list items.

   ```
   <a href="#mixing"><li>Mixing</li></a>
   <a href="#spraying"><li>Spraying</li></a>
   <a href="#cleanup"><li>Cleanup</li></a>
   ```

5. Save the file, and then refresh the Internet Explorer display.

6. Click each of the hyperlinks in the bulleted list; click the **Back** button after each one to return to the top of the page.

As you click each link, the browser scrolls down the page to display the corresponding heading at the top of the window. The exception is Cleanup, which does not appear at the very top because it is so near the bottom of the page; instead, the lower portion of the page appears when the Cleanup link is clicked.

7. Open the *index* file in Notepad.

8. Under *HTML version*, link each of the bulleted list items to the corresponding anchor point you created in the *spray* file.

```
<ul><li><a href="spray.htm">HTML version</a>
    <ul><a href="spray.htm#equipment"><li>Equipment</li></a>
    <a href="spray.htm#mixing"><li>Mixing</li></a>
    <a href="spray.htm#spraying"><li>Spraying</li></a>
    <a href="spray.htm#cleanup"><li>Cleanup</li></a></ul></li>
```

9. Save the file, and then refresh the Internet Explorer display.

10. Click each of the hyperlinks. Click the **Back** button after each one to return to the referring Web page.

 CLEAN UP Close the Notepad and Internet Explorer windows.

Hyperlinking to Other Content

A hyperlink can reference any file, not just a Web document. You can take advantage of this to link to other content such as Microsoft Office documents, compressed archive files such as .zip files, and even executable program files such as setup utilities for programs that you want to provide to your visitors. The procedure for linking to other content is the same as for linking to a Web page; the only difference is the file name you enter in the hyperlink.

Note You can create hyperlinks to pictures, but linking to a picture by using the <*a*> tag opens the picture in its own window rather than displaying it on the Web page. You will learn in Chapter 9 how to place pictures on the pages themselves.

Before you create a link to non-HTML content, you need to remember that not everyone has the same software. At first, it might seem like a great idea to provide a set of reports as Word documents, for example, but what about people who don't have Word installed? Some browsers have a feature that automatically tries to download an appropriate viewer, player, or plug-in (an extension to the browser for handling a certain type of file) for anything it can't display as native content. That's a great feature when it works, but it's not reliable because not all your Web visitors will have a browser with this capability. If you don't provide an HTML alternative for a proprietary-format file, you should at least provide a hyperlink to a free viewer that can display that file type. This is especially important with audio and video clips, which you will learn about in Chapter 15, "Incorporating Sound and Video."

Here are some of the popular viewers and the addresses where they can be downloaded:

- Adobe Reader:

    get.adobe.com/reader

- Microsoft Download Center, offering Microsoft Office viewers (PowerPoint, Excel, Word) and trial versions of Microsoft Office

    http://www.microsoft.com/downloads/en/default.aspx

Tip After the 60-day trial period, the Office trial version software operates in reduced functionality mode that still allows users to view documents created with Word, Excel, and PowerPoint.

In this exercise, you will create a hyperlink to a Microsoft Word file, and to the Microsoft Download Center page.

SET UP Use the *index.htm, spray.htm,* and *spray.doc* files in the practice file folder for this topic. These files are located in the Documents\Microsoft Press\HTML5 SBS\05Links\LinkingOther folder. Open the *index* file in Notepad and in Internet Explorer.

1. In the *index* file, locate the list item *Microsoft Word version* and enclose it with an *<a>* tag that points to the *spray* document.

   `<li><a href="spray.doc">Microsoft Word version</a></li>`

2. After the hyperlink to the Word document, add a hyperlink that references the downloadable Microsoft Word viewer.

   `<li><a href="spray.doc">Microsoft Word version</a> - <a href="`
   `http://www.microsoft.com/downloads/en/default.aspx ">(Download free Word`
   `viewer)</a></li>`

3. Save the file, and then refresh the Internet Explorer display.

4. In Internet Explorer, click **Download free Word viewer** and confirm that the Microsoft Download Center page appears. If it does not, you have probably made a typographical error in the hyperlink; make corrections if needed.

5. Click the **Back** button to return to the referring page, and then click Microsoft Word version.

6. If a dialog box appears prompting you to save or open the file, click **Open in Word 97 - 2003**, or whatever variant of **Open** the dialog box shows.

Depending on the Windows version and browser, the dialog box wording might vary. Here's how it looks in Windows 7 with Internet Explorer 9:

The *spray* document opens in Word.

 CLEAN UP Close the Notepad and Internet Explorer windows and exit Word.

Key Points

- To create a hyperlink, use the *<a>* tag with the *href=* attribute. The *<a>* tag is two-sided, so add *</a>* after the text that you use as the hyperlink.

- Use absolute paths (that is, paths containing the full location of the file) when referring to content outside your own Web site. Use relative paths when referring to files in the same folder as the current page, or in a parent or child folder.

- To open a hyperlink target in a new window, include the *target="_blank"* attribute in the *<a>* tag.

- To create a hyperlink that opens a pre-addressed e-mail message, precede the address with *mailto:*, for example, *mailto:support@microsoft.com*.

- To create an anchor point, use the *name=* attribute with the *<a>* tag, for example, *<a name="equipment">*.

- To reference an anchor point, reference the anchor point name, but remember to precede the name with a pound symbol (#) in the *href=* attribute, as in *<a href="#equipment">*.

- You can create hyperlinks to other types of content besides Web pages, but you should include hyperlinks to viewers for any content types that might not be supported by all browsers, and/or make HTML or plain-text alternative versions available.

- To provide a viewer for a type of content, create a hyperlink that points to a site from which it can be downloaded, or store the viewer on your own Web site and provide a link to it.

Part 2

Style Sheets and Graphics

Chapter at a Glance

Create classes and IDs for applying styles, **page 93**

Apply styles to hyperlinks, **page 96**

Create and link to external stylesheets, **page 98**

6 Introduction to Style Sheets

In this chapter, you will learn how to

- ✔ Understand styles.
- ✔ Construct style rules.
- ✔ Create styles for nested tags.
- ✔ Create classes and IDs for applying styles.
- ✔ Apply styles to hyperlinks.
- ✔ Create and link to external style sheets.

After you learn about cascading style sheets, you will wonder how anybody ever had the patience to create large Web sites without them. Cascading style sheets can save you a tremendous amount of time by standardizing the formatting of an entire Web page or group of pages.

A *cascading style sheet* (CSS) is code that specifies formatting based on styles. You can store the CSS code in the *<head>* section of the Web page to which you want it to apply, or you can store it in a separate file with a .css extension (which works well if you want the same CSS to apply to more than one Web page). The formatting then "cascades" down to the individual instances of each tag. You can also place a style directly within an individual tag if desired, as you did in Chapter 4, "Using Lists and Backgrounds."

In this chapter, you'll learn how to construct style sheets, and how to attach them to a document—either by placing them within the document itself, or by linking to them as a separate file. You'll learn how to define a style and how to apply it. The next several chapters will include further opportunities to practice with various style types.

See Also Do you need only a quick refresher on the topics in this chapter? See the Key Points section at the end of this chapter.

> **Practice Files** Before you can use the practice files provided for this chapter, you need to download and install them from the book's companion content location. See "Using the Practice Files" at the beginning of this book for more information.

Understanding Styles

In simplest terms, a *style* is a formatting rule. That rule can be applied to an individual tag, to all instances of a certain tag within a document, or to all instances of a certain tag across a group of documents.

In Chapter 4, you saw how to use the *style=* attribute for ordered and unordered lists. For example, to use a square bullet character in an unordered list, you would use the *style=* attribute with the *<ul>* tag like this:

```
<ul style="list-style-type: square">
```

But suppose you have several unordered lists in your document, and you want them all to use the same square bullet character. You could type the style attribute into the opening *<ul>* tag for each one, but that's a lot of work. Instead, you can create a *<style>* section within the *<head>* section that creates a global style rule for all *<ul>* tags in the document. The *<style>* section might look like this:

```
<style type="text/css">
ul {
list-style-type: square
}
</style>
```

Don't worry about the line breaks; they are simply a means of making your code more readable. Many third-party CSS editing programs format style rules with the extra line breaks. However, the preceding code could also be written like this:

```
<style type="text/css">ul {list-style-type: square}</style>
```

Notice that the *<ul>* tag does not have angle brackets. Also, note that the rules for the tag appear in curly braces. Other than those two minor differences, the syntax is exactly the same as when applied directly to a specific *<ul>* tag. You don't need to include the *style=* attribute because the entire definition is enclosed in a *<style>* tag.

You can define multiple rules within one *<style>* section. For example, if you want to expand this example to also specify that ordered lists are labeled with lowercase letters rather than numbers, use the following:

```
<style type="text/css">
ul {
    list-style-type: square
}
ol {
    list-style-type: lower-alpha
}
</style>
```

Now further suppose that you want these specifications to apply to all the bulleted and numbered lists in all documents, in your entire Web site. You can create an external cascading style sheet, and then refer to that style sheet in the *<head>* section of each document to which it should apply. For example, here's the entire text of an external cascading style sheet (a plain text file with a .css extension) that would apply the specified rules.

```
ul {
    list-style-type: square;
}
ol {
    list-style-type: lower-alpha;
}
```

It's the same code that was enclosed within the *<style>* tag in the previous example. When style rules appear in a separate file, you don't need the *<style>* tag.

A cascading style sheet can get very complex if it includes a lot of rules, but the principles are always the same as in these examples. The remainder of this chapter explores how to construct style rules within both embedded and external style sheets.

Constructing Style Rules

An embedded style sheet consists of a two-sided *<style>* tag placed in the *<head>* section of a document. Between the *<head>* and *</head>* tags, you define the rules for the various styles.

A style rule begins with the name of the tag or other element to which the style applies. For example, if you are creating a rule that will apply to all instances of the *<h1>* tag, start the rule with *h1* (no brackets):

```
<style>
h1
</style>
```

No brackets are necessary around *h1* because it's already enclosed in the *<style>* tag.

Next, type a set of curly braces (you can place them on separate lines for greater read-ability, if you want). Then place the rule inside the braces. For example, to create a rule that makes the text of a first-level heading red, use the following:

```
<style>
h1 {
color: red
}
</style>
```

If you have more than one rule to apply, such as a color plus a typeface, separate the rules with semicolons within the curly braces. It is customary but not required to write each rule on its own line. For example, to specify that the heading text must be both red and 14 pixels in height, include the following in your rule:

```
<style>
h1 {
    color: red;
    font-size: 14px;
}
</style>
```

If multiple tags should have the same rule applied to them, you can list them together and separate them by commas. For example, if all heading styles *<h1>* through *<h6>* should be red, you could write:

```
<style>
h1, h2, h3, h4, h5, h6 {
color: red
}
</style>
```

In this exercise, you will create an embedded style sheet governing the appearance of horizontal lines.

 SET UP Use the *index.htm* file in the practice folder for this topic. This file is located in the Documents\Microsoft Press\HTML5 SBS\06Styles\ConstructingRules folder. Open the *index* file in Notepad and in Internet Explorer.

1. In Internet Explorer, examine the horizontal lines in the index file.

2. In Notepad, in the *<head>* section, add the following:

```
<style>
hr {
color: green;
background-color: green;
height: 3
}
</style>
```

3. In the *<body>* section, locate the first instance of an *<hr>* tag. Remove all the attributes from it, leaving only this:

```
<hr>
```

4. Repeat step 3 for the other *<hr>* tag (near the bottom of the file).

5. Save the file, and then refresh the Internet Explorer display.

   The appearance of the horizontal lines does not change. You have not changed the lines; you've simply moved the definition of their appearance into an embedded style sheet.

6. In Notepad, in the *<head>* section, modify the style so that the lines are red, 50% of the browser window in width, 10 pixels in height, and left-aligned, as follows:

```
<style>
hr {
color: red;
background-color: red;
height: 10px;
width: 50%;
text-align: left;
}
</style>
```

Note Notice that you use the text-align attribute to align the horizontal line, even though it is not text. That's because there is no separate alignment attribute for elements that do not contain text.

7. Save the file, and then refresh the Internet Explorer display.

The appearance of both lines has changed.

The Garden Company

Helping you help your gardens grow since 1975

Welcome to **The Garden Company**! We hope you will find our site a useful resource for becoming a better gardener.

Recent Articles

- Diagnosing Foliage Problems
- Spraying Techniques for Fruit Trees
  - HTML version
    - Equipment
    - Mixing
    - Spraying
    - Cleanup
  - Microsoft Word version - (Download free Word viewer)
- Glossary of Terms

Copyright © 2012 *The Garden Company*™
No material may be reproduced without written permission
Contact the Webmaster

 CLEAN UP Close the Notepad and Internet Explorer windows.

Creating Styles for Nested Tags

Sometimes you might want to apply a specific formatting only when one tag is nested within another. For example, perhaps you want a bulleted list that's nested within another bulleted list to use a different bullet character.

If you simply created a rule for the entire tag, all text to which this tag has been applied would be formatted the same way. For example, if you created a style for the *<ul>* tag, all bulleted items would use the same bullet character. Instead, you must specify that you want to apply a rule only to the nested tag. To do this, instead of using a single style name at the beginning of the rule, specify that the item is nested by listing the parent style name followed by the descendent (child) style name. For example, to use round bullets for all bulleted lists that are nested within numbered lists, specify the following:

```
ol ul {list-style-type: circle}
```

This technique works with multiple nested levels. For example, to apply this formatting only to bulleted lists nested within other bulleted lists that are nested within numbered lists, specify the following:

```
ol ul ul {list-style-type: circle}
```

You can do this with any text attributes, not just those pertaining to the bullet or number type. For example, to make all the bold text that appears in unordered lists appear blue, specify the following:

```
ul b {color: blue}
```

In this exercise, you will apply different bullet characters to a nested list by creating styles in the *<style>* area of a document.

 SET UP Use the *index.htm* file in the practice folder for this topic. This file is located in the Documents\Microsoft Press\HTML5 SBS\06Styles\CreatingNested folder. Open the *index* file in Notepad and in Internet Explorer.

1. Examine the *index* file in Internet Explorer.

   Notice that the first-level bullet characters are discs, the second-level bullet characters are circles, and the third-level bullet characters are squares.

2. In Notepad, in the *<style>* section, create a style rule specifying that first-level unordered lists have a square bullet character.

```
<style>
hr {
color: green;
background-color: green;
height: 3px;
}
ul {
list-style-type: square
}
</style>
```

Caution Make sure that you place the new style rule *outside* of the curly braces of the existing rule.

3. Create a style rule specifying that second-level unordered lists have a disc bullet character.

```
<style>
hr {
color: green;
background-color: green;
height: 3px;
}
ul {
list-style-type: square
}
ul ul {
list-style-type: disc
}
</style>
```

4. Create a style rule specifying that third-level unordered lists have a circle bullet character.

```
<style>
hr {
color: green;
background-color: green;
height: 3px;
}
ul {
list-style-type: square
}
ul ul {
list-style-type: disc
}
ul ul ul {
list-style-type: circle
}
</style>
```

5. Save the file, and then refresh the Internet Explorer window.

The bullet characters change.

 CLEAN UP Close the Notepad and Internet Explorer windows.

Creating Classes and IDs for Applying Styles

As you have just seen, style rules can modify the built-in tags in HTML by redefining their formatting. Styles don't stop there, however. You can make your own styles by creating classes and IDs.

Classes and *IDs* mark certain elements so that you can refer to them in your style sheet. A class can be applied to multiple selections, whereas an ID uniquely identifies a specific selection within a document. (Different documents can use the same ID.)

For example, suppose you have an unordered list of products, and you want new products to appear in red. One way to do it would be to manually add the *style="color: red"* attribute to each of the list items, like this:

```
<li style="color: red">Spraying Techniques for Fruit Trees</li>
```

However, this method is not optimal because if you change your mind and decide to make the new items blue instead, you would need to make the change manually for each instance. A better way is to create a class called *new* and define formatting for it in the *<style>* area. Then you could apply the *new* class to each bullet point you want to spotlight.

To apply a class style, add a *class=* attribute to the opening tag for the element. For example, to make a list item part of the *new* class, use the following:

```
<li class="new">Spraying Techniques for Fruit Trees</li>
```

Then in the *<style>* area, add a style that defines the class as red. The only difference between defining a class and redefining a standard tag is that you put a period in front of a class name, as shown here:

```
<style>
.new {
color: red
}
</style>
```

IDs work the same way, except that you can apply them only once per document. For example, you might apply an ID to a unique heading. To create an ID, add an *id=* attribute to the tag, like this:

```
<li id="special">Spraying Techniques for Fruit Trees</li>
```

Then define the ID in the *<style>* area, preceding the ID name with a hash symbol (#), like this:

```
<style>
#special {
color: red
}
</style>
```

In this exercise, you will create two classes and apply them to items in a list. Then you'll change the items' formatting by applying different styles to the classes.

 SET UP Use the *bestsellers.htm* file in the practice folder for this topic. This file is located in the Documents\Microsoft Press\HTML5 SBS\06Styles\CreatingClasses. Open the *bestsellers* file in Notepad and in Internet Explorer.

1. Apply a class named *appleton* to all the Appleton Acres items.

```
<ol>
   <li>Sampson & Company All-Natural Pesticide</li>
   <li>Vickers and Vickers Fertilizer Sticks</li>
   <li class="appleton">Appleton Acres Big Sack of Bulbs, Tulips</li>
   <li>Jackson and Perkins Climbing Rosebushes</li>
   <li>Easton Create-Your-Own Paving Stones Kit</li>
   <li class="appleton">Appleton Acres Big Sack of Bulbs, Daffodils</li>
   <li class="appleton">Appleton Acres Big Sack of Bulbs, Hyacinths</li>
   <li class="appleton">Appleton Acres Big Sack of Bulbs, Crocuses</li>
   <li>Hawthorne Hills Hosta, 3-Pack</li>
   <li>Sampson & Company All-Natural Herbicide</li>
</ol>
```

2. Apply a class named *sampson* to the Sampson & Company items.

```
<ol>
   <li class="sampson">Sampson & Company All-Natural Pesticide</li>
   <li>Vickers and Vickers Fertilizer Sticks</li>
   <li class="appleton">Appleton Acres Big Sack of Bulbs, Tulips</li>
   <li>Jackson and Perkins Climbing Rosebushes</li>
   <li>Easton Create-Your-Own Paving Stones Kit</li>
   <li class="appleton">Appleton Acres Big Sack of Bulbs, Daffodils</li>
   <li class="appleton">Appleton Acres Big Sack of Bulbs, Hyacinths</li>
   <li class="appleton">Appleton Acres Big Sack of Bulbs, Crocuses</li>
   <li>Hawthorne Hills Hosta, 3-Pack</li>
   <li class="sampson">Sampson & Company All-Natural Herbicide</li>
</ol>
```

3. In the *<style>* area, create a style rule that makes items in the *appleton* class green.

```
<style>
hr {color: green; background-color: green; height: 3}
.appleton {color: green}
</style>
```

Note Each style rule here is run in as a single line, whereas in earlier examples, rules were broken into multiple lines for readability. It makes no difference which way you do it. The one-line method is more compact, but the multi-line method is easier to browse when editing code. From this point on in the book, most style rules will be written in the more compact form to save space.

4. In the *<style>* area, create a style rule that makes items in the *sampson* class blue.

```
<style>
hr {color: green; background-color: green; height: 3}
.appleton {color: green}
.sampson {color: blue}
</style>
```

5. Save the file, and then refresh the Internet Explorer display.

Items 1 and 10 are blue, and items 3, 6, 7, and 8 are green.

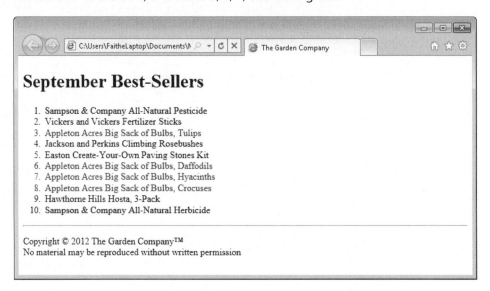

 CLEAN UP Close the Notepad and Internet Explorer windows.

Applying Styles to Hyperlinks

By default in most browsers, textual hyperlinks appear as underlined blue text, and *visited* hyperlinks (that is, hyperlinks to pages you have already visited) appear as underlined purple text. You have probably seen Web sites where this wasn't the case, though, and perhaps you wondered how they did it.

You can control hyperlink formatting by placing attributes in the *<a>* tag for each link, although it's tedious to do so. For example, to make an individual hyperlink magenta, use the following:

```
<a href="foliage.htm" style="color: magenta">Diagnosing Foliage Problems</a>
```

You could apply a class to all hyperlinks, as you learned in the preceding section, but that method does not provide a way to distinguish between the visited and the unvisited links. Ideally you would want them to be different colors, and that's not possible when you use a class to define them. To apply different colors, you can use *pseudo-classes*. A pseudo-class is a class that uses a variable to determine membership. HTML defines pseudo-classes called *link* and *visited* for unvisited and visited hyperlinks respectively.

You do not need to apply anything to the individual hyperlink tags within the *<body>* section to use pseudo-classes. Simply create the style rule in the *<style>* section for the pseudo-classes, and the browser will apply that rule throughout the document. For example, to make all visited links magenta and all unvisited links black:

```
<style>
a:link {color: black}
a:visited {color: magenta}
</style>
```

There are three additional pseudo-classes that you can use with hyperlink styles:

- **focus** This is used for links that are selected by using the keyboard but not yet activated. This is not an issue when you select a link with the mouse because clicking a link both selects it and activates it. This pseudo-class is not commonly used because so few people navigate pages by using the keyboard that it is not worthwhile to go to the trouble.

- **hover** This is used to change the appearance of a link when the mouse is positioned over it. You can use this pseudo-class to make a link change color, become bold, and so on when the user points at it.

- **active** This is used for a link when it is clicked. Immediately after being clicked, the link changes to the visited state. You might use this pseudo-class if you have set the link and visited states to the same value but want the link to change momentarily when clicked.

Caution A link can be in more than one state at once. For example, a link can be visited, but also in the hover state if a mouse pointer is positioned over it. Therefore, the order in which you list the style rules for links is significant, because later rules will override earlier ones. Define them in the following order to avoid any confusion: *link, visited, focus, hover, active*.

In this exercise, you will create style rules for various hyperlink states.

 SET UP Use the *foliage.htm*, *glossary.htm*, *index.htm*, and *spray.htm* files in the practice folder for this topic. These files are located in the Documents\Microsoft Press\HTML5 SBS\06Styles\StylingHyperlinks folder. Open the *index* file in Notepad and in Internet Explorer.

1. In Internet Explorer, click the **Diagnosing Foliage Problems** hyperlink, and then click **Back** to return to the referring page.

   Different colors identify visited and unvisited links.

2. In Notepad, in the *<style>* area, add these rules:

```
a:link {color: blue}
a:visited {color: green}
a:hover {color: lime}
a:active {color: red}
```

3. Save the file, and then refresh the Internet Explorer display.

4. Position the mouse pointer over each hyperlink.

Notice that hyperlink text is lime green when you position the mouse pointer over it. Diagnosing Foliage Problems is red because it is the active link.

5. Click the hyperlink **Glossary of Terms**.

Notice that the hyperlink text color changes to red immediately before the Glossary page loads. The Glossary page loads in its own separate window.

6. Close the Glossary page window.

Notice that the Glossary of Terms hyperlink is still red because it is still active. It was made active when you clicked it in step 5, and will remain so until you click something else.

7. Click the hyperlink **HTML Version**, and then click **Back**.

Notice that HTML Version is now red (active), but Glossary of Terms is green (visited).

 CLEAN UP Close the Notepad and Internet Explorer windows.

Creating and Linking to External Style Sheets

Embedded style sheets work well for single-page Web sites, but to really take advantage of what cascading style sheets can do, you need to create an *external style sheet*. A single external style sheet can be linked to multiple documents, ensuring complete consistency even in a large site. An external style sheet also makes it easy to change the formatting of your site after the pages have been constructed. Rather than having to edit each page individually, you can simply change the style sheet.

An external style sheet is a plain text file, just like an HTML file. The only difference is that you assign it a .css rather than an .htm extension. It contains anything you would place within the *<style>* tag if you were creating the style sheet internally. You do not need the *<style>* and *</style>* tags themselves.

After creating the style sheet, you create a link to it in the *<head>* area of each document that will use it. For example, if the style sheet is named default.css, you would link to it by inserting this code in the document's *<head>* area, as shown in the following:

```
<link rel="stylesheet" type="text/css" href="default.css" />
```

Note The name "default.css" is common, but not required. You can name your style sheet anything you like, as long as the name ends with a .css extension.

An embedded style sheet takes precedence over an external one. For example, if your external style sheet specifies Roman numerals for ordered lists but your embedded style sheet specifies uppercase letters, ordered lists will be labeled with uppercase letters. Furthermore, any tag-specific styles you apply take precedence over both embedded and external style sheets. So, if you add a style rule to an individual *<ol>* tag, that setting will override any style sheet settings.

In this exercise, you will create an external style sheet and link a Web page to it.

 SET UP Use the *index.htm* file in the practice folder for this topic. This file is located in the Documents\Microsoft Press\HTML5 SBS\06Styles\CreatingExternal folder. OPEN the *index* file in Notepad and in Internet Explorer.

1. Select all the text between *<style>* and *</style>* but do not include those tags in the selection.

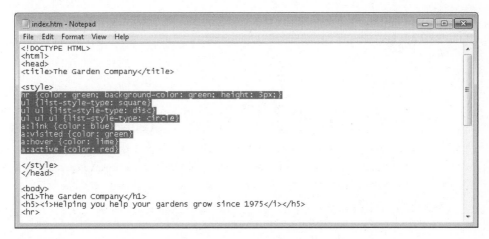

2. Press **Ctrl+X** to cut the text from the document and store it in the Clipboard.

3. Save the file, and then start a new document in Notepad.

4. Press **Ctrl+V** to paste the text from the Clipboard into the new document.

5. Save the new document as **default.css** in the practice file folder for this exercise (Documents\Microsoft Press\HTML5 SBS\06Styles\CreatingExternal).

```
hr {color: green; background-color: green; height: 3px;}
ul {list-style-type: square}
ul ul {list-style-type: disc}
ul ul ul {list-style-type: circle}
a:link {color: blue}
a:visited {color: green}
a:hover {color: lime}
a:active {color: red}
```

6. Return to the *index* file in Notepad, and then delete the *<style>* and *</style>* tags.

7. Add this line to the *<head>* section:

```
<link rel="stylesheet" type="text/css" href="default.css">
```

8. Save the file, and then refresh the Internet Explorer display.

   The file does not appear to change, but the styles are now defined in the external style sheet rather than in the embedded style sheet.

   Note One way to quickly check whether the style sheet is applied is to position the mouse pointer over a hyperlink. If the style sheet is working, the hyperlink text will turn lime green.

✖ CLEAN UP Close the Notepad and Internet Explorer windows.

Key Points

- Styles can define the formatting for specific instances of a tag, for all uses of a tag within a document, or for all uses of a tag within a group of documents.

- A cascading style sheet is a list of style rules applied to tags within an HTML document. This list can either be internal (embedded) or external to the document (a linked file).

- When rule conflicts occur, they are resolved as follows (from highest priority to lowest):

   ○ Styles applied to individual tags

   ○ Styles applied using an internal style sheet (with highest priority going to the entries nearest the bottom of that style sheet)

   ○ Styles applied using an external style sheet (again, with highest priority to the entries nearest the bottom)

- There are three ways to apply a style. You can use the *style=* attribute within an individual tag, you can create an embedded style sheet, or you can create an external style sheet.

- You place an embedded style sheet in the *<head>* section of the file and enclose it in a *<style>* tag. An external style sheet is a separate plain text file with a .css extension.

- A style sheet consists of one or more style rules. A style rule is the tag, class, or ID name followed by curly braces in which the specifications are placed.

- Each specification takes the format of name: value. For example, *list-style-type: square*.

- Separate multiple specifications within a rule by using semicolons. To define two or more tags the same way, include both tags (with a comma between them) before the opening curly brace, like this: *h1, h2 {color: black}*. If you omit the comma, two tag names in a row refer to nested styles in a rule. For example, *ol ul {color: green}* refers to unordered lists nested within ordered lists.

- You can assign a class to multiple elements. You can define a style based on a class. Precede a class's name in a style sheet with a period, like this: *.new {color: red}*.

- An ID must be uniquely assigned within a document. You can define a style based on an ID. Precede the ID in a style sheet with a hash symbol (#), like this: *#special {color: red}*.

- Apply a class or ID to a tag by including the *class=* or *ID=* attribute within its opening tag, like this: *<ol class="new">*.

- To apply styles to hyperlinks, use a pseudo-class of the hyperlink type. You can apply the *link, visited, hover, active*, or *focus* pseudo-class like this: *a:visited {color: red}*.

- To create an external style sheet, start a new Notepad document and place all the style rules within it. Then refer to it from the *<head>* section of each document to which that style sheet should apply, by using the tag *<link rel="stylesheet" type="text/css" href="default.css">*, where *default.css* is the name of your style sheet.

Chapter at a Glance

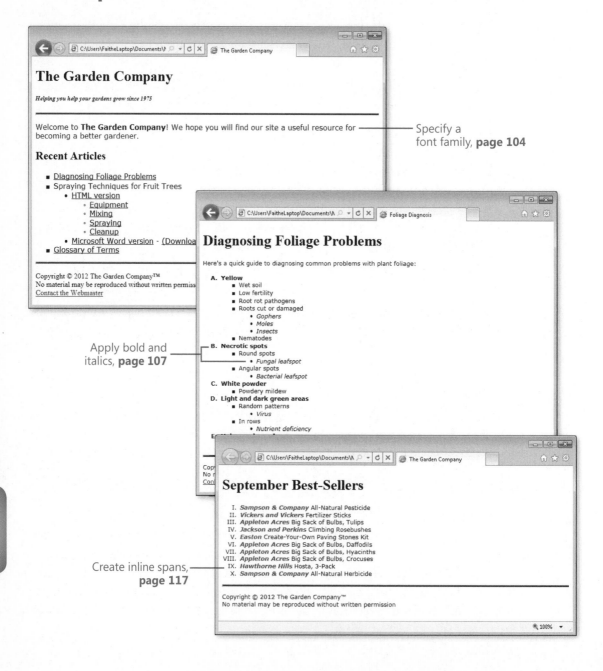

Specify a
font family, **page 104**

Apply bold and
italics, **page 107**

Create inline spans,
page 117

7 Formatting Text by Using Style Sheets

In this chapter, you will learn how to

✔ Specify a font family.

✔ Specify a font size and color.

✔ Apply bold and italics.

✔ Apply strikethrough and underlining.

✔ Create inline spans.

✔ Adjust spacing between letters.

Learning how to create style rules opens up a whole new world in HTML formatting. Virtually anything that you can do in a word-processing program, you can do in HTML by using styles.

You might be wondering whether the simple text-formatting tags you learned about in Part 1 of the book, such as the *<b>* and *<i>* tags, are still relevant. They are—to a degree. The W3C is increasingly focused on applying text formatting by using styles, which means you should try to use the style-based formatting that you'll learn in this chapter (and the next). However, those old tags still work perfectly well when you create HTML5 documents, and Web browsers will continue to support tag-based formatting for a long time. If you've already created an extensive Web site that uses formatting tags, there's no big rush to recreate the existing pages by using styles. For new pages, however, it's a good idea to do it "right" from the start by using styles for all your formatting.

In this chapter, you'll learn about character-based formatting—that is, formatting that makes individual characters look a certain way. You'll learn how to specify fonts, sizes, and colors; how to use styles to apply bold, italic, strikethrough, or underline styling to your text; and how to add a background to text and adjust the spacing between letters. In Chapter 8, "Formatting Paragraphs by Using Style Sheets," you'll learn about paragraph formatting features such as line spacing, indentation, and alignment.

See Also Do you need only a quick refresher on the topics in this chapter? See the Key Points at the end of this chapter.

> **Practice Files** Before you can use the practice files provided for this chapter, you need to install them from the book's companion content page to their default locations. See "Using the Practice Files" in the beginning of this book for more information.

Specifying a Font Family

Specifying a certain font to appear on a page can be tricky because not everyone has the same fonts installed. Even fonts that come with Microsoft Windows, such as Courier New and Arial, are not universally acceptable because not everyone who has access to the Web uses a Windows-based computer.

To work around this issue, you can specify a *font family* rather than an individual font. A font family is a set of fonts listed in order of preference. If the computer displaying your page does not have the first font in the list, it checks for the second, and then the third, and so on until it finds a match. For example, here's how to specify a font family in a style rule:

```
p {font-family: "Arial", "Helvetica", sans-serif}
```

Although no font is universally available on all PCs, there are a few generic font types that are nearly so: serif, sans-serif, cursive, fantasy, and monospace. Those font types are not specified with quotation marks around them, as is the case in the preceding example. Here's how each of those fonts renders on a Web page.

Serif

Sans-serif

Cursive

Fantasy

Monospace

Note In the preceding example, the Cursive font does not appear as you might expect from its name; it doesn't look like cursive handwriting. In most browsers, cursive appears as a rounded version of sans-serif.

By specifying a generic font type as the final font in the family, you can virtually guarantee that you'll at least get your last choice. If the browser can't use any of your preferences, it will simply render the text using its default font. Here are some common font families, grouped by their similar appearances:

- Arial Black, Helvetica Bold
- Arial, Helvetica, sans-serif
- Verdana, Geneva, Arial, Helvetica, sans-serif
- Times New Roman, Times, serif
- Courier New, Courier, monospace
- Georgia, Times New Roman, Times, serif
- Zapf-Chancery, cursive
- Western, fantasy

You can also add a *font-family* attribute to individual tags to ensure that the text stands out. Here's how you might set an individual paragraph to the second font family from the preceding list.

```
<p style="font-family: Arial, Helvetica, sans-serif">
```

Notice that there are no quotation marks around any of the font names when applied in this way. Instead, the quotation marks are placed around the entire style rule.

In this exercise, you will assign a default font to all the *<p>* tags in a document, and then you'll override that font choice on a specific paragraph.

 SET UP Use the *index.htm* and *default.css* files in the practice folder for this topic. These files are located in the Documents\Microsoft Press\HTML5 SBS\07Text\ SelectingFont folder. Open the *default.css* style sheet file in Notepad and open the *index* file in Internet Explorer.

1. In the *default.css* style sheet, add a style rule that defines a font family of Verdana, Arial, Helvetica, and sans-serif for the *<p>* tag and the *<li>* tag, as shown in the following:

   ```
   p, li {font-family: "Verdana", "Arial", "Helvetica", sans-serif}
   ```

2. Save the file, and then refresh the Internet Explorer display.

   The font of all the text in paragraphs and lists changes.

3. Open the *index* file in Notepad. Change the tag for the copyright notice at the bottom of the page to use the Times New Roman, Times, or serif font.

```
<p style="font-family: Times New Roman, Times, serif">
Copyright &copy; 2012 The Garden Company&trade;<br>
No material may be reproduced without written permission<br>
<a href="mailto:webmaster@contoso.com?subject=Question/Comment"
 title="webmaster@contoso.com">Contact the Webmaster</a></p>
```

4. Save the file, and then refresh the Internet Explorer display.

Font determined by style rule defined in default.css —

Font rule overridden by style attribute in the *<p>* tag —

Because each page of the Web site has a copyright notice, it might be better to create a class (as you learned in Chapter 6, "Introduction to Style Sheets") and change the font for the class. That's what we'll do next.

5. In Notepad in *index.htm*, remove the *style=* attribute you just applied to the copyright notice, and instead apply a class called *copyright* to that paragraph, as follows:

```
<p class="copyright">
Copyright &copy; 2012 The Garden Company&trade;<br>
No material may be reproduced without written permission<br>
<a href="mailto:webmaster@contoso.com?subject=Question/Comment"
title="webmaster@contoso.com">Contact the Webmaster</a></p>
```

6. Save the file, and then refresh the Internet Explorer display.

   The copyright notice has reverted to the default font set for <p> tags in the default.css style sheet because no special formatting has been defined for the copyright class.

7. In Notepad, in the *default.css* file, define the *copyright* class to use the Times New Roman, Times, or serif font.

   ```
   .copyright {font-family: "Times New Roman", "Times", serif}
   ```

8. Save the file, and then refresh the Internet Explorer display.

✖ CLEAN UP Close the Notepad and Internet Explorer windows.

Specifying a Font Size and Color

There are many ways to set the font size in HTML, but all the methods use one of two strategies: either specify an absolute size or specify a size in relation to the parent tag.

To specify an absolute size, you use a number followed by a unit of measurement. The most common unit of measurement for Web pages is *px*, which stands for pixels. (An average size for text is 10 pixels.) Pixels are the native unit of measurement for computer monitor display modes. HTML also accepts inches (in), centimeters (cm), millimeters (mm), points (pt), and picas (pc), but those units are most appropriate when working with a page designed to be printed.

The size of a pixel depends on the display resolution of the monitor. For example, suppose someone views your page using a 17-inch monitor at 800 × 600 resolution. The monitor's size is measured diagonally, so it's about 13.6 inches wide and 10.2 inches tall. If 10.2 inches high represents 600 pixels, there are about 60 pixels per inch vertically. Therefore, a 15-pixel character height translates into about 1/4 of an inch onscreen. Now suppose the display resolution is 1024 × 768. That means there are about 77 pixels per inch vertically; a 15-pixel character height translates into about 1/5 of an inch onscreen.

Note HTML does not usually accept a numeric size without a unit of measurement. There are a few exceptions, though; one is the line-height style you will learn about in Chapter 8.

To specify a relative size, you use a relational description: xx-small, x-small, small, medium, large, x-large, or xx-large. The exact size of each of those specifications depends on the base size within the parent tag. Here are some examples of fonts at those various sizes.

xx-small
x-small
small
medium (the default)
large

x-large

Note There is not a big difference between xx-small and x-small, especially in Internet Explorer 9.

You can define a font size for an entire tag in the style sheet like this:

```
p {font-size: 12px}
```

Or, embed it in a single paragraph's tag like this:

```
<p style="font-size: x-small">This text is extra-small.</p>
```

You can also specify relative sizing as a percentage of the base size, such as 120%. Another way to specify relative sizing is in ems. An *em* is a multiplier of the base font; for example, 2 em is two times the base size, or 200%.

For example, you could make text tagged as *<h3>* twice the size of the base font by including this in the style sheet, as shown in the following:

```
h1 {font-size: 2em}
```

Or, you could set the size for an individual heading, like this:

```
<p style="font-size: 2em">This text is twice the base size.</p>
```

To specify a font color, use the *color* attribute that you learned in previous chapters. For example, to make text in all *<p>* tags blue, place this style rule in the style sheet, as shown this example:

```
p {color: blue}
```

To include the `color` attribute for a single tag, include it in the *style=* attribute like this:

```
<p style="color: blue">This is blue text.</p>
```

You can use the basic or extended color names, as described in Chapter 4, "Using Lists and Backgrounds," or use hexadecimal or RGB naming. Refer to the colors.htm, extended.htm, and websafe.htm files in the Reference folder of the downloadable companion content for full-color swatches of these groups of colors.

Remember from Chapter 4 that the *color* attribute refers to the foreground color, or the color of the text. You can also set a background color for the text. This is different from the background color in the document itself. The *color* attribute refers only to the text within the tag in which it is applied. For example, you could use foreground and background color selections to create reverse text (set white text on a dark background). To do this, in the style sheet, use the *background-color* attribute, such as the following:

```
p {background-color: yellow}
```

Or, for an individual instance, like this:

```
<p style="background-color: yellow">This text has a yellow background.</p>
```

In this exercise, you will assign a font size to certain tags in an external style sheet. You will also set a background color and text color for a class.

SET UP Use the *index.htm* and *default.css* files in the practice folder for this topic. These files are located in the Documents\Microsoft Press\HTML5 SBS\07Text\ SelectingSize folder. Open the *default.css* style sheet file in Notepad and open the *index.htm* file in Internet Explorer.

1. In the default style sheet, change the style rule for the *<p>* and *<li>* tags so they include a font size of **13px**.

   ```
   p, li {font-family: "Verdana", "Arial", "Helvetica", sans-serif; font-size:
   13px}
   ```

   Note Don't forget to add the semicolon after *sans-serif* to separate the *font-family* rule from the *font-size* rule.

2. Change the style rule for the *copyright* class to make the text white.

   ```
   .copyright {font-family: "Times New Roman", "Times", serif; color: white}
   ```

3. Change the style rule for the *copyright* class to make the background green.

   ```
   .copyright {font-family: "Times New Roman", "Times", serif; color: white;
   background-color: green}
   ```

Add a font size

```
default.css - Notepad
File  Edit  Format  View  Help
hr {color: green; background-color: green; height: 3px;}
ul {list-style-type: square}
ul ul {list-style-type: disc}
ul ul ul {list-style-type: circle}
a:link {color: blue}
a:visited {color: green}
a:hover {color: lime}
a:active {color: red}
ol {list-style-type: upper-roman}
p, li {font-family: "Verdana", "Arial", "Helvetica", sans-serif; font-size: 13px}
.copyright {font-family: "Times New Roman", "Times", serif; color: white; background-color:
green}
```

Add a color and
a background color

4. Save the file, and then refresh the Internet Explorer display to view the effect of the changes.

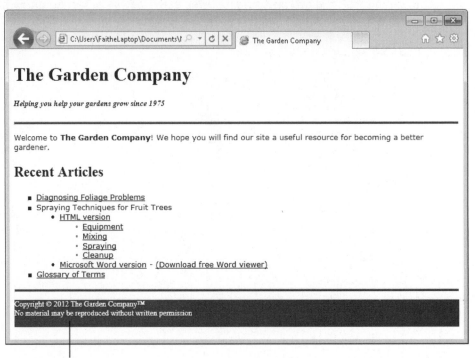

Hyperlink not visible

Notice that because the background color is the same color as the visited hyperlink color, the *Contact the Webmaster* hyperlink is no longer visible at the bottom of the page. (If you have not yet visited this hyperlink on your PC, the hyperlink might appear blue instead of being invisible.) This occurs because an *a:visited* style rule has a higher priority than the *a* class in the style sheet. To force the hyperlink to be white, you must enter a style in an internal style sheet for the document (that is, a style sheet created in the *<head>* section of the page, as you learned in Chapter 6), or create an attribute for the individual instance's tag.

5. In the *<a>* tag for the *mailto* hyperlink at the bottom of the file, add a *style=* attribute that forces the hyperlink to be white.

```
<a href="mailto:webmaster@contoso.com?subject=Question/Comment" title=
"webmaster@contoso.com" style="color: white">Contact the Webmaster</a></p>
```

6. Save the file, and then refresh the Internet Explorer display.

Copyright © 2012 The Garden Company™
No material may be reproduced without written permission
Contact the Webmaster

 CLEAN UP Close the Notepad and Internet Explorer windows.

Applying Bold and Italics

You learned how to apply bold and italic formatting by using the *<b>* and *<i>* tags in Part 1 of this book. You can continue to use those tags to format individual words and phrases, but you can't use them in internal or external style sheets.

To include boldface in a style, use the *font-weight* attribute. For example, you might create a class called *boldface* in your style sheet like this:

```
.boldface {font-weight: bold}
```

You can apply the boldface class to all text elements of a specified type, for example, all paragraphs, in style sheets.

```
p {font-weight: bold}
```

You can also apply it by using a *style=* attribute in an individual paragraph.

```
<p style="font-weight: bold">This text is bold.</p>
```

One of the advantages of using a style for bold formatting instead of the *<b>* tag is that you can control the intensity of the effect. You can specify *bolder*, *lighter*, or a numeric value from *100* (the lightest) to *900* (the darkest) to indicate the amount of bold formatting. However, the differences in the effects are noticeable only when using a font that supports multiple levels of boldface. Because most fonts have only two weights (normal and bold), not all the numeric values render differently. The following image shows the various settings in Arial, which has three weights. Look specifically at the difference in the bold formatting applied to the 600 and 700 entries versus the 800 and 900.

This is normal text.

This is bold applied with the b tag.

This is font-weight: bold

This is font-weight: bolder

This is font-weight: lighter

This is font-weight: 100

This is font-weight: 200

This is font-weight: 300

This is font-weight: 400

This is font-weight: 500

This is font-weight: 600

This is font-weight: 700

This is font-weight: 800

This is font-weight: 900

To apply italic formatting, use the *font-style* attribute. The font style can be *normal* (not italic), *italic*, or *oblique*. Oblique is also called "false italics" because it is a right-tilted version of normal (non-italic) text. Some fonts have a separate set of characters for italic, so there is a difference between oblique and italic; for fonts that do not, there is no difference. Most people prefer to use italic. You can apply italic formatting in a style rule for paragraphs.

```
p {font-style: italic}
```

This rule would make all the *<p>* text within the document italicized. If you then wanted make a certain paragraph appear without italic formatting, you might include a style tag in that paragraph's *<p>* tag like this:

```
<p style="font-style: normal">This paragraph is not italicized.</p>
```

In this exercise, you will apply bold and italic styles to ordered and unordered lists.

 SET UP Use the *foliage.htm* file in the practice folder for this topic. This file is located in the Documents\Microsoft Press\HTML5 SBS\07Text\ApplyingBold folder. Open the *foliage* file in Notepad and in Internet Explorer.

1. In the *<style>* section, add bold formatting to the definition of an ordered list.

   `ol {list-style-type: decimal; `**`font-weight: bold`**`}`

2. Save the file, and then refresh the Internet Explorer display to see the change.

   The text of the entire list becomes bold.

3. Create a new style rule for unordered lists, setting the font weight to normal.

   `ul {font-weight: normal}`

4. Save the file, and then refresh the display in Internet Explorer.

   The unordered list items are no longer bold, but the ordered list items are.

5. Create a new style rule for unordered lists within unordered lists, setting the font style to italic.

   `ul ul {font-style: italic}`

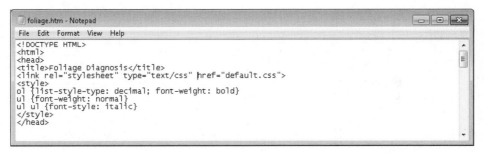

6. Save the file, and then refresh the display in Internet Explorer.

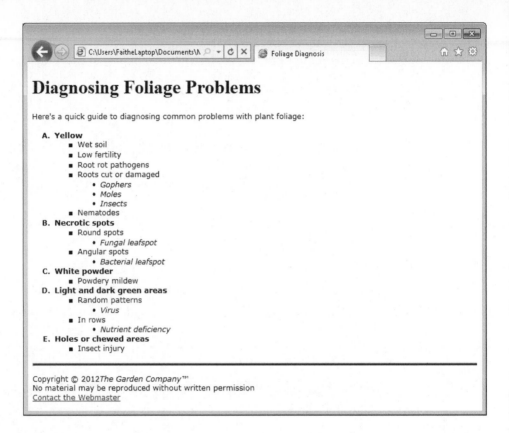

CLEAN UP Close the Notepad and Internet Explorer windows.

Applying Strikethrough and Underlining

Strikethrough formatting is typically used to denote text that has changed. For example, if you have marked down the price of an item, you might strike through the original price.

List price: ~~$24.00~~ <u>Now only $9.99</u>

Most Web designers don't use underlining as a formatting technique because hyperlinks are underlined, and it is considered poor design to confuse your users with text that looks "clickable" but is not. In the example just shown, for instance, you might think that the text *Now only $9.99* is a hyperlink, but it's not; it's just underlined.

If you simply want to underline or strike through a few words of text in one specific instance that probably won't recur elsewhere on your page (or site), it's easiest to use the *<ins>* tag for underlining or the *<del>* tag for strikethrough. These tag names come from the logical functions that underlining and strikethrough often serve in an edited document; insertions are commonly underlined, and deletions are commonly struck through. Here's the code for the preceding example:

```
<p>List price: <del>$24.00</del> <ins>Now only $9.99</ins></p>
```

Note In early HTML versions, there was a *<strike>* or *<s>* tag for strikethrough and a *<u>* tag for underlining, but both were deprecated in HTML4 and removed completely in HTML5. The *<ins>* and *<del>* tags will probably become deprecated at some point, but for now they are still in use.

To strike through or underline text by using a style (a more modern and "correct" method, although it requires a little more typing), use the *text-decoration* attribute. This attribute accepts several keywords:

- underline
- overline (line over the text)
- line-through (strikethrough)
- blink (flashing text)
- none (removes all inherited decoration)

Caution Do not use blinking text if at all possible. It is quite annoying. Visitors to your site will probably dislike it so much that they will leave your site and never return.

You can use the *none* keyword to remove the underlining from text that would ordinarily be underlined automatically, such as a hyperlink. Be careful, though, because if you remove the underline from a hyperlink, many people will not realize they can click it. Here are some examples applied to individual paragraphs:

```
<p style="text-decoration: underline">This looks clickable, but isn't.</p>
<p style="text-decoration: line-through">This is struck-through.</p>
<p style="text-decoration: blink">Congratulations, you win!</p>
```

Here's an example of underlining applied within a style sheet to a class called underlined:

```
.underlined {text-decoration: underline}
```

In this exercise, you will remove the underlining from a hyperlink.

 SET UP Use the *index.htm* file in the practice folder for this topic. This file is located in the Documents\Microsoft Press\HTML5 SBS\07Text\ApplyingStrike folder. Open the *index* file in Notepad and in Internet Explorer.

1. In the *<a>* tag for the Contact the Webmaster hyperlink at the bottom of the document, add a *text-decoration* attribute that removes the underline.

   ```
   <a href="mailto:webmaster@contoso.com?subject=Question/Comment" title=
   "webmaster@contoso.com" style="color: white; text-decoration:none">Contact
   the Webmaster</a></p>
   ```

2. Save the file, and then refresh the Internet Explorer display.

   The hyperlink is no longer underlined, but you can still point at it to see its Screen-Tip, indicating it is still a live hyperlink.

3. Use the *<del>* tag to strike through the word *Webmaster*, and insert **Master Gardener** in boldface following it. (Use the *<b>* tag for the boldface.)

   ```
   <a href="mailto:webmaster@contoso.com?subject=Question/Comment" title=
   "webmaster@contoso.com" style="color: white; text-decoration:none">Contact
   the <del>Webmaster</del><b>Master Gardener</b></a></p>
   ```

4. Save the file, and then refresh the Internet Explorer display.

   Copyright © 2012 The Garden Company™
   No material may be reproduced without written permission
   Contact the ~~Webmaster~~**Master Gardener**

 CLEAN UP Close the Notepad and Internet Explorer windows.

Creating Inline Spans

Part of the problem with replacing the old style tags like *<b>*, *<i>*, and *<del>* with styles for individual items is that the *style=* attribute must be placed within an existing tag. For example, in the following sentence, how would you avoid using *<b>* to make only one word bold?

```
<p>I had a <b>great</b> time.</p>
```

The word *great* does not have any container tags surrounding it, so there's no place to put a *style=* attribute. The solution is to use an *inline span*. A span is simply a shell into which you can place any attributes you need. For example, the preceding example could be written as follows to use a style:

```
<p>I had a <span style="text-weight: bold">great</span> time.</p>
```

That's an awful lot of typing, but there's a good reason for it. By using a span, you can apply a class, and by applying a class you can create consistency. For example, suppose you know that you want to make new vocabulary words stand out somehow, but you haven't yet decided whether you want to make them bold, italicized, or both. You can create a class called *vocabulary*, and apply that class to each vocabulary word.

```
<span class="vocabulary">Deciduous</span>
```

Then in your style sheet, you can define the class with the formatting you want. Suppose, for example, that you decide to make vocabulary words italicized. Simply create a style that defines *vocabulary* as italic:

```
.vocabulary {font-style: italic}
```

If you later change your mind, you need to make the change in only one place—the style sheet.

In this exercise, you will format text by using inline spans.

SET UP Use the *bestsellers.htm* file in the practice folder for this topic. This file is located in the Documents\Microsoft Press\HTML5 SBS\07Text\CreatingSpan folder. Open the *bestsellers* file in Notepad and in Internet Explorer.

1. Create a span around the company name in each of the list items, and assign a class called *company* to each one.

```
<ol>
    <li><span class="company">Sampson & Company </span>All-Natural
Pesticide</li>
    <li><span class="company">Vickers and Vickers </span>Fertilizer
Sticks</li>
    <li><span class="company">Appleton Acres </span>Big Sack of Bulbs,
Tulips</li>
    <li><span class="company">Jackson and Perkins </span>Climbing
Rosebushes</li>
    <li><span class="company">Easton </span>Create-Your-Own Paving Stones
Kit</li>
    <li><span class="company">Appleton Acres </span>Big Sack of Bulbs,
Daffodils</li>
    <li><span class="company">Appleton Acres </span>Big Sack of Bulbs,
Hyacinths</li>
    <li><span class="company">Appleton Acres </span>Big Sack of Bulbs,
Crocuses</li>
    <li><span class="company">Hawthorne Hills </span>Hosta, 3-Pack</li>
    <li><span class="company">Sampson & Company </span>All-Natural
Herbicide</li>
</ol>
```

Tip Use the Clipboard to copy and paste the opening and closing *<span>* tags to save time. They are identical for each entry.

Note In the above example, the space following the text in each span is included within the span. The space could have gone outside of the span instead. If the class applied to the span specifies a very different font size than used outside the span, the placement of the space inside versus outside could make a difference in how the text appears onscreen; in this exercise's example, it makes no difference.

2. In the *<style>* section of the document, create a style that defines the company class as bold, italic, and red.

```
.company {font-style: italic; font-weight: bold; color: red}
```

3. Save the file, and then refresh the Internet Explorer display.

 CLEAN UP Close the Notepad and Internet Explorer windows.

Adjusting Spacing Between Letters

In many desktop publishing applications, you can fine-tune the spacing between letters to subtly change the appearance of a paragraph. Thanks to styles, you can do the same thing in HTML.

There are two types of spacing you can control in HTML: word spacing and letter spacing. Word spacing controls the amount of space between each word, and letter spacing controls the amount of space between each letter. The default is 0 for each; positive numbers increase the space and negative numbers decrease it. Usually, one or two pixels in either direction is plenty.

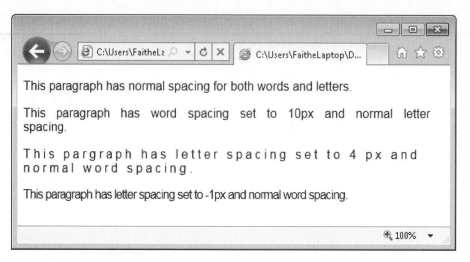

To apply word and/or letter spacing, add spacing to the *style=* attribute for a specific tag.

```
<p style="letter-spacing: 4px">This text has increased letter spacing.</p>
```

You can also add spacing to a style rule in the style sheet.

```
p {letter-spacing: 4px}
```

In this exercise, you will increase the word and letter spacing for all paragraphs and headings in a document.

SET UP Use the *spray.htm* file in the practice folder for this topic. This file is located in the Documents\Microsoft Press\HTML5 SBS\07Text\AdjustingSpacing folder. Open the *spray* file in Notepad and in Internet Explorer.

1. Examine the document in Internet Explorer. Note the overall look and the spacing between words and letters.

2. In the *<head>* section, create the following *<style>* section:

```
<style>
h1, h2, p {word-spacing: 1px; letter-spacing: 1px}
</style>
```

3. Save the file, and then refresh the Internet Explorer display.

   Notice the spacing difference. It's not very attractive, but it's different. The difference is also enhanced by the fact that this document does not yet have the cascading style sheet applied to it.

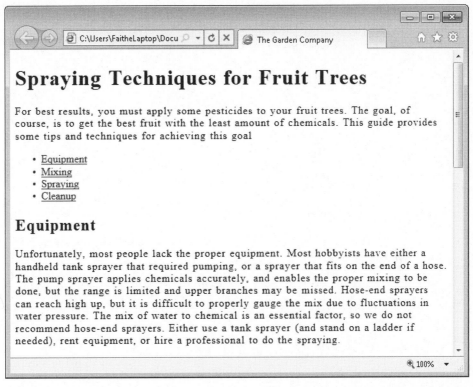

4. Apply the *default.css* cascading style sheet to the document by inserting the following code in the *<head>* section (but not within the *<style>* tag):

   ```
   <link rel="stylesheet" type="text/css" href="default.css">
   ```

5. Edit the embedded style sheet to decrease the line spacing and word spacing to **0.5px**.

   ```
   h1, h2, p {word-spacing: 0.5px; letter-spacing: 0.5px}
   ```

6. Save the file, and then refresh the Internet Explorer display.

   Now it looks more attractive, and is more consistent with the rest of the pages for this Web site.

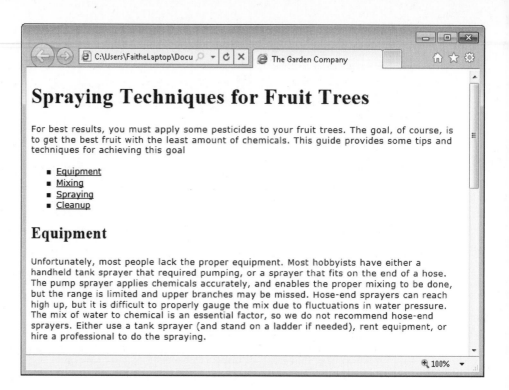

 CLEAN UP Close the Notepad and Internet Explorer windows.

Key Points

- Font families are sets of fonts, listed in order of preference. Because not all Web visitors have the same fonts installed on their computers, you should use the *font-family* attribute to help ensure that your Web site appears the way you want.

- Font size is typically measured in pixels (px) for onscreen display. To specify size, use the *font-size* attribute.

- You can define font color by using any color description method, including RGB, hexadecimal, and color names. Use the color attribute to define font color.

- To set the background color for text, use the *background-color* attribute. To set the background color for a paragraph, insert a *style= attribute* in the *<p>* tag.

- You can still use the *<b>* tag to apply bold formatting and the *<i>* tag to apply italic formatting. In style sheets, you can also apply bold formatting by using the *font-weight: bold* attribute, and italic formatting by using the *font-style: italic* attribute.

- For individual instances of strikethrough formatting, you can use the *<del>* tag; for individual instances of underlining, use the *<ins>* tag. To apply this formatting by using styles, use *font-decoration: line-through* and *font-decoration: underline*.

- Inline spans create tags that serve as containers for attributes. Use the *<span>* tag to surround any amount of text to be marked in some way.

- Use the *word-spacing* attribute to define an amount of space between words. Use *letter-spacing* to define space between letters. The default amount is 0; specify a positive number to increase spacing or a negative number to decrease it.

Chapter at a Glance

Clean the tank, sprayer, and all protective gear with clean water. Use soap on your protective gear and rinse with running water, and then allow them to air-dry.

Apply a border to a paragraph, **page 130**

Specify the horizontal alignment of a paragraph, **page 135**

Specify vertical space within a paragraph, **page 137**

8 Formatting Paragraphs by Using Style Sheets

In this chapter, you will learn how to

✔ Indent paragraphs.

✔ Apply a border to a paragraph.

✔ Specify the horizontal alignment of a paragraph.

✔ Specify vertical space within a paragraph.

In Chapter 7, "Formatting Text by Using Style Sheets," you learned how to use style rules to apply character formatting, including font style, size, and color. Now you can go a step further and apply those concepts to paragraph formatting.

Paragraph formatting refers to the layout of entire paragraphs, not the placement or spacing of individual characters. For example, a paragraph can be double-spaced, but an individual character cannot. You saw some style-based paragraph formatting in Chapter 4, "Using Lists and Backgrounds," when you applied bullet characters and numbering styles. Later, in Chapter 6, "Introduction to Style Sheets," you worked with several ordered and unordered list items. The same principles apply when formatting other types of paragraphs.

In this chapter, you'll learn how to control indentation and spacing around a paragraph, and how to specify a paragraph's alignment. You'll also learn how to set the line height for a paragraph (that is, the space between lines of text) and how to place and format a border around a paragraph.

See Also Do you need only a quick refresher on the topics in this chapter? See the Key Points at the end of this chapter.

> **Practice Files**   Before you can use the practice files provided for this chapter, you need to install them from the book's companion content page to their default locations. See "Using the Practice Files" in the beginning of this book for more information.

Indenting Paragraphs

You can indent any paragraph-level element in HTML. Such elements include regular paragraphs, list items, definitions, quotations, and headings. *Indenting* is the process of offsetting text from its usual position, either to the right or to the left. You can apply three types of indentation in HTML:

- **First-line indent**   This indents only the first line of a paragraph. Use the *text-indent* attribute. For in-line styling of a single paragraph, specify this style:

  ```
  <p style="text-indent: 20px">
  ```

  In a style sheet, specify a rule similar to this:

  ```
  p {text-indent: 20px}
  ```

- **Padding**   This adds a specified amount of space between the border of an element and its contents (*inside* of the element). It applies equally to all lines of text in the paragraph. Use the *padding* attribute to create this space. For in-line styling of a single paragraph, specify this style:

  ```
  <p style="padding: 20px">
  ```

  In a style sheet, specify a rule like this:

  ```
  p {padding: 20px}
  ```

- **Margin**   This adds a specified amount of white space around an element, on the *outside* of the element. It applies equally to all lines of text in the paragraph. Use the *margin* attribute to create this space. For a single paragraph, specify this style:

  ```
  <p style="margin: 20px">
  ```

  In a style sheet, specify the following rule:

  ```
  p {margin: 20px}
  ```

The difference between applying the *padding* and *margin* attributes is most apparent when the paragraph has a visible border, or when the paragraph's background contrasts with the surrounding area. You'll learn how to apply borders later in this chapter, but here's a quick comparison. Padding adds space between the text and the border.

Equipment

> Unfortunately, most people lack the proper equipment. Most hobbyists have either a handheld tank sprayer that required pumping, or a sprayer that fits on the end of a hose. The pump sprayer applies chemicals accurately, and enables the proper mixing to be done, but the range is limited and upper branches may be missed. Hose-end sprayers can reach high up, but it is difficult to properly gauge the mix due to fluctuations in water pressure. The mix of water to chemical is an essential factor, so we do not recommend hose-end sprayers. Either use a tank sprayer (and stand on a ladder if needed), rent equipment, or hire a professional to do the spraying.

Padding: added space is inside

In contrast, margins add space outside the border.

Equipment

> Unfortunately, most people lack the proper equipment. Most hobbyists have either a handheld tank sprayer that required pumping, or a sprayer that fits on the end of a hose. The pump sprayer applies chemicals accurately, and enables the proper mixing to be done, but the range is limited and upper branches may be missed. Hose-end sprayers can reach high up, but it is difficult to properly gauge the mix due to fluctuations in water pressure. The mix of water to chemical is an essential factor, so we do not recommend hose-end sprayers. Either use a tank sprayer (and stand on a ladder if needed), rent equipment, or hire a professional to do the spraying.

Margins: added space is outside

By default, *margin* and *padding* attributes apply to all four sides of an element, but you can add *-top*, *-right*, *-bottom*, or *-left* arguments to restrict the formatting to one or more specific sides.

```
p style="padding-left: 10px; padding-top: 5px; padding-bottom: 5px}
```

You can use either pixels (*px*) or percentage (%) as the unit of measure. For example, the following line indents the first line of a paragraph by 10 percent of its total width:

```
<p style="text-indent: 10%">
```

To apply the same formatting using a style sheet, specify the following rule:

```
p {text-indent: 10%}
```

In this exercise, you will indent the first line of each paragraph in an article and add padding to the left and right sides of all paragraphs. Then you will create a CSS class that removes the first-line indent and applies that class style to some individual paragraphs.

SET UP Use the *spray.htm* file in the practice file folder for this topic. This file is located in the Documents\Microsoft Press\HTML5 SBS\08Paragraphs\Indenting folder. Open the *spray.htm* file in Notepad and in Internet Explorer.

1. In the *<style>* area, create a style for the *<p>* tag that inserts 20 pixels of padding at the left and indents the first line by 20 pixels.

   ```
   p {padding-left: 20px; text-indent: 20px}
   ```

2. Create a new class called *first*. Define it as having no first-line indent.

   ```
   .first {text-indent: 0px}
   ```

3. Apply the new class to the first paragraph beneath each heading.

   ```
   <h1>Spraying Techniques for Fruit Trees</h1>
   <p class="first">For best results, you must apply some pesticides to your
   fruit trees.
   ...

   <a name="equipment"><h2>Equipment</h2></a>
   <p class="first">Unfortunately, most people lack the proper equipment. Most
   ...

   <a name="mixing"><h2>Mixing</h2></a>
   <p class="first">When mixing pesticides, make sure you follow directions
   ...

   <a name="spraying"><h2>Spraying</h2></a>
   <p class="first">It is important to cover all surfaces uniformly, while not
   ...

   <a name="cleanup"><h2>Cleanup</h2></a>
   <p class="first">Clean the tank, sprayer, and all protective gear with clean
   ...
   ```

4. Save the file, and then refresh the Internet Explorer display.

   The difference between the first and subsequent paragraphs is apparent in the *Spraying* section.

5. Scroll to the bottom of the page and view the copyright notice.

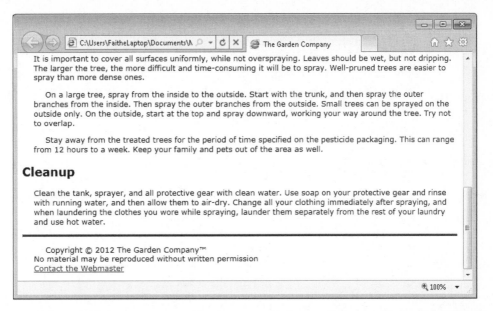

It is indented like other paragraphs, but you don't want it to be. This is an excellent example of an unintended consequence stemming from making a global change to a tag's style rules. There are several ways of removing the unwanted indentation: you could create a new class for the single line you don't want indented; you could create a span; or you could override that line's settings in its *<p>* tag. Because this situation occurs only once in the document, use the third option—change the *<p>* tag directly.

6. In the *<p>* tag for the copyright notice, add the following:

```
<p style="text-indent:0; padding:0">Copyright &copy; 2012 The Garden Company&trade;<br>
```

7. Save the file, and then refresh the Internet Explorer display.

The copyright notice now has no indentation or padding.

Copyright © 2012 The Garden Company™
No material may be reproduced without written permission
Contact the Webmaster

 CLEAN UP Close the Notepad and Internet Explorer windows.

Applying a Border to a Paragraph

You can apply a border style rule to almost any two-sided tag. Border style rules are used most commonly with regular paragraphs, but they also work with headings, lists, and even spans. You can also apply a border to a division (*<div>*) tag to differentiate one area of the screen from another, as you will see in Chapter 11, "Creating Division-Based Layouts."

Specifying a Border Style

To select the line type for the border, use the *border-style* attribute along with one of the arguments listed in the table on the following page.

Argument	Example
solid	Clean the tank, sprayer, and all protective gear with clean water. Use soap on your protective gear and rinse with running water, and then allow them to air-dry.
dotted	Clean the tank, sprayer, and all protective gear with clean water. Use soap on your protective gear and rinse with running water, and then allow them to air-dry.
dashed	Clean the tank, sprayer, and all protective gear with clean water. Use soap on your protective gear and rinse with running water, and then allow them to air-dry.
double	Clean the tank, sprayer, and all protective gear with clean water. Use soap on your protective gear and rinse with running water, and then allow them to air-dry.
groove	Clean the tank, sprayer, and all protective gear with clean water. Use soap on your protective gear and rinse with running water, and then allow them to air-dry.
ridge	Clean the tank, sprayer, and all protective gear with clean water. Use soap on your protective gear and rinse with running water, and then allow them to air-dry.

Argument	Example
inset	Clean the tank, sprayer, and all protective gear with clean water. Use soap on your protective gear and rinse with running water, and then allow them to air-dry.
outset	Clean the tank, sprayer, and all protective gear with clean water. Use soap on your protective gear and rinse with running water, and then allow them to air-dry.
none	Clean the tank, sprayer, and all protective gear with clean water. Use soap on your protective gear and rinse with running water, and then allow them to air-dry.

To apply a border style to an individual instance of a tag, use the following:

```
<p style="border-style: solid">
```

To apply the same formatting using a style sheet, specify the following rule:

```
p {border-style: solid}
```

Setting Border Padding

A border encloses the element very tightly by default. You will usually want to add a little more spacing. Create the spacing using the *padding* attribute. To apply padding using a style sheet, specify the following rule:

```
p {border-style: solid; padding: 15px}
```

To apply the same formatting to an individual instance of a tag, use the following:

```
<p style="border-style: solid; padding: 15px">
```

Specifying Border Width and Color

By default, a border is black and 4 pixels wide. To change these attributes, use the *border-color* and *border-width* attributes. The color can be any basic or extended color name or any RGB or hexadecimal color number. (See the discussion of color choices in Chapter 4 if you need to review the color options in HTML.) For example, to decrease the border width and color it blue using a style sheet, write a rule like this:

```
p {border-style: solid; border-width: 2px; border-color: blue}
```

To apply the same formatting to an individual instance of a tag, use this:

```
<p style="border-style: solid; border-width: 2px; border-color: blue">
```

Note The default border style is *none*—and that doesn't change just because you specify a border width and color. Don't forget to turn a border on by including the *border-style* attribute in addition to specifying the border's color and width.

Formatting Border Sides Individually

By default, border attributes apply to all four sides of the border unless you specify otherwise. To specify that a certain side of the border has special formatting, include the *-top*, *-right*, *-left*, or *-bottom* argument between the word *border* and the property being set. For example, to set a color other than black for the top border using a style sheet, use the following:

```
p {border-style: solid; border-top-color: blue}
```

To apply the same formatting to an individual instance of a tag, use this:

```
<p style="border-style: solid; border-top-color: blue">
```

You can use this technique not only with *border-color,* but with *style, padding,* and *width* attributes as well. For example, the following rule applies a dotted line and 15 pixels of padding to only the top and bottom of a paragraph:

```
<p style="border-top-style: dotted; border-bottom-style: dotted; padding-top:
15px; padding-bottom: 15px">
```

Here's how the rendered paragraph looks:

••

Clean the tank, sprayer, and all protective gear with clean water. Use soap on your
protective gear and rinse with running water, and then allow them to air-dry.

••

There's a shortcut for specifying arguments for each side of the border. Rather than writing each one out individually, you can simply include four different settings for the argument. Specify them in clockwise order, starting at the top: *top, right, bottom, left*. Using this method, the example you just saw could be written like this:

```
<p style="border-style: dotted none dotted none; padding: 15px 0px 15px 0px">
```

Specifying fewer than four arguments applies the formatting differently. Specifying two arguments sets the top and bottom border attributes, while specifying three arguments sets the top, bottom, and left/right (same settings for both) border attributes.

Setting All Border Attributes at Once

A similar shortcut lets you specify border attributes for all four sides at once. Use the *border* attribute, and then specify all the settings together in the following order: *size*, *color*, *style*.

```
<p style="border: 2px green solid">
```

You can use the single *border* attribute when all sides are the same, but you cannot combine it with individual border-formatting attributes. For example, the following would *not* work:

```
<p style="border: 2px green dotted none dotted none">
```

In this next exercise, you will add top and bottom borders to a paragraph.

SET UP Use the *spray.htm* file in the practice file folder for this topic. This file is located in the Documents\Microsoft Press\HTML5 SBS\08Paragraphs\AddingBorders folder. Open the *spray* file in Notepad and in Internet Explorer.

1. In the *spray.htm file*, locate the following paragraph (about three-quarters of the way down the document).

   ```
   <p>Stay away from the treated trees for the period of time specified on the
   pesticide packaging. This can range from 12 hours to a week. Keep your fam-
   ily and pets out of the area as well.</p>
   ```

2. Add dotted top and bottom borders to the paragraph.

   ```
   <p style="border-top-style: dotted; border-bottom-style: dotted">Stay away
   from the treated trees for the period of time specified on the pesticide
   packaging. This can range from 12 hours for a week. Keep your family and
   pets out of the area as well.</p>
   ```

3. Save the file, and then refresh the Internet Explorer display.

4. Locate the bordered paragraph in the *Spraying* section.

   Notice that the paragraph still has its first-line indent, and the border is close to the top and bottom of the paragraph text.

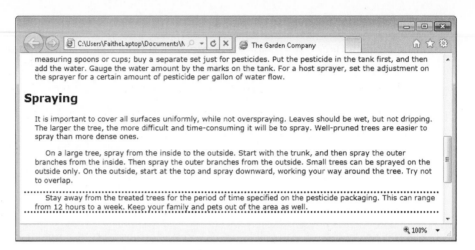

5. Add **5px** (five pixels) of padding to the top and bottom of the border, and remove the first-line indent from the paragraph.

```
<p style="border-top-style: dotted; border-bottom-style: dotted; padding-top: 5px; padding-bottom: 5px; text-indent: 0">Stay away from the treated trees for the period of time specified on the pesticide packaging. This can range from 12 hours to a week. Keep your family and pets out of the area as well.</p>
```

6. Change the width of the border to **6px** (six pixels), and set its color to **green**.

```
<p style="border-top-style: dotted; border-bottom-style: dotted; padding-top: 5px; padding-bottom: 5px; text-indent: 0; border-width: 6px; border-color: green">Stay away from the treated trees for the period of time specified on the pesticide packaging. This can range from 12 hours to a week. Keep your family and pets out of the area as well.</p>
```

7. Save the file, and then refresh the Internet Explorer display.

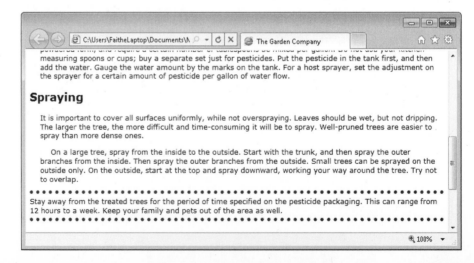

8. Rewrite the border specification to be as concise as possible.

   ```
   <p style="border: 6px green; border-style: dotted none dotted none; padding:
   5px 0px 5px 0px; text-indent: 0">Stay away from the treated trees for the
   period of time specified on the pesticide packaging. This can range from 12
   hours to a week. Keep your family and pets out of the area as well.</p>
   ```

9. Save the file, and then refresh the Internet Explorer display. Even though the HTML code changed, the screen should look the same.

✖ **CLEAN UP** Close the Notepad and Internet Explorer windows.

Specifying the Horizontal Alignment of a Paragraph

Alignment refers to the placement of a paragraph within its container. You can specify horizontal alignment in a style using the *text-align* attribute. You can apply alignment only to block-level elements, such as paragraphs, list items, headings, and so on. (A *block-level element* is one that occupies a complete paragraph or more.) The default alignment setting is *left*; the other choices are *center*, *right*, and *justify*, as shown in the following example:

This paragraph is left-aligned. The edges align neatly at the left, and the right edge is ragged. This paragraph is left-aligned. The edges align neatly at the left, and the right edge is ragged.

This paragraph is centered. The midpoints of each line are centered on the page, with ragged edges at left and right. This paragraph is centered. The midpoints of each line are centered on the page, with ragged edges at left and right.

This paragraph is right-aligned. The edges align neatly at the right, and the left edge is ragged. This paragraph is right-aligned. The edges align neatly at the right, and the left edge is ragged.

This paragraph is justified. The edges align neatly at both the left and right, and extra space is inserted between words to make that happen. This paragraph is justified. The edges align neatly at both the left and right, and extra space is inserted between words to make that happen.

Notice that the *justify* option aligns all lines of the paragraph (except the last one) at both the right and left. The last line of a justified paragraph is always left-aligned. Justified text can sometimes result in awkwardly spaced lines, especially when the text column is fairly narrow, such as in the following example:

```
This  paragraph is
justified.     The
edges         align
neatly    at   both
the left and right,
and  extra  space
is         inserted
between      words
to   make     that
happen.      This
paragraph       is
justified.     The
edges         align
neatly    at   both
the left and right,
and  extra  space
is         inserted
between      words
to   make     that
happen.
```

On a full-size Web page, justified paragraphs should not be a problem, because there is enough text to ensure even spacing. However, when you start working with table-based or division-based page layouts (such as those presented in Part 3 of this book) you might have some narrow columns of text like the one in the previous example. Avoid using justified alignment for text in narrow columns whenever possible.

In this exercise, you will change the alignment of certain elements by editing the embedded style sheet.

 SET UP Use the *spray.htm* file in the practice file folder for this topic. This file is located in the Documents\Microsoft Press\HTML5 SBS\08Paragraphs\Indenting folder. Open the *spray* file in Notepad and in Internet Explorer.

1. In the *<style>* area, create the following style rule:

   `h1, h2, {text-align: center}`

2. Save the file, and then refresh the Internet Explorer display.

3. Change the style definition for the *<p>* tag to use justified alignment.

   `p {text-indent: 20px; padding-left: 20px; text-indent: 20px; `**`text-align: justify}`**

4. Save the file, and then refresh the Internet Explorer display.

 CLEAN UP Close the Notepad and Internet Explorer windows.

Specifying Vertical Space within a Paragraph

The line height is the amount of space between each line. This is also referred to as *leading* (pronounced like the metal). You can use this setting to make paragraphs easier to read. You are not limited to just single-spacing or double-spacing like on a typewriter; you can specify any amount of space you like.

You can express line height either as a number or as a percentage. If you use a number, it's a fixed measurement (usually in pixels). If you later increase or decrease the font size, the line height will not change. If you use a percentage, the browser multiplies the line height percentage by the font size to derive a spacing amount. For example, you can specify 200 percent to make a paragraph double-spaced. If you later change the font size, the line height will be recalculated using the new font size. To specify the line height in a style sheet, set the *line-height* attribute, as follows:

```
p {line-height: 150%}
```

To specify the same formatting in an individual tag, use the following:

```
<p style="line-height: 150%">
```

In this exercise, you will change the line height of certain elements by editing the embedded style sheet.

 SET UP Use the *spray.htm* file in the practice file folder for this topic. This file is located in the Documents\Microsoft Press\HTML5 SBS\08Paragraphs\Indenting folder. Open the *spray* file in Notepad and in Internet Explorer.

1. In the *<style>* area, modify the style rule for the *<p>* tag by setting the line height to **150%**.

   ```
   p {text-indent: 20px; padding-left: 20px; text-indent: 20px; text-align:
   justify; line-height: 150%}
   ```

2. Create a style rule. Set the line height of list items to **125%**.

   ```
   li {line-height: 125%}
   ```

3. Save the file, and then refresh the Internet Explorer display to see the results.

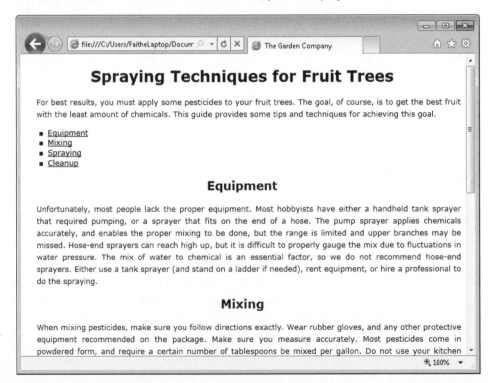

 CLEAN UP Close the Notepad and Internet Explorer windows.

Key Points

- You can indent the first line of paragraphs using the *text-indent* attribute.

- The *Padding* attribute sets the amount of space between an element and its border; the *margin* attribute sets the amount of space around the outside of an element.

- The *Border-style* attribute places a border around a paragraph. To specify the appearance of the border, use one of the following arguments: *solid, dotted, dashed, double, groove, ridge, inset, outset,* or *none*.

- To set the width of a border, use the *border-width* attribute followed by the width in pixels (*px*).

- To set the color of a border, use the *border-color* attribute followed by the color name or the RGB or hexadecimal notation for the color.

- To format each side of a border individually, specify four arguments, in clockwise order from the top: *top, right, bottom, left*. For example, *border-style: solid none solid bottom*.

- To specify the style, color, and size of a border in a single command, use the *border* attribute and specify the arguments in this order: *size, color, style*. For example, *border: 2px green dotted*.

- To set paragraph alignment, use the text-align attribute with one of these arguments: *left, center, right,* or *justify*.

- To set the line height, use the *line-height* attribute followed by the height expressed in pixels or as a percentage of the font height.

Chapter at a Glance

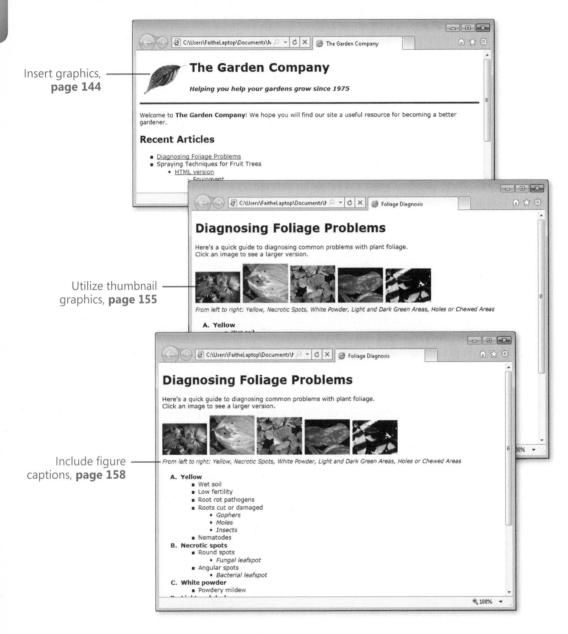

Insert graphics, **page 144**

Utilize thumbnail graphics, **page 155**

Include figure captions, **page 158**

9 Displaying Graphics

In this chapter, you will learn how to

✔ Select a graphics format.

✔ Prepare graphics for use on the Web.

✔ Insert graphics.

✔ Arrange elements on the page.

✔ Control image size and padding.

✔ Hyperlink from graphics.

✔ Utilize thumbnail graphics.

✔ Include alternate text for graphics.

✔ Add figure captions.

So far in this book, you have created text-only Web pages. They're perfectly functional, but a bit dull. Web pages are more interesting and attractive when they include graphics.

Note Graphic or image? The HTML5 specification uses the term *images*, but the term *graphic* is more popular in everyday usage. This book uses the two terms interchangeably.

In a word-processing program such as Microsoft Word, you embed graphics directly into the document. When you distribute a document to others, the graphics are included with the file. In HTML, however, each graphic displayed on a Web page is stored in a separate file which must reside on the Web server or somewhere the Web server can reach it.

In this chapter, you'll learn how to include images on a Web page and how to format and size the images. You will learn how to hyperlink from a graphic and how to create thumbnail images. You'll learn how to create alternate text that will appear if the graphic cannot load. Finally, you'll learn how to use the new HTML5 *<figure>* and *<figurecaption>* tags.

See Also Do you need only a quick refresher on the topics in this chapter? See the Key Points at the end of this chapter.

Practice Files   Before you can use the practice files provided for this chapter, you need to install them from the book's companion content page to their default locations. See "Using the Practice Files" in the beginning of this book for more information.

Selecting a Graphics Format

There are dozens of graphics formats, but most Web browsers can display only a few. The most commonly accepted formats are GIF, JPG, and PNG, so most Web designers stick to those.

Graphics formats differ from each other in the following ways:

- **Color depth**   The higher the color depth (that is, the more bits used to uniquely describe the color of each pixel), the more realistic a photo will look. Color depth is not a major issue for drawings. Full color is 24-bit; if a graphic uses more bits per pixel than that, the extra bits are typically used to further define the color (not really necessary for Web use) and/or to set special image attributes, such as transparency.

- **Compression/file size**   Graphics files tend to be large, so there are compression schemes that decrease their file size. *Lossless compression* makes a file smaller without losing any image quality; *lossy compression* shrinks a file at the expense of some quality. When the image is displayed on a computer monitor, however, the difference is minimal.

- **Animation**   Some graphics formats support a very primitive kind of animation, in which several versions of a graphic are stored in a single file, and the Web page displaying the file cycles through the images. Simple animations displayed on a Web page are usually animated graphics rather than video clips.

- **Transparency**   Some graphics formats can make the background of an image transparent. When you place the image in a document, the background color of the document shows through the transparent portions of the image. You can use this to create interesting effects. For example, when you place an image with a transparent background in a document containing text, the text wraps around the image. Delving into that technique is beyond the scope of this book, but you might want to experiment with transparency in Photoshop or some other graphics-editing program on your own.

Tip To create your own animated graphics, use a graphics program that supports that feature, such as Photoshop or Paint Shop Pro.

Different graphics formats have different color depths and compression types, so you might find that one format is appropriate in one situation but not in another. To convert a graphic to a different format, open it in any graphics program that saves in multiple formats, and then save it in a different format.

The following table lists the differences between the major Web-supported graphics formats.

Name	Color Depth	Compression	Animation	Transparency
Graphics Interchange Format (GIF)	8-bit (256 colors)	Lossless	Yes	Yes
Joint Photographic Experts Group (JPEG, JPG)	24-bit (1.6 million colors)	Lossy	No	No
Portable Network Graphics (PNG)	24-bit or 48-bit	Lossless	Yes	Yes

Preparing Graphics for Web Use

After you decide which graphics format to use for a particular image, your next decision is how large the graphic should be—that is, how many pixels it should contain. This is called the image's *resolution*, and it is expressed in width and height, always in that order. For example, an image that is 800 × 600 is 800 pixels wide and 600 pixels tall.

A graphic's *file size*—how many bytes the file will take up on disk—has a direct relationship to its resolution: the more pixels in a graphic, the larger the file. You must strike a balance between making the resolution of a graphic high enough to display optimally and low enough to download quickly when users load your page.

There are two ways of controlling the size (in pixels) of a graphic on a Web page:

- One method is to use a graphics-editing program to resize it before using it on the Web page. This method results in the smallest file size possible, which will allow your page to load more quickly. It is also more work, though, and it prevents anyone visiting your page from downloading a high-quality copy of your graphic. (That could be a good or bad thing, depending on the purpose of your page.) The exercise in "Inserting Graphics," on page 144 uses a graphic that has already been resized in this manner.

- The other way is to use attributes within the HTML code to specify the height and width at which the graphic is displayed. The Web browser will scale the graphic down to the specified size when it displays the page. With this method, the file size is larger, so the page takes longer to load. (With the popularity of broadband access these days, that shouldn't make much of a difference for most users.) This method is also useful if you need to reuse a graphic at various sizes in multiple instances. For example, perhaps you use the same graphic as a small thumbnail image in one spot and as a large featured photo in another spot. You will practice using these sizing attributes in "Controlling Image Size," on page 149.

Another consideration for graphics preparation is the color palette. If anyone viewing your page has an 8-bit display on his or her computer (that is, a display with only 256 colors), your photos will probably not look very good to them. Most graphics-editing programs, such as Photoshop and Paint Shop Pro, have features you can use to shift the colors in your photo to those that are web-safe. You might lose a bit of the image's original quality by doing this, though, so consider it only if you think that a large segment of your audience is using very old computer equipment.

Inserting Graphics

Inserting a graphic on a Web page is as simple as placing an *<img>* tag where you want the graphic to appear, like this:

```
<img src="logo.gif">
```

Note HTML5 also supports a *<figure>* tag for inserting images that is discussed later in this chapter on page 158. However *<figure>* is not a replacement for the *<img>* tag; it's a container tag into which you place an *<img>* tag. You can then use the *<figurecaption>* tag to assign a caption to the figure; the caption stays with the image wherever it floats on the page.

As you saw in Chapter 5, "Creating Hyperlinks and Anchors," when a file resides in the same folder as the HTML document that references it, you can refer to that file using the file name only, without any additional path information. If you want to store your graphics in a subfolder of the folder containing the text files (to organize your files in a more tidy fashion), you must refer to the graphic using the subfolder name, like this:

```
<img src="images/logo.gif">
```

To refer to a file that is up one level in the folder structure, use two periods and a forward slash (../), such as the following:

```
<img src="../logo.gif">
```

To refer to an image that is stored somewhere else—perhaps on your company's main Web server or at a partner's server—use the complete absolute URL to the file, as shown in the following:

```
<img src="http://i2.microsoft.com/h/all/i/ms_masthead_8x6a_ltr.jpg">
```

By default, unless you place the image within a block-level tag such as a paragraph or heading, an image blocks off all the horizontal space across the rest of the page—even if the image itself takes up only a fraction of the available horizontal space.

To force an image to render on the left or right side of the screen and wrap surrounding text around the image, apply a *float* style rule that uses a *left* or *right* attribute, like this:

```
<img src="logo.gif" style="float: left">
```

You could also create a style rule in the *<style>* area of the document or in a separate cascading style sheet that would make all images float unless otherwise specified, as shown in the following:

```
img {float: left}
```

Here's what the earlier example looks like when you float the leaf image to the left.

Here it is to the right.

Notice that floating to the right moves the image all the way to the right end of the page, not simply to the right of the text. If you want to place the image in a precise location, see the section "Positioning Divisions," in Chapter 11, "Creating Division-Based Layouts."

In this exercise, you will insert a graphic located in a subfolder and set it to float to the left of the text.

SET UP Use the *index.htm* file in the practice file folder for this topic. This file is located in the Documents\Microsoft Press\HTML5 SBS\09Graphics\InsertingImages folder. Open the *index* file in Microsoft Notepad and in Microsoft Internet Explorer.

Important If you copy the practice files for this exercise to some other location, you must also copy the default.css file and the images folder for the practice files to work properly.

1. Immediately after the opening *<body>* tag, add the following:

   ```
   <img src="images/leaf.gif">
   ```

2. Save the file, and then refresh Internet Explorer.

3. Modify the code to float the image to the left.

   ```
   <img src="images/leaf.gif" style="float: left">
   ```

4. Save the file, and then refresh Internet Explorer to check your work.

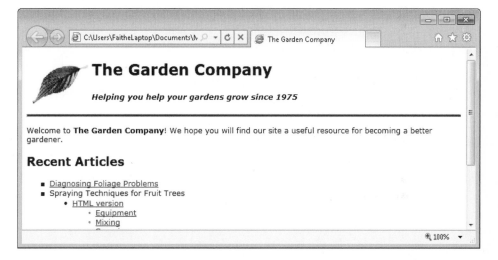

 **CLEAN UP** Close the Notepad and Internet Explorer windows.

Arranging Elements on the Page

The image in the preceding exercise was carefully prepared to be the correct size to fit in the space where it was to be inserted. But what if the image is larger?

Perhaps that's the look you want; but perhaps not. However, the example could certainly be improved by changing the placement of the *Recent Articles* heading. It should be at the left margin, aligned with the company name, and not wrapped around the graphic.

To move text down vertically until the space occupied by the graphic becomes "clear," use the clear style rule. You apply this rule to the text's tag, not to the graphic's tag. For example:

```
<h2 style="clear: left">Recent Articles</h2>
```

In this exercise, you will move the top horizontal line, and everything following it, below the graphic.

 SET UP Use the *index.htm* file in the practice file folder for this topic. This file is located in the Documents\Microsoft Press\HTML5 SBS\09Graphics\ClearingImages folder. Open the *index* file in Notepad and in Internet Explorer.

Important If you copy the practice files for this exercise to some other location, you must also copy the default.css file and the images folder for the practice files to work properly.

1. Examine the document in Internet Explorer. Notice the placement of the text in relation to the graphic.

2. In Notepad, add a *clear* style rule to the *<hr>* tag near the top:

   `<hr style="clear: left">`

3. Save the file, and then refresh Internet Explorer.

   The horizontal line, and everything that follows it, appears below the graphic.

 CLEAN UP Close the Notepad and Internet Explorer windows.

Of course, this isn't a look that you would want to keep, because there's too much white space around the graphic. But in the next exercise, you will learn how to specify the graphic's size to fix that.

Controlling Image Size and Padding

Image size is expressed in pixels. If you want, you can specify only the width; the height will be resized proportionally, or vice versa. But you also have the option to specify both the width and the height. For example, suppose the following is your original image, which is 150 pixels high:

You could add a *height="75"* attribute to the *<img>* tag, without specifying a width, like this:

```
<img src="tree.gif" style="float: left" height="75">
```

When you view the page, the image shrinks proportionally, like this:

However, if you specify both height and width of 75, like this:

```
<img src="tree.gif" style="float: left" height="75" width="75">
```

The image will be distorted, like this:

Like text, images can have margins and/or padding to separate them from surrounding elements. For example, in the example just shown, notice how close the text is to the graphic. It would be better if the text were moved slightly to the right.

As you learned in Chapter 8, "Formatting Paragraphs by Using Style Sheets," the *padding* attribute controls the space around content, on the inside of the element, and the *margin* attribute controls the space surrounding the element. You can use either attribute for an image. When the image has a border, however, it is better to use the *margin* attribute.

To increase the space around the example, you can insert a right margin specification within the style rule, like this:

```
<img src="tree.gif" style="float: left; margin-right: 10px" height="75"
width="75">
```

Notice that the margin measurement was added to the existing *style* attribute for the tag, not inserted as a separate attribute.

In this exercise, you will set the size, padding, and margin for a graphic.

SET UP Use the *index.htm* and *spray.htm* files in the practice file folder for this topic. These files are located in the Documents\Microsoft Press\HTML5 SBS\09Graphics\ SizingImages folder. Open the index file in Notepad and in Internet Explorer.

Important If you copy the practice files for this exercise to some other location, you must also copy the default.css file and the images folder for the practice files to work properly.

1. In Notepad, edit the *<img>* tag for the graphic so that the image is exactly 70 pixels in height.

   ```
   <img src="images/lg-leaf.gif" style="float: left" height="70">
   ```

2. Add a margin of five pixels to the image.

   ```
   <img src="images/lg-leaf.gif" style="float: left; margin: 5px" height="70">
   ```

3. Save the file, and then refresh Internet Explorer.

4. Open the *spray* file in Notepad and in Internet Explorer.

Notice in Internet Explorer that the graphic is too large, and the text wraps around it too tightly.

5. Edit the *<img>* tag so that the image is 350 pixels in width and has 15 pixels of padding.

```
<img src="images/apple.png" style="float: left; padding: 15px" width="350">
```

Note You could use *margin* instead of *padding* in this step.

6. Save the file, and then refresh Internet Explorer.

7. Edit the *<img>* tag so that the image floats to the right.

```
<img src="images/apple.png" style="float: right; padding: 15px" width="350">
```

8. Save the file, and then refresh Internet Explorer.

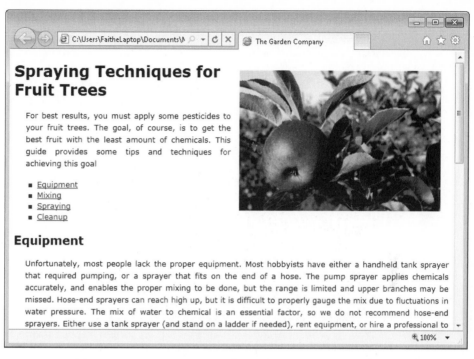

Note Because the first paragraph of the story is now narrower, the justified alignment causes the text to look a little odd. In situations like this, you might want to left-align the paragraph text to make it more readable. To do so, remove the *text-align* attribute in the *<p>* style's definition in the *<styles>* area at the top of the file.

 **CLEAN UP** Close the Notepad and Internet Explorer windows.

Hyperlinking from Graphics

In Chapter 5, you learned how to create text hyperlinks using the *<a>* tag. Recall that you place the URL in the opening *<a>* tag, and then you place the hyperlink text between the *<a>* and *</a>* tags. You create a graphical hyperlink in much the same way, by placing an *<img>* tag in an *<a>* tag like this:

```
<a href="http://www.contoso.com" title="Home page">
<img src="images/leaf.gif" style="float: left; margin: 5px">
</a>
```

The graphic appears as usual in the document, but when the user moves the mouse pointer over it, the pointer changes to a hand, indicating that the graphic is a hyperlink. By default, hyperlinked graphics have a border that is the same color as hyperlinked text.

You can remove the border by adding *border: none* to the style rule for the graphic, like this:

```
<a href="http://www.contoso.com" title="Home page">
<img src="images/leaf.gif" style="float: left; margin: 5px; border: none">
</a>
```

In this exercise, you will set up a graphic to be a hyperlink.

SET UP Use the *index.htm* file in the practice file folder for this topic. This file is located in the Documents\Microsoft Press\HTML5 SBS\09Graphics\ CreatingHyperlinks folder. Open the *index* file in Notepad and in Internet Explorer.

Important If you copy the practice files for this exercise to some other location, you must also copy the default.css file and the images folder for the practice files to work properly.

1. In Notepad, add an *<a>* tag around the *<img>* tag that hyperlinks to *www.contoso. com*. Specify a link title of **Home page**, as shown in bold text in the following:

   ```
   <a href="http://www.contoso.com" title="Home page">
   <img src="images/lg-leaf.gif" style="float: left; margin: 5px;" height="70">
   </a>
   ```

2. Save the file, and then refresh Internet Explorer.

3. In Internet Explorer, move the mouse over the graphic to display the ScreenTip. Notice that the graphic has a border around it.

4. Remove the border by adding *border: none* to the style rule.

   ```
   <a href="http://www.contoso.com" title="Home page">
   <img src="images/lg-leaf.gif" style="float: left; margin: 5px; border: none" height="70">
   </a>
   ```

5. Save the file, and then refresh Internet Explorer.

Mouse pointer

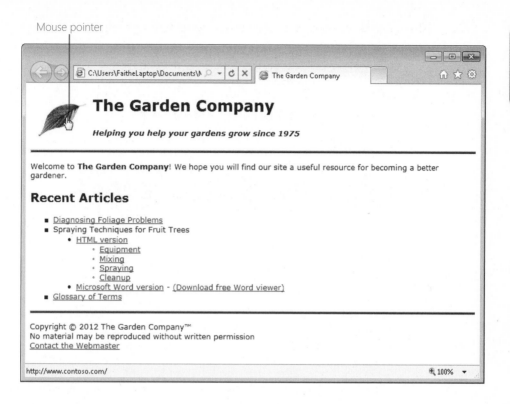

 CLEAN UP Close the Notepad and Internet Explorer windows.

Using Thumbnail Graphics

High-resolution graphics can make a page load slowly, but avoiding high-resolution graphics altogether can limit your site's effectiveness in delivering content. A compromise is to include thumbnail images, which are low-resolution copies of the images that are linked to the larger, high-resolution versions.

Note Some Web development programs create thumbnail images automatically when you set up a photo album page.

To create a thumbnail, you will need small versions of each of the graphics. You can create them by opening the original graphic in a program like Photoshop or Paint Shop Pro, and then using that program to scale the picture to a lower resolution (for example, 100 pixels high). Then save the file under a different name. For example, if the original is *tree.jpg*, you might call the thumbnail *sm-tree.jpg*. Then you place the thumbnail images on the page and create hyperlinks to the larger files. Set each of the larger files to open in its own window by using the *target="_blank"* attribute, as shown in the following.

```
<a href="tree.jpg" target="_blank"><img src="sm_tree.jpg"></a>
```

Thumbnails are most useful when you have a lot of images to display, as shown here.

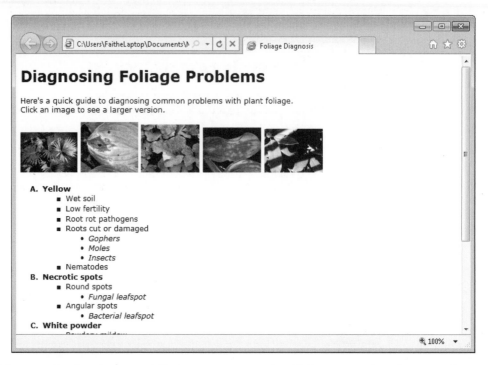

In this example, the pictures might have more meaning if they were placed next to the outline point they represent. However, doing that requires a bit more HTML layout skill than you have at this point, so let's save that topic for Part 3 of this book.

In this exercise, you will hyperlink thumbnails of several images to full-size versions that will open in a separate window.

SET UP Use the *foliage.htm* file in the practice file folder for this topic. This file is located in the Documents\Microsoft Press\HTML5 SBS\09Graphics\UsingThumbnails folder. Open the *foliage* file in Notepad and in Internet Explorer.

Important If you copy the practice files for this exercise to some other location, you must also copy the default.css file and the images folder for the practice files to work properly.

1. In Notepad, enclose each of the images in a hyperlink that opens its full-size counterpart in a new window.

```
<a href="images/yellow.jpg" target="_blank"><img src="images/sm_yellow.jpg"
style="border: none"></a><a href="images/necrotic.jpg" target="_blank"><img
src="images/sm_necrotic.jpg" style="border: none"></a>
```

```
<a href="images/powder.jpg" target="_blank"><img src="images/sm_powder.jpg"
style="border: none"></a><a href="images/lightdark.jpg" target="_blank"><img
src="images/sm_lightdark.jpg" style="border: none"></a>
<a href="images/holes.jpg" target="_blank"><img src="images/sm_holes.jpg"
style="border: none"></a>
```

2. Save the file, and then refresh Internet Explorer. Test each graphic's hyperlink to make sure it works.

3. Add a ScreenTip to each hyperlink by inserting a *title* attribute:

```
<a href="images/yellow.jpg" target="_blank" title="Yellow"><img src="images/
sm_yellow.jpg" style="border: none"></a>
<a href="images/necrotic.jpg" target="_blank" title="Necrotic spots"><img
src="images/sm_necrotic.jpg" style="border: none"></a>
<a href="images/powder.jpg" target="_blank" title="White powder"><img
src="images/sm_powder.jpg" style="border: none"></a>
<a href="images/lightdark.jpg" target="_blank" title="Light and dark green
areas"><img src="images/sm_lightdark.jpg" style="border: none"></a>
<a href="images/holes.jpg" target="_blank" title="Holes or chewed
areas"><img src="images/sm_holes.jpg" style="border: none"></a>
```

4. Save the file, and then refresh Internet Explorer. Hover your mouse over each graphic to make sure the correct ScreenTip appears.

Screen Tip

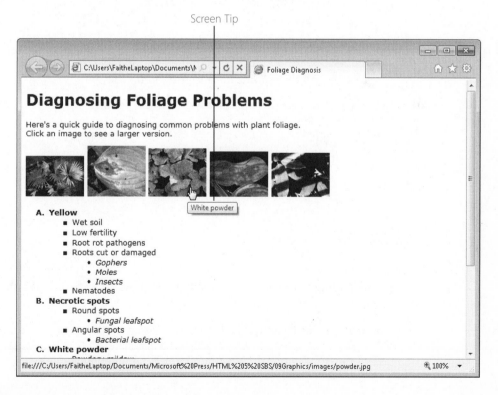

CLEAN UP Close the Notepad and Internet Explorer windows.

Including Alternate Text for Graphics

Placing an *alt* attribute (traditionally called an *alt tag*, although it isn't really a tag) in an *<img>* tag creates alternate text for the graphic. This alternate text is a pop-up box that contains a text explanation of the graphic, much like the title does for a hyperlink.

Alternate text is not just for decoration; it serves an important purpose for users who might not be able to view your graphics for some reason. This might include visually-impaired users who are accessing your page through the use of a screen-reading pro-gram, or people who browse using handheld devices.

Alternate text is simple to include; just place an *alt="text"* attribute in the *<img>* tag, like this:

```
<img src="leaf.gif" alt="Leaf logo">
```

In this exercise, you will add alternate text to a picture.

SET UP Use the *spray.htm* file in the practice file folder for this topic. This file is located in the Documents\Microsoft Press\HTML5 SBS\09Graphics\UsingAlt folder. Open the *spray* file in Notepad and in Internet Explorer.

Important If you copy the practice files for this exercise to some other location, you must also copy the default.css file and the images folder for the practice files to work properly.

1. In Notepad, add an *alt* attribute to the *<img>* tag.

```
<img src="images/apple.png" style="float: right; padding: 15px" width="350"
alt="Apples on tree">
```

2. Save your work.

CLEAN UP Close the Notepad and Internet Explorer windows.

Adding Figure Captions

HTML5 includes a new tag for marking figures: *<figure>*. It is not a replacement for *<img>*, rather it is a container into which you place an *<img>* tag, like this:

```
<figure>
<img src="images/diagram.gif">
</figure>
```

If the browser does not support HTML5, the *<figure>* tag is ignored.

The main advantage to using *<figure>* is that you can then use the *<figurecaption>* tag to associate a caption with the image. That caption will then stick with the image no matter where it floats in your layout. The following example shows how to use it:

```
<figure>
<img src="/images/diagram.gif">
<figurecaption>This diagram shows the life cycle of the product.</figcaption>
</figure>
```

Another advantage to using *<figure>* is that you can assign styles and other attributes to the *<figure>* element via an external or internal style sheet, just as you do for any other container tag.

You can also assign a single caption to a group of images, such as shown in the following:

```
<figure>
<img src="/images/stage1.jpg">
<img src="/images/stage2.jpg">
<img src="/images/stage3.jpg">
<figcaption>The three stages of the life cycle</figcaption>
</figure>
```

In this exercise, you will add a single caption to a group of pictures.

SET UP Use the *foliage.htm* file in the practice file folder for this topic. This file is located in the Documents\Microsoft Press\HTML5 SBS\09Graphics\CaptioningFigures folder. Open the *foliage* file in Notepad and in Internet Explorer.

Important If you copy the practice files for this exercise to some other location, you must also copy the default.css file and the images folder for the practice files to work properly.

1. In Notepad, add an opening *<figure>* tag immediately above the first image's tag.

   ```
   <figure>
   <a href="images/yellow.jpg" target="_blank" title="Yellow"><img src="images/
   sm_yellow.jpg" style="border: none"></a>
   ```

2. Add a closing *</figure>* tag immediately below the last image's tag.

   ```
   <a href="images/holes.jpg" target="_blank" title="Holes or chewed
   areas"><img src="images/sm_holes.jpg" style="border: none"></a>
   </figure>
   ```

3. Add a *
* and a *<figurecaption>* tag immediately above the closing *</figure>* tag.

```
<a href="images/holes.jpg" target="_blank" title="Holes or chewed
areas"><img src="images/sm_holes.jpg" style="border: none"></a>
<br>
<figurecaption>From left to right: Yellow, Necrotic Spots, White Powder,
Light and Dark Green Areas, Holes or Chewed Areas</figurecaption>
</figure>
```

4. In the *<style>* tag in the document's *<head>* section, add the following line:

```
figurecaption {font-size: 12px; font-style: italic}
```

5. Save the file, and then refresh Internet Explorer to check your work.

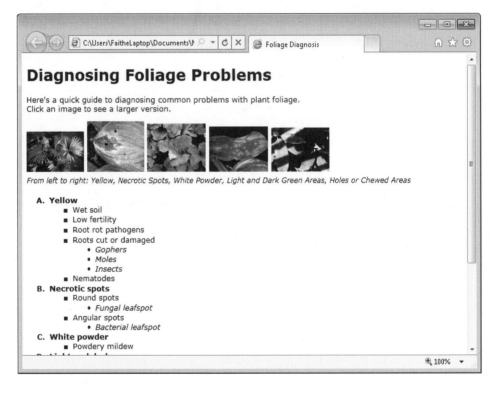

CLEAN UP Close the Notepad and Internet Explorer windows.

Key Points

- Valid graphics formats for Web use are GIF, PNG, and JPG.

- When possible, use graphics files that are as close as possible in resolution to the size at which they will be displayed on the Web page. Use a photo-editing program to change the resolution.

- Use the *<img>* tag to insert an image. The *src* attribute specifies the image file name.

- To refer to a graphic in a subfolder, precede the name with the subfolder name and a slash (/).

- To allow a graphic to float to the left or right of the text, use a *style="float: left"* or *style="float: right"* attribute within the *<img>* tag.

- To force text to be positioned below an image, add *style="clear: left"* or *style="clear: right"* to the opening tag of the text.

- To size an image proportionally, specify a height or width for it as an attribute in the *<img>* tag. To size an image and distort it if needed, specify both a height and a width.

- To make a graphic into a hyperlink, enclose it in an *<a>* tag.

- To use thumbnail images, create a smaller, low-resolution version of each image, and then hyperlink it to the high-resolution version.

- As a contingency in the event that an image cannot be viewed, you can include a text explanation of the image in a pop-up box by inserting an *alt* attribute to specify alternate text.

- Enclose an image, or a group of images that should have a single collective caption, in a two-sided *<figure>* container. This allows you to then assign a caption with the *<figurecaption>* tag.

Part 3

Page Layout and Navigation

Chapter at a Glance

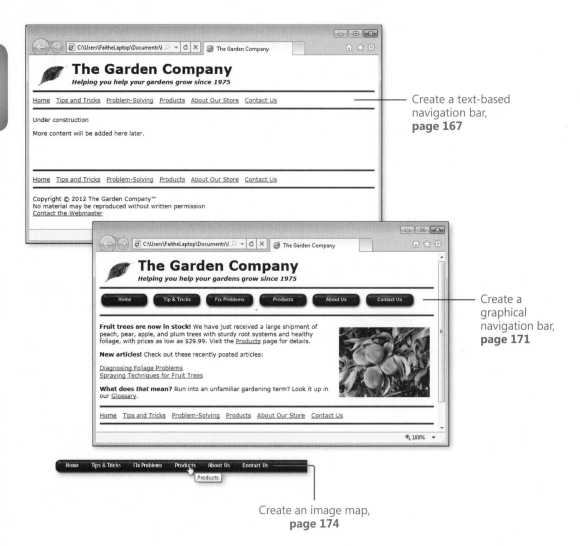

Create a text-based navigation bar, **page 167**

Create a graphical navigation bar, **page 171**

Create an image map, **page 174**

10 Creating Navigational Aids

In this chapter, you will learn how to

- ✔ Plan your site's organization.
- ✔ Create a text-based navigation bar.
- ✔ Create a graphical navigation bar.
- ✔ Create an image map.
- ✔ Redirect to another URL.

If you worked through the exercises in Parts 1 and 2 of this book, you have acquired most of the basic skills you need to create simple Web sites. Now it's a matter of putting all these skills together to make attractive and easy-to-use sites, and that's what you'll focus on in Part 3.

One way to make your Web site easily accessible is to place a consistent navigation bar on each page. A *navigation bar* is a set of hyperlinks that connect to the major pages of your Web site. These hyperlinks can be either text-based or graphical. You already saw how to create both kinds of hyperlinks in Chapters 5, "Creating Hyperlinks and Anchors," and Chapter 9, "Displaying Graphics," so creating a navigation bar is a logical next step. You'll learn how to plan your site's organization, and then create a suitable navigation bar to match it.

This chapter also explains a couple of other useful techniques to help users navigate your site. You'll learn how to redirect users from one page to another and how to create an image map that hyperlinks defined areas of a graphic to specific pages.

See Also Do you need only a quick refresher on the topics in this chapter? See the Key Points at the end of this chapter.

Practice Files Before you can use the practice files provided for this chapter, you need to install them from the book's companion content page to their default locations. See "Using the Practice Files" in the beginning of this book for more information.

Planning Your Site's Organization

Navigation bars can be easy to create, but they require some planning to be effective. Up to this point in the book, you've been creating single pages with a common theme for eventual inclusion in a Web site, but you probably have not yet given a lot of thought to how the pages fit together. So before creating a navigation bar, you want to consider the overall structural plan for the site.

A navigation bar should contain links to the most important sections of the Web site, plus a link to the Home page.

The Garden Company
Helping you help your gardens grow since 1975

Home   Tips and Tricks   Problem-Solving   Products   About Our Store   Contact Us

The navigation bar should not contain hyperlinks to every page in the site unless the site is extremely small and simple. Although there is no hard-and-fast rule about the number of items a navigation bar can contain, most people try for somewhere between four and seven. With fewer than four, your site doesn't look very content-rich; with more than seven, the navigation bar becomes crowded and confusing. In addition, on low-resolution displays or in narrow browser windows, your navigation bar might wrap to a second (or even third) line if it's a horizontal bar, or it might force the user to scroll down if it's a vertical bar. This chapter discusses only horizontal bars, but you'll learn how to make vertical navigation bars in Chapter 12, "Creating Tables."

Note Some Web sites have navigation bars in which each hyperlink opens a menu of options when the user points to it or clicks it. You can't create that with plain HTML; those are constructed with JavaScript or another Web-based programming language.

Before building your navigation bar, create a diagram that outlines the site's planned structure. It doesn't matter if you haven't created all the pages yet. You can be as fancy or as plain as you want with your chart. It can be scrawled on the back of a napkin or built using SmartArt (through a Microsoft Office application), Microsoft Visio, or some other charting tool. Choose file names for each planned page, so you can start referring to them in hyperlinks even if they don't exist yet.

The organization of The Garden Company's site, which you've been creating pages for in this book's examples, might look something like this.

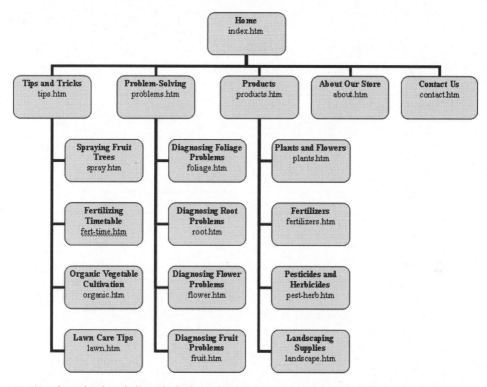

Notice that the level directly below the Home page consists of five pages. The navigation bar will contain hyperlinks to each of these pages. Three of these are introductory pages for larger sections of content; the introductory pages of those sections will link to each page within that section. This Web site is modest in scope initially, but there is plenty of room for future expansion. You could add dozens of additional tips, problem-solving techniques, and products. You could even create subsections within one of the main areas if the content becomes too overwhelming for a single page.

Notice also that not every page referenced from the navigation bar is a major section. Three of them—Home, About Our Store, and Contact Us—are simply pages that are important for visitors to be able to access quickly from any page.

Creating a Text-Based Navigation Bar

A text-based navigation bar is the simplest and easiest, and it is also very user-friendly. On simple Web pages, text-based navigation bars are usually placed at the top of the page, in a single horizontal line. Some Web designers also place a copy at the bottom of each page so visitors don't need to scroll back up to the top of a page to access the links.

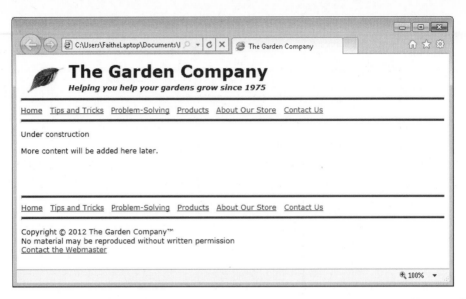

Tip When you place a navigation bar at the bottom of a page, it is customarily a text-based bar rather than a graphical one.

HTML5 includes a *<nav>* tag, a two-sided container tag in which you can optionally place the code for a navigation bar. The *<nav>* tag is designed to help browsers and style sheets identify sets of links as a navigational element, and handle them appropriately. If the browser does not support the *<nav>* tag, it is ignored. You'll use the *<nav>* tag in this chapter because it's good practice to start including HTML5 tags in your code, but you won't be doing anything special with the *<nav>* tag's attributes. However, in sites you create yourself, you are free to define style attributes for the *<nav>* tag in internal or external style sheets; this can be a way to help ensure consistency among the navigation bars throughout all the pages in your Web site.

In this exercise, you will add a text-based navigation bar to the top and bottom of a Web page.

 SET UP Be sure to use the files provided specifically for this exercise, and not earlier versions. Use the *index.htm* and *default.css* files in the practice folder for this topic. These files are located in the Documents\Microsoft Press\HTML5 SBS\10Navigation\ CreatingTextBar folder. Open the *index* file in Microsoft Notepad and in Microsoft Internet Explorer.

1. At the first *<hr>* tag, add a *<nav>* container and add the text for a navigation bar.

```
<nav>
<hr>
<p>Home Tips and Tricks Problem-Solving Products About Our Store Contact
Us</p>
</nav>
```

2. Save the file, and then refresh Internet Explorer.

The text of the intended navigation bar appears, but the items are not clearly separated.

Home Tips and Tricks Problem-Solving Products About Our Store Contact Us

HTML ignores multiple spaces, so you must instead use the nonbreaking space code (* *) if you want to insert extra spaces between words without creating a table or some other structural container.

3. Insert a nonbreaking space (and a normal space following it) between each section title, like this:

```
<p>Home   Tips and Tricks   Problem-Solving   Products
  About Our Store   Contact Us</p>
```

4. Save the file, and then refresh Internet Explorer.

5. To help set off the navigation bar from the rest of the text, insert a second horizontal line below the navigation bar text, but above the closing *</nav>* tag.

```
<nav>
<hr>
<p>Home   Tips and Tricks   Problem-Solving   Products  
About Our Store   Contact Us</p>
<hr>
</nav>
```

6. Save the file, and then refresh Internet Explorer.

Home   Tips and Tricks   Problem-Solving   Products   About Our Store   Contact Us

---

The horizontal spacing looks okay, but the navigation bar would look better if the green lines were closer to it at the top and bottom.

7. Set the margin for the paragraph to zero.

```
<p style="margin:0px">Home   Tips and Tricks   Problem-Solving
  Products   About Our Store   Contact Us</p>
```

8. Save the file, and then refresh Internet Explorer.

Now the lines are closer to the text.

Home   Tips and Tricks   Problem-Solving   Products   About Our Store   Contact Us
---

9. Add hyperlinks to each of the six items in the navigation bar to the corresponding pages.

Note Line breaks are added in the following code for ease of reading, but they are not required.

```
<nav>
<hr>
<p style="margin:0px">
<a href="index.htm">Home</a>  
<a href="tips.htm">Tips and Tricks</a>  
<a href="problems.htm">Problem-Solving</a>  
<a href="products.htm">Products</a>  
<a href="about.htm">About Our Store</a>  
<a href="contact.htm">Contact Us</a></p>
<hr>
</nav>
```

10. Save the file, and then refresh Internet Explorer.

The navigation bar is complete.

Home   Tips and Tricks   Problem-Solving   Products   About Our Store   Contact Us
---

11. Select the code for the entire navigation bar, including the *<nav>* and *</nav>* tags, and press **Ctrl+C** to copy it to the Clipboard.

12. Select the *<hr>* tag at the bottom of the document, and press **Ctrl+V** to replace it with a copy of the navigation bar.

13. Save the file, and then refresh Internet Explorer.

Two navigation bars appear, one above and one below the main content of the page.

 CLEAN UP Close the Notepad and Internet Explorer windows.

Creating a Graphical Navigation Bar

Text hyperlinks are clear and unambiguous, but not all that attractive. You might prefer to create a navigation bar that uses buttons or other graphics instead of text links. You can create the graphics yourself in a graphics-editing program. If you do create your own, it's a good idea to follow these guidelines:

● Keep the size of each button small (150 pixels wide at the most).

● Make each button the same size and shape. They only variation should be in the text that they present.

● Save each button as a separate file in GIF or JPG format.

If you have no talent or inclination for art projects, search the Web; there are thousands of sites with free graphical buttons that you can download. Make several copies of a button you like, and then use a text tool in a graphics-editing program to place different text on each copy. Here are a couple of links to free button sites to get you started:

- *http://www.aaa-buttons.com*
- *http://www.eosdev.com/eosdev_Buttons.htm*

Most professional Web site designers do not create their own buttons, nor do they acquire them from others; instead they use *button-creation programs* to generate them. Such programs make it very easy to create groups of identical buttons with different text on each one. There are both commercial standalone programs that make buttons, and also free Web utilities. Here are a few sites; you can find many more with a simple Web search.

- *http://www.crystalbutton.com*
- *http://www.buttongenerator.com*

Note The buttons provided for the exercises in this book were created with Crystal Button.

You set up a graphical navigation bar just like a text-based navigation bar, but instead of hyperlinks from the text, you hyperlink from the graphic by placing the *<img>* tag within the *<a>* tag, like this:

```
<a href="product.htm"><img src="product_button.gif"></a>
```

In this exercise, you will convert a text-based navigation bar to a graphics-based one.

SET UP Be sure to use the files provided specifically for this exercise, and not earlier versions. Use the *index.htm* file in the practice folder for this topic. This file is located in the Documents\Microsoft Press\HTML5 SBS\10Navigation\CreatingGraphicBar folder. Open the *index* file in Notepad and in Internet Explorer.

1. In Notepad, in the upper navigation bar, change the hyperlinks so that they reference the button graphics in the */images* folder rather than displaying text.

```
<nav>
<hr>
<p style="margin:0px">
<a href="index.htm"><img src="images/btn_home.gif" style="border:none"></a>
<a href="tips.htm"><img src="images/btn_tips.gif" style="border:none"></a>
```

```
<a href="problems.htm"><img src="images/btn_problem.gif"
style="border:none">
</a>
<a href="products.htm"><img src="images/btn_products.gif" style=
"border:none"></a>
<a href="about.htm"><img src="images/btn_about.gif" style="border:none"></a>
<a href="contact.htm"><img src="images/btn_contact.gif" style="border:none">
</a></p>
<hr>
</nav>
```

Note The preceding code also removes the spaces you previously placed between the links, because the spacing is now provided by the graphics themselves.

2. Save the file, and then refresh Internet Explorer to view your work.

CLEAN UP Close the Notepad and Internet Explorer windows.

Creating an Image Map

You have seen how to make an image function as a hyperlink, but sometimes you might want different areas of the image to hyperlink to different locations. For example, suppose you have a map of the United States, and you want the user to be able to click individual states to view a page containing information specific to her location. To create such an effect, you must use an *image map*.

An image map is an overlay for a graphic that assigns hyperlinks to specifically defined areas (*hotspots*) on the image. The hotspots can be rectangular, circular, or irregularly shaped (called a *poly* hotspot).

The position of a rectangular hotspot is defined by two points: its upper-left and lower-right corners. Each point is expressed as a pair of numbers that represent the horizontal and vertical distance (in pixels) from the upper-left corner of the image. For example, in the following image, the shed door is defined as a hotspot. The upper-left corner of the shed door is located at 284,170—in other words, 284 pixels to the right and 170 pixels down from the upper-left corner of the image. The lower-right corner of the shed door is at 352,314. Therefore, the code for defining this particular hotspot is as follows:

```
<area shape="rect" coords="284,170,352,314" href="enter.htm">
```

Click the potting shed door to enter the members-only area...

Top left corner of the image: 0,0

Top left corner of hot spot: 284,170

Mouse pointer changes when over a hot spot

Hot spot area (invisible)

Bottom right corner of hot spot: 352,314

To define a circular hotspot, you use three coordinates: two for the circle's center point (horizontal and vertical values), and one for the radius of the circle.

```
<area shape="circle" coords="270,364,144" href="index.htm">
```

Click the ball to enter the Dog Toy Zone...

Radius of the circle is 270 pixels

The center of the circle is 270,364

To define a poly hotspot, you use as many coordinates as are needed to define all the vertexes of the shape. Poly hotspots consist of straight lines that connect each of the points you define. For example, here's one with four vertices:

```
<area shape="poly" coords="287,71,413,286,314,446,188,267" href="index.htm">
```

Click the moth to see the Pesticides area... 287,71

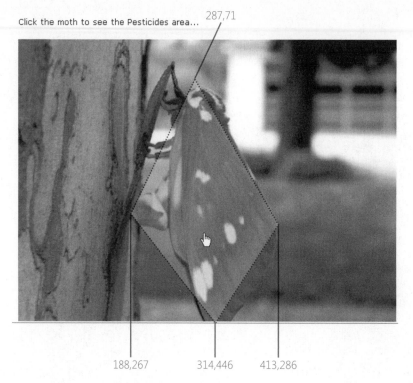

188,267   314,446   413,286

The easiest way to determine the coordinates of various points is to open the image in a graphics-editing program such as Paint Shop Pro, which displays the mouse pointer position in the status bar as you work. Move the mouse pointer over any spot on the image, and the program will display its coordinates.

Mouse pointer position

If you don't have access to a graphics-editing program, you can use trial-and-error to position the points.

To construct an image map, start with a two-sided *<map>* tag. In it, place *name* and *id* attributes. The name and ID can be the same; you need the *name* for the map itself, and you can use the *id* to refer to the image map in the style sheet, if desired.

```
<map name="moth" id="moth">
</map>
```

Then within the *<map>* tag, insert the points for the areas:

```
<map name="moth" id="moth">
<area shape="poly" coords="287,71,413,286,314,446,188,267" href="index.htm">
</map>
```

Just as with hyperlinks, you can include a *title* attribute in an *<area>* tag to make a ScreenTip appear when a user hovers the mouse over it. This is especially helpful when there is no text in the area, such as on a map or a photo.

```
<map name="moth" id="moth">
<area shape="poly" coords="287,71,413,286,314,446,188,267" href="index.htm"
title="Home page">
</map>
```

Finally, reference the map's name in the *<img>* tag for the image with the *usemap* attribute. You must include a pound or hash sign (#) before the map name, as shown in the following:

```
<img src="moth.jpg" usemap="#moth" style="border:none">
```

In this exercise, you will create an image map that uses one graphic as a navigation bar with multiple hyperlinks.

 SET UP Be sure to use the files provided specifically for this exercise, and not earlier versions. Use the *index.htm* file in the practice folder for this topic. This file is located in the Documents\Microsoft Press\HTML5 SBS\10Navigation\CreatingImageMap folder. Open the *index* file in Notepad and in Internet Explorer.

1. Immediately after the *<img>* tag that contains the *bar.jpg* graphic, add an image map definition.

```
<nav>
<img src="images/bar.jpg" style="border:none">
<map>
</map>
</nav>
```

2. Name the map **navbar**, and then set its ID to **navbar**.

```
<nav>
<img src="images/bar.jpg" style="border:none">
<map name="navbar" id="navbar">
</map>
</nav>
```

3. Within the *<map>* tag, create the following hotspots:

```
<nav>
<img src="images/bar.jpg" style="border:none">
<map name="navbar" id="navbar">
<area shape="rect" coords="0,0,60,30" href="home.htm">
<area shape="rect" coords="70,0,155,30" href="tips.htm">
<area shape="rect" coords="165,0,250,30" href="problem.htm">
```

```
<area shape="rect" coords="260,0,325,30" href="products.htm">
<area shape="rect" coords="335,0,400,30" href="about.htm">
<area shape="rect" coords="410,0,490,30" href="contact.htm">
</map>
</nav>
```

4. In the *<img>* tag, reference the name of the image map.

   ```
   <img src="images/bar.jpg" usemap="#navbar" style="border: none">
   ```

5. Save the file, and then refresh Internet Explorer. Position the mouse pointer over each name in the navigation bar. Notice that the URL displays in the browser's status bar.

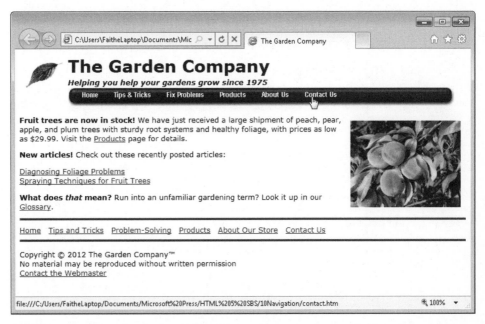

Note Depending on your screen resolution and browser window size, the entire URL might not be visible in the status bar. After you publish the site to a Web server, however, the URL shown in the status bar will be much shorter and easier to read.

6. Edit each hyperlink to display a ScreenTip when the mouse pointer is positioned over it.

   ```
   <nav>
   <img src="images/bar.jpg" usemap="#navbar" style="border:none">
   <map name="navbar" id="navbar">
   <area shape="rect" coords="0,0,60,30" href="home.htm" title="Home">
   <area shape="rect" coords="70,0,155,30" href="tips.htm" title="Tips
   &amp; Tricks">
   ```

```
<area shape="rect" coords="165,0,250,30" href="problem.htm" title="Fix
Problems">
<area shape="rect" coords="260,0,325,30" href="products.htm" title=
"Products">
<area shape="rect" coords="335,0,400,30" href="about.htm" title= "About Us">
<area shape="rect" coords="410,0,490,30" href="contact.htm" title=
"Contact Us">
</map>
</nav>
```

Note Even though ScreenTips simply display the text that the user is clicking, they are still useful because they indicate that the text is clickable.

Notice the *&* used in the second hotspot definition. Remember that HTML uses the ampersand as a special character, so to display an ampersand, you must use *&* so that it will render as an ordinary symbol.

7. Save the file, and then refresh Internet Explorer. Position the mouse pointer over each name in the navigation bar to display the ScreenTips.

 CLEAN UP Close the Notepad and Internet Explorer windows.

Redirecting to Another URL

After you have managed your own Web site for a while, you might decide you want to restructure its organization by renaming some pages, placing pages in folders, or hosting your site at a different location with a different URL. All that is fine, but what about the people who bookmarked the original page? They'll be faced with an unfriendly *Page Not Found* message if you remove the old content entirely, and they won't have any way of finding the page in its new location.

To help your past visitors find the new page, you can leave the old page in place and replace its text with a hyperlink that tells them where the new page is located. You already know how to create a hyperlink—that's simple. But you can take it one step further and set up the old page to actually *redirect* to the new page. In other words, you can make the old page automatically display the new page.

It is customary for a redirection to include five seconds of delay, so users can cancel the redirect operation if desired. It is also customary to include a text hyperlink to the new page, in case the redirect operation fails for some reason (such as the browser not supporting it, although this is uncommon).

You implement a redirect operation by adding an attribute to a *<meta>* tag in the *<head>* section of the page (as you learned in Chapter 2, "Setting Up the Document Structure"). You must create a new *<meta>* tag for this operation; you cannot add the attributes to any existing *<meta>* tag that the document might have. For example, to redirect to the page *support.microsoft.com* after a five-second delay, use the following:

```
<meta http-equiv="refresh" content="5; url=http://support.microsoft.com">
```

Be sure to use a semicolon (not a comma) between the delay (the *content* attribute) and the *url* attribute.

In this exercise, you will redirect one page to another page automatically after five seconds.

 SET UP Be sure to use the files provided specifically for this exercise, and not earlier versions. Use the *foliage.htm* file in the practice folder for this topic. This file is located in the Documents\Microsoft Press\HTML5 SBS\10Navigation\Redirecting folder. Open the *foliage* file in Notepad and Internet Explorer.

1. In the *<head>* section, add a new *<meta>* tag as follows:

   ```
   <meta http-equiv="refresh" content="5; url=foliage-new.htm">
   ```

2. In the *<body>* section, make the text *click here* into a hyperlink to *foliage-new.htm*.

   ```
   <p>This page has been moved. <br>
   If your browser supports automatic redirection, the new page will appear in
   5 seconds. <br>
   If the new page does not appear, <a href="foliage-new.htm">click here
   </a>.</p>
   ```

3. Save the file, and then refresh Internet Explorer.

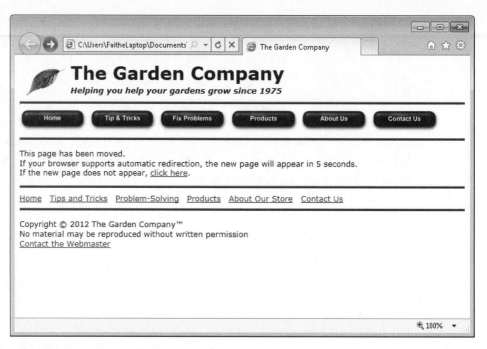

After five seconds, the *foliage-new* page appears.

4. Click the browser's **Back** button, and then quickly click the **Click here** hyperlink to test it.

✖ CLEAN UP Close the Notepad and Internet Explorer windows.

Key Points

- A navigation bar contains a list of hyperlinks to the major pages on your site. It need not include every page in the site. The optimal number of links is between four and seven.

- In HTML5, you can use the *<nav>* tag as a container to indicate that a group of links constitutes a navigation element.

- Plan your site's organization before you create the navigation bar. Draw a diagram of all the pages and their connections to one another, and choose a file name for each page.

- Navigation bars are traditionally placed at the top or left side of a page. Placing a bar to the side requires the use of layout techniques discussed later in this book.

- Many Web designers place a text version of their navigation bar at the bottom of each page for user convenience.

- A text-based navigation bar is simply a series of hyperlinks.

- A graphical navigation bar uses small graphics for the hyperlinks. You can create these graphics using a graphics program such as Photoshop or a utility designed specifically for creating Web buttons.

- To redirect a page to a different URL, create a *<meta>* tag in the *<head>* section with the *http-equiv* attribute, like this: *<meta http-equiv="refresh" content="5; url=http://support.microsoft.com">* .

- You use an image map to specify individual sections of a single graphic that should act as hyperlinks. Use the *<map>* tag to create the map. Within it, define hotspots with *<area>* tags, and then reference the map as an attribute in the *<img>* tag.

- To create image areas for your image maps, remember that points in an image are defined by their distances from the upper-left corner of the graphic. For example, the coordinates 10,15 refer to a point on the graphic that is 10 pixels to the right and 15 pixels below the upper-left corner.

Chapter at a Glance

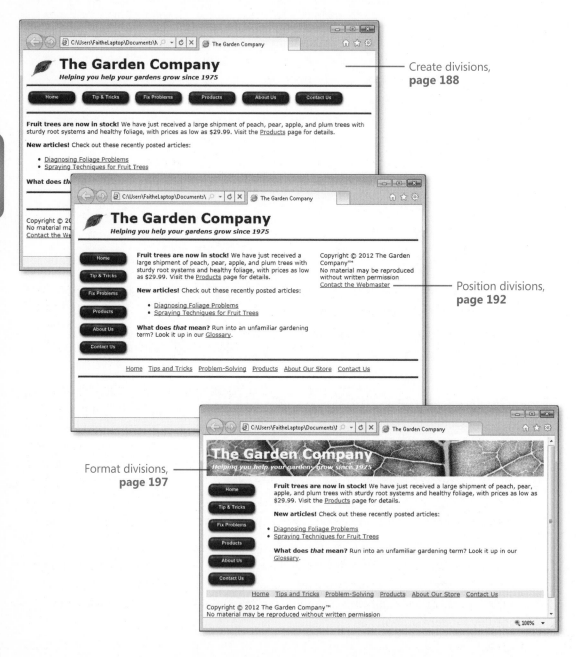

Create divisions,
page 188

Position divisions,
page 192

Format divisions,
page 197

11 Creating Division-Based Layouts

In this chapter, you will learn how to
- ✔ Understand HTML5 semantic tags.
- ✔ Begin to think in divisions.
- ✔ Create divisions.
- ✔ Create an HTML5 semantic layout.
- ✔ Position divisions.
- ✔ Format divisions.

Until a few years ago, tables were the most popular way of structuring a Web page. You'll learn about tables and their formatting in Chapter 12, "Creating Tables," and Chapter 13, "Formatting Tables," in case that's the route you want to go with your site's design. However, as Web designers move increasingly toward separating style and content, division-based layouts are becoming more appealing.

A *division-based layout* defines the area of a page with *<div>* tags, or some of the new HTML5 semantic tags such as *<article>* and *<aside>*, and then applies formatting to each area using styles. One big advantage of division-based layouts is that you can place the styles in an external style sheet, and then make style changes to many pages at once simply by modifying the style sheet. For example, moving the navigation bar from the left to the right on a dozen pages is easy with a division-based layout that uses an external style sheet, but it's a huge chore with a table-based layout. Another advantage is that division-based layouts reduce the number of lines of code needed to produce a page.

In this chapter, you will learn how to create a separate area of a page (a *division*) in a document, and how to control division and element positions. Then you'll learn how to format a division (which is mostly a matter of applying the same formatting styles that you've learned about in previous chapters) and how to overcome any problems introduced by the formatting.

See Also Do you need only a quick refresher on the topics in this chapter? See the Key Points at the end of this chapter.

> **Practice Files** Before you can use the practice files provided for this chapter, you need to install them from the book's companion content page to their default locations. See "Using the Practice Files" in the beginning of this book for more information.

Understanding HTML5 Semantic Tags

HTML5 adds some *semantic tags* to define layouts in more intuitive ways than the generic *<div>* tag is capable of. A semantic tag is one in which the name of a tag reflects its purpose.

Here are the major semantic tags you should know:

- **<header>** Defines the masthead or other header information on the page. Typically the header is repeated on every page of a site, although that is not required.

- **<footer>** Defines the text at the bottom of a page, such as the copyright or contact information. Again, it is typically repeated on every page of the site.

- **<article>** Defines a block of text that represents a single article, story, or message. An article can be distinguished from other text in that it can logically stand alone. For example, on a news site, each news story is an article.

- **<aside>** Defines a block of text that is tangential to the main discussion, such as a note, tip, or caution. An aside can be distinguished from other text in that it could be pulled out and discarded without disrupting the main document in which it appears.

- **<section>** Defines a generic content or application section. Examples of sections would be book chapters or the numbered sections of a thesis; a site's home page could be split into sections such as Introduction, News, and Contact Information. A section begins with a heading such as *<h1>* followed by other content. A general rule is to use *<section>* if the area being defined would be included in an outline of the document or page.

Note The *<section>* tag might sound similar to the *<div>* tag, but the HTML5 standard differentiates them, saying that *<section>* should not be used merely to define formatting. A section defines a particular type of meaningful content, not just a block of contiguous text that should be formatted the same way.

If you use semantic tags to structure your page and someone views it with a browser that doesn't support HTML5, the page might not look the way you want it to; the browser will ignore the tags it doesn't understand. That's why, for the time being, creating the page structure using *<div>* tags is the safest way to go. However, it's important that you learn the HTML5 semantic tags too, for future reference.

In this chapter, you'll learn to mark up a document both ways: with generic *<div>* tags that are readable in any browser, and with the new HTML5 semantic tags.

Beginning to Think in Divisions

In an effective division-based layout, each part of the page you want to format separately should be a *division*. For now, don't think about whether the division will be a vertical or horizontal area on the page, or how large or small it will be; just think about the content. For example, look at the following Web page. How many natural divisions do you see here?

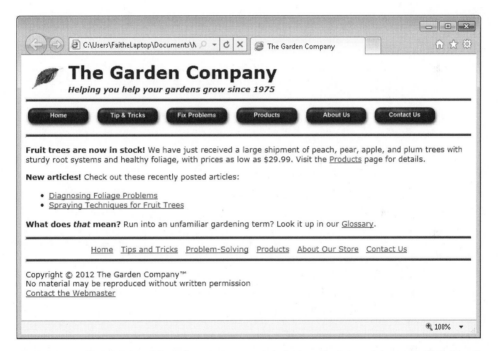

If you were designing with *<div>* tags, you might break down this page like this: the masthead, the top navigation bar, the body text, the bottom navigation bar, and the copyright notice.

If you were designing with HTML5 semantic tags, you might break it down like this: *<header>* for the masthead, *<nav>* for the navigation bars, and *<footer>* for the copyright notice. Formatting each of the paragraphs in the body with its own *<article>* tag might be overkill for this page, but in a page with more content, you might use *<article>*, *<aside>*, or *<section>* to break content down into manageable pieces.

Creating Divisions

You use an *id* attribute to give a name to a division, like this:

```
<div id="masthead">
```

Each ID must be unique within the document, but multiple documents can use the same division names. Such reuse is good, in fact, because it lets you define the formatting of multiple documents with a single style sheet.

In this exercise, you will create divisions within a page. Then in later exercises, you will position and format those divisions.

SET UP Use the *index.htm* file in the practice file folder for this topic. This file is located in the Documents\Microsoft Press\HTML5 SBS\11Divisions\CreatingDivisions folder. Open the *index* file in Microsoft Notepad and Microsoft Internet Explorer.

1. Enclose the logo, company name, and tagline in a *<div>* tag, and name the tag **masthead**.

   ```
   <body>
   <div id="masthead">
   <a href="http://www.contoso.com" title="Home page">
   <img src="images/leaf.gif class="logo""></a>
   <h1 class="pagetitle">The Garden Company</h1>
   <h5 class="tagline"><i>Helping you help your gardens grow since 1975</i></
   h5>
   </div>
   ```

2. Enclose the top navigation bar in a *<div>* tag, and name the tag **topnav**.

   ```
   <div id="topnav">
   <hr>
   <a href="index.htm"><img src="images/btn_home.gif"
   style="border:none"></a>
   <a href="tips.htm"><img src="images/btn_tips.gif" style="border:none"></a>
   <a href="problems.htm"><img src="images/btn_problem.gif"
   style="border:none"></a>
   <a href="products.htm"><img src="images/btn_products.gif"
   style="border:none"></a>
   <a href="about.htm"><img src="images/btn_about.gif"
   style="border:none"></a>
   <a href="contact.htm"><img src="images/btn_contact.gif"
   style="border:none"></a>
   <hr>
   </div>
   ```

   Note Make sure that you include the *<hr>* tags in the topnav division.

Note As you learned in Chapter 10, "Creating Navigational Aids," the *<nav>* tag is an HTML5 semantic tag that serves the same purpose as defining a *<div>* tag, but it is intended for a navigation bar. You'll use *<nav>* in the next exercise in the chapter, where you apply HTML5 semantic tags.

3. Enclose the body paragraphs in a *<div>* tag, and name the tag **main**.

```
<div id="main">
<p><b>Fruit trees are now in stock! </b>We have just received a large
shipment of peach, pear, apple, and plum trees with sturdy root systems
and healthy foliage, with prices as low as $29.99. Visit the <a href=
"products.htm">Products</a> page for details.</p>
<p><b>New articles!</b> Check out these recently posted articles:
<ul>
<li><a href="foliage.htm">Diagnosing Foliage Problems</a></li>
<li><a href="spray.htm">Spraying Techniques for Fruit Trees</a></li>
</ul>
<p><b>What does <i>that</i> mean?</b> Run into an unfamiliar gardening term?
Look it up in our <a href="glossary.htm" target="_blank">Glossary</a>.</p>
</div>
```

4. Enclose the bottom navigation bar in a *<div>* tag, and name the tag **bottomnav**.

```
<div id="bottomnav">
<hr>
<p style="margin:0px; text-align: center">
<a href="index.htm">Home</a>  
<a href="tips.htm">Tips and Tricks</a>  
<a href="problems.htm">Problem-Solving</a>  
<a href="products.htm">Products</a>  
<a href="about.htm">About Our Store</a>  
<a href="contact.htm">Contact Us</a></p>
<hr>
</div>
```

5. Enclose the copyright notice in a *<div>* tag, and name the tag **copy**.

```
<div id="copy">
<p>Copyright &copy; 2012 The Garden Company&trade;<br>
No material may be reproduced without written permission<br>
<a href="mailto:webmaster@contoso.com?subject=Question/Comment" title=
"webmaster@contoso.com">Contact the Webmaster</a></p>
</div>
```

6. Save the file.

Note You do not need to view your work in Internet Explorer this time because you have not made any changes that change the rendering or appearance of the page. You will do that later in the chapter.

 CLEAN UP Close the Notepad and Internet Explorer windows.

Creating an HTML5 Semantic Layout

If you prefer to use the HTML5 semantic tags to create your layout, you choose the appropriate tags based on the *purpose* of the text. It's conceptually very much the same as using a *<div>* tag with an *id* attribute, but the tag itself provides the context. For example, instead of the *<div id="masthead>* tag, you would use the *<header>* tag.

In this exercise, you will change a division-based document to one that uses semantic tags to define the layout.

SET UP Use the *index2.htm* file in the practice file folder for this topic. This file is located in the Documents\Microsoft Press\HTML5 SBS\11Divisions\UsingSemantic folder. Open the *index2* file in Microsoft Notepad and Microsoft Internet Explorer.

1. Replace the *<div id="masthead">* tag with *<header>*, and change its closing *</div>* tag to *</header>*.

   ```
   <body>
   <header>
   <a href="http://www.contoso.com" title="Home page">
   <img src="images/leaf.gif class="logo""></a>
   <h1 class="pagetitle">The Garden Company</h1>
   <h5 class="tagline"><i>Helping you help your gardens grow since
   1975</i></h5>
   </header>
   ```

2. Replace the *<div id="topnav">* tag with *<nav>*, and change its closing *</div>* tag to *</nav>*.

   ```
   <nav>
   <hr>
   <a href="index.htm"><img src="images/btn_home.gif"
   style="border:none"></a>
   <a href="tips.htm"><img src="images/btn_tips.gif" style="border:none"></a>
   <a href="problems.htm"><img src="images/btn_problem.gif"
   style="border:none"></a>
   <a href="products.htm"><img src="images/btn_products.gif"
   style="border:none"></a>
   <a href="about.htm"><img src="images/btn_about.gif"
   style="border:none"></a>
   <a href="contact.htm"><img src="images/btn_contact.gif"
   style="border:none"></a>
   <hr>
   </nav>
   ```

   Note Because the bottom navigation bar should be formatted differently than the top one, leave it formatted as a division. That way you can use the *<nav>* tag to define the formatting for only the top navigation bar.

3. Delete the *<div id="main">* tag and its closing *</div>* tag.

4. Enclose the first paragraph of the body text with an *<article>* tag.

<article>
```
<p><b>Fruit trees are now in stock! </b>We have just received a large
shipment of peach, pear, apple, and plum trees with sturdy root systems
and healthy foliage, with prices as low as $29.99. Visit the <a href=
"products.htm">Products</a> page for details.</p>
```
</article>

Note In practical usage, the individual paragraphs of body text on this page would probably not warrant their own semantic tags because this page contains so little content overall. However, for example purposes, you will mark them up anyway.

5. Enclose the second paragraph and the bulleted list that follows it with an *<article>* tag.

<article>
```
<p><b>New articles!</b> Check out these recently posted articles:
<ul>
<li><a href="foliage.htm">Diagnosing Foliage Problems</a></li>
<li><a href="spray.htm">Spraying Techniques for Fruit Trees</a></li>
</ul>
```
</article>

6. Enclose the last body paragraph with an *<aside>* tag.

<aside>
```
<p><b>What does <i>that</i> mean?</b> Run into an unfamiliar gardening term?
Look it up in our <a href="glossary.htm" target="_blank">Glossary</a>.</p>
```
</aside>

Leave the bottom navigation bar's *<div>* tag as is.

7. Replace the *<div id="copy">* tag with *<footer>*, and change its closing *</div>* tag to *</footer>*.

<footer>
```
<p>Copyright &copy; 2012 The Garden Company&trade;<br>
No material may be reproduced without written permission<br>
<a href="mailto:webmaster@contoso.com?subject=Question/Comment" title=
"webmaster@contoso.com">Contact the Webmaster</a></p>
```
</footer>

8. Save the file.

Note You do not need to view your work in Internet Explorer this time because the changes you have made do not change the rendering.

 CLEAN UP Close the Notepad and Internet Explorer windows.

Positioning Divisions

There are two ways of positioning a division (or equivalent semantic-tagged block): you can use the *float* style rule, as you did with pictures in Chapter 9, "Displaying Graphics", or you can use the *position* style rule. The following sections explain each of these methods.

Note In the rest of this chapter, for simplicity, I use the term *division* generically to mean both the *<div>* tag and the HTML5 semantic tags. In most cases, browsers handle the formatting and positioning the same way.

Floating a Division to the Right or Left

The easiest way to place one division beside another is to use the *float* style rule. For example, to make a navigation bar that floats to the left of the main body text, you can set the navigation bar's division to a certain width (perhaps 150 pixels or so), and then float it like this:

```
<div id="topnav" style="width: 150px; float: left">
```

Alternatively, if you were using the *<nav>* tag for the navigation bar, it would look like this:

```
<nav style="width: 150px; float: left">
```

Because the main advantage of using divisions is to promote consistency across documents, you would probably want to set up the style rule in an external style sheet rather than in the individual division tag or an internal style sheet.

In a style sheet, you precede the names of unique elements such as divisions with a pound sign (#), as shown in the following:

```
#topnav {width: 150px; float: left}
```

Alternatively, if you were using the *<nav>* tag for the navigation bar, the style rule in the style sheet would look like this:

```
nav {width: 150px; float: left}
```

Positioning a Division on the Page

If you need a division to be in a specific spot on the page, use the *position* style rule, which has three possible values:

- *position: absolute*   This value specifies a fixed position with respect to the parent element. Unless the element is within some other tag, the parent element is generally the *<body>* tag; in this case, the element would have a fixed position relative to the upper-left corner of the page.

- *position: relative*   This value specifies an offset from the element's natural position. Other elements on the page are not affected, even if the new position causes elements to overlap.

- *position: fixed*   This value specifies a fixed position within the browser window that doesn't change even when the display is scrolled up or down. Internet Explorer does not support this setting.

You must use each of these values in conjunction with a *top*, *right*, *bottom*, and/or *left* style rule that specifies the location to which the *position* rule refers. For example, to position a division called *main* exactly 100 pixels from the top of the page and 200 pixels from the left side, create this style rule in the style sheet:

```
#main {position: absolute; top: 100px; left: 200px}
```

Note When using semantic tags, you won't have one that defines the entire main body of the page content, so you might want to create a division for that purpose if you want to specify an exact position for all the body text on the page. As this example illustrates, it's okay to mix up semantic tags and *<div>* tags in your work. The *<div>* tag is not deprecated in HTML5; it's still perfectly valid.

You can combine positioning with a *width* specification to position each division in a precise rectangular area on the screen. For example, to place the top navigation bar exactly 100 pixels from the top of the page and make it 150 pixels wide, use the following:

```
#topnav {position: absolute; top: 100px; width: 150px}
```

Or, if you are using the *<nav>* tag instead, use this:

```
nav {position: absolute; top: 100px; width: 150px}
```

The *position* style rule results in positioning that does not take into regard other elements on the page. This can get you in trouble because elements can potentially overlap unattractively, but it can also be used to intentionally create overlapping elements. For example, you can use this feature to overlay text on a photo.

In this exercise, you will specify a size and position for several divisions by creating rules that refer to those divisions in an external style sheet. This example file uses a mixture of HTML5 semantic tags and generic *<div>* tags.

SET UP Use the *default.css* and *index3.htm* files in the practice file folder for this topic. These files are located in the Documents\Microsoft Press\HTML5 SBS\11Divisions\PositioningDivisions. Open the *default.css* style sheet in Notepad, and open the *index3.htm* file in Internet Explorer.

1. In Internet Explorer, view the *index3* file. Note the position of the top navigation bar.

2. In Notepad, in *default.css*, add the following style rule:

   nav {float: left; width: 150px; padding-top: 15px}

   Note You can add the style rule anywhere in default.css; adding it at the end of the file is fine.

3. Save the file, and then refresh Internet Explorer.

   The navigation bar now appears at the left side of the page.

Note Notice that when the navigation bar is laid out vertically, the horizontal rule below it looks awkward.

4. Open *index3.htm* in Notepad and remove the *<hr>* tag immediately before the *</nav>* tag. Save your work, and then refresh Internet Explorer to view the change.

5. Reopen *default.css* in Notepad if necessary. Add a style rule that limits the width of the main division to 500 pixels.

   `#main {width: 500px}`

6. Save the file, and then refresh Internet Explorer.

   Notice that the body text begins higher on the page than the top button, which looks a bit awkward. We'll fix that next.

7. Specify an absolute position for the top of the main division that is 85 pixels from the top and 140 pixels from the left

   `#main {width: 500px; position: absolute; top: 85px; left: 140px}`

8. Save the file, and then refresh Internet Explorer.

   Notice that the text in the main division now aligns nicely with the top of the buttons.

9. (Optional) Experiment with the top and left settings in *default.css*, saving your work and refreshing Internet Explorer to see the changes. Return the style rule to **top: 85px** and **left: 140px** when you are finished experimenting.

10. Position the upper-left corner of the *<footer>* section 85 pixels from the top and 500 pixels from the left side of the page.

    `footer {position: absolute; top: 85px; left: 500px}`

11. Save the file, and then refresh Internet Explorer.

    Notice that the main and copy divisions overlap.

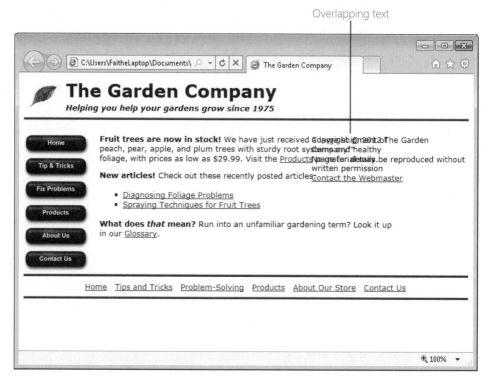

Overlapping text

12. Modify the style rules for the main division and the footer tag so that the main division is only 400 pixels wide, and the footer starts at 550 pixels from the left:

    `#main {width: 400px; position: absolute; top: 85px; left: 140px}`

    `footer {position: absolute; top: 85px; left: 550px}`

13. Save the file, and then refresh Internet Explorer.

    Now the divisions share the horizontal space more attractively.

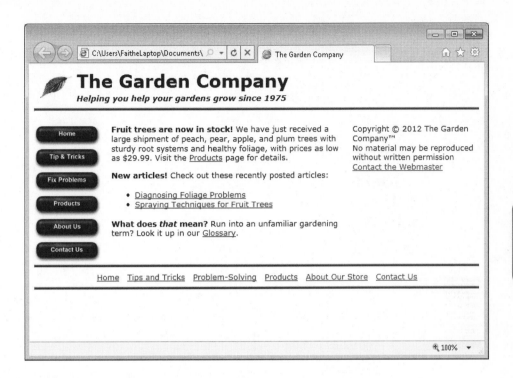

 CLEAN UP Close the Notepad and Internet Explorer windows.

Formatting Divisions

You format divisions as you would any other elements. You can use styles to specify the font family, font style, font weight, alignment, color, and everything else covered so far in this book.

You can change the background color of a division with the *background-color* style rule. For example, to add a khaki-colored background to the navigation bar, use the following:

```
nav {float: left; width: 150px; padding-top: 15px; background-color: khaki}
```

When you start applying colors to divisions, however, you might uncover some underlying problems with your page. For example, the page for The Garden Company from the previous example looks pretty good when everything has a white background, but watch what happens when you add that khaki background to the navigation bar, as shown in the image that follows.

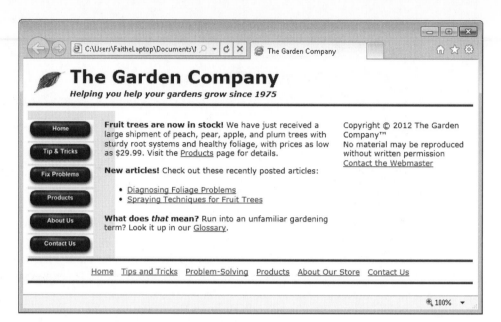

There are several problems with this layout. One is that the *main* division, which has an absolute position, is overlapping the navigation bar. The root cause is that the navigation bar is wider than it needs to be. Also, the button graphics in the navigation bar have a rectangular white background—a fact that was not obvious until now.

You can fix the size and positioning issues easily enough by modifying the styles. For example, you could decrease the width of the navigation bar to 100 pixels, as shown in the following:

```
nav {float: left; width: 100px; padding-top: 15px; background-color: khaki}
```

Unfortunately, you can't fix the button background problem with HTML; you'd need to edit the button graphics in a program that supports transparency, setting each button's background to be transparent. If your graphics-editing program does not support transparency, one solution is to change each button's background color to khaki. That method is not as good, though, because you might decide to make the navigation bar some other color later. With a transparent background, the buttons will blend nicely into any background color.

Note Recall from Chapter 9 that GIF and PNG graphics formats support transparency, but JPG does not.

In this exercise, you will apply a colored background to a division and edit that division's formatting to fine-tune it.

SET UP Use the *default.css* and *index3.htm* files in the practice file folder for this topic. These files are located in the Documents\Microsoft Press\HTML5 SBS\11Divisions\FormattingDivisions folder. Open the *default.css* style sheet in Notepad, and open the *index3.htm* file in Internet Explorer.

1. In the *default.css* style sheet, add the khaki background color to the footer.

```
footer {position: absolute; top: 85px; left: 550px; background-color: khaki}
```

2. Save the file, and then refresh Internet Explorer.

3. Open the *index3 file* in Notepad and delete the *<hr>* tags from the *bottomnav* division.

4. Save the file, and then refresh Internet Explorer.

Oops! Look what has happened. Those horizontal lines were holding that division at the bottom of the page, where it belongs. Without them, the text shifted up. The browser ignores all the other divisions except the masthead because they are all absolutely positioned.

Bottom navigation bar has shifted up

At this point you have two choices: you can set an absolute position for the *bottomnav* division, or you can get rid of the absolute positioning for all the divisions and go back to a simple float for the top navigation bar. Let's do the latter.

5. In the *default.css* style sheet, delete the *main* division's style rule as well as the style rules for the *footer*.

6. Add a style rule that changes the bottom navigation bar to khaki.

```
#bottomnav {background-color: khaki}
```

7. Save the file, and then refresh Internet Explorer.

Now the bottom navigation bar is back down at the bottom of the page, but it doesn't clear the navigation bar at the left.

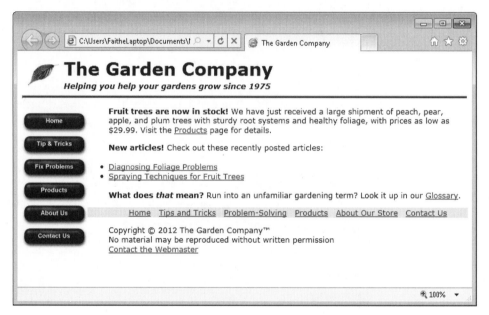

8. In the *default.css* style sheet, set the *bottomnav* division to clear any items positioned to its left.

```
#bottomnav {background-color: khaki; clear: left}
```

9. Save the file, and then refresh Internet Explorer.

Now give the site a new look by getting rid of the graphic and horizontal line in the masthead and inserting a background image in the *masthead* division.

10. In the *index3* file, in the header, delete the *<img>* tag for the leaf and its associated *<a>* hyperlink. Delete the horizontal line, as well. This leaves the *<header>* looking like this:

```
<header>
<h1 class="pagetitle">The Garden Company</h1>
<h5 class="tagline"><i>Helping you help your gardens grow since 1975</i></
h5>
</header>
```

Some browsers don't interpret *<header>* correctly, and the masthead is a fairly important page element to get right, so in the interest of compatibility, turn that *<header>* back into a division whose name is *header* before going any further.

11. Change the *<header>* tag to a *<div>* tag.

```
<div id="header">
<h1 class="pagetitle">The Garden Company</h1>
<h5 class="tagline"><i>Helping you help your gardens grow since 1975</i></
h5>
</div>
```

12. Save the file.

13. In the *default.css* style sheet, add a style rule for the header division that applies an image as its background:

`#header {background-image: url(images/leaf-green.jpg)}`

14. Save the file, and then refresh Internet Explorer.

The new masthead looks interesting, but you need to add some padding and make the text easier to read.

15. Modify the style rule for the header division to use white text and to add 10 pixels of padding on all sides:

`#header {background-image: url(images/leaf-green.jpg); padding: 10px; color: white}`

16. Save the file, and then refresh Internet Explorer to see the new masthead.

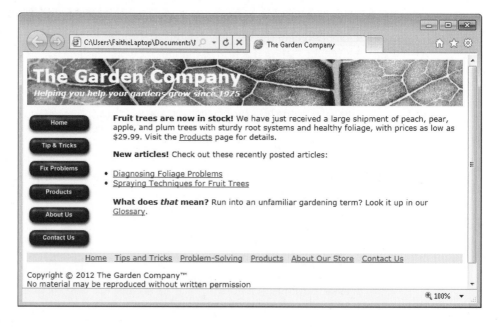

 CLEAN UP Close the Notepad and Internet Explorer windows.

Key Points

- To create a division, surround a section of a page with a *<div>* tag.

- HTML5 uses semantic tags to define sections of a page. Some of the most common of these are *<header>*, *<footer>*, *<nav>*, *<article>*, *<aside>*, and *<section>*. Not all browsers support these tags yet. Internet Explorer 9.0 and higher does, as do the current versions of Google Chrome and Firefox.

- Each division tag has an *id* attribute that should be unique within that document. Multiple documents can have the same division names, though, and in fact, this is encouraged so that one external style sheet can format multiple documents.

- One way to position a division is with a *float* attribute. For example, to place a division at the left (for use as a navigation bar), use *float: left*.

- Another way to position a division is with a position attribute. The valid values are *absolute*, *relative*, and *fixed*. When you use the *position* attribute, you must also use a *top*, *bottom*, *left*, and/or *right* attribute to specify the numeric value for the position.

  - With absolute positioning, the element is positioned absolutely within its parent element, which is usually the *<body>* tag, so the element is positioned absolutely on the page.

  - With relative positioning, the element is positioned in relation to its default position.

  - With fixed positioning, the element is positioned in relation to the browser window.

- Divisions can be formatted by using the same character, paragraph, and page formatting styles you learned throughout the book, including *background-color* and *background-image*.

Chapter at a Glance

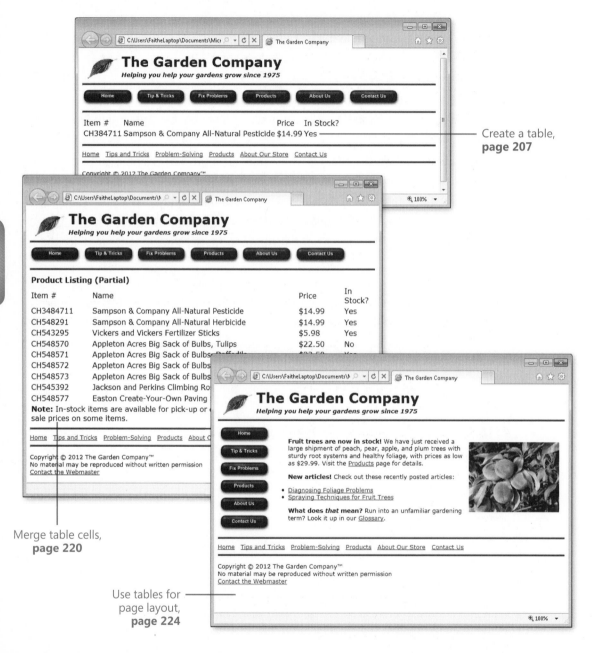

Create a table,
page 207

Merge table cells,
page 220

Use tables for
page layout,
page 224

12 Creating Tables

In this chapter, you will learn how to

✔ Create a simple table.

✔ Specify the size of a table.

✔ Specify the width of a column.

✔ Merge table cells.

✔ Use tables for page layout.

If you've used a word-processing program before, you're probably already familiar with the task of creating tables. A *table* is a grid of rows and columns, the intersections of which form *cells*. Each cell is a distinct area, into which you can place text, graphics, or even other tables.

HTML handles tables very well, and you can use them to organize and present complex data to your site visitors. For example, you could display your store's inventory in a table.

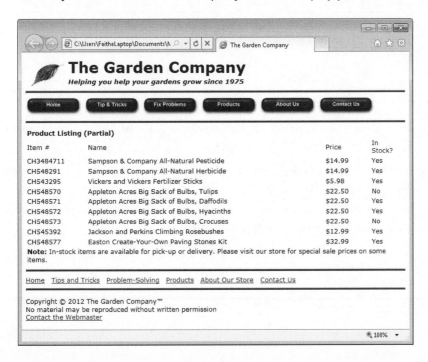

The most popular use of tables in HTML, however, is as a page-layout tool. You can create a large table that occupies the entire page, and then place content into the cells to position that content on the page. In the following figure, for example, each of the sections (the masthead, the navigation bar, the body, and the footer) resides in its own separate table cell. You will create this layout later in the chapter, learning the details of how it's done.

Note   Now that division-based layouts are becoming more common (see Chapter 11, "Creating Division-Based Layouts"), some experts will tell you that table-based design is on its way out. However, for a small, non-professional Web site for personal or organizational use, tables are still a very viable way of laying out your pages.

In this chapter, you'll learn the basic HTML for creating tables, rows, and cells. You'll also learn how to specify cell sizes and merge cells to create larger areas. After you master these skills, you'll put them to work by creating a table-based page layout grid. Then, in the next chapter, you'll learn how to format tables.

See Also   Do you need only a quick refresher on the topics in this chapter? See the Key Points at the end of this chapter.

Creating a Simple Table

> **Practice Files**   Before you can use the practice files provided for this chapter, you need to install them from the book's companion content page to their default locations. See "Using the Practice Files" in the beginning of this book for more information.

Creating a Simple Table

The *<table>* tag creates an HTML table. Within that tag, you include one or more *<tr>* tags, which define the table's rows, and within each *<tr>* tag, you define one or more *<td>* tags, which define the cells.

```
<table>
   <tr>
      <td>Cell 1</td>
      <td>Cell 2</td>
   </tr>
   <tr>
      <td>Cell 3</td>
      <td>Cell 4</td>
   </tr>
</table>
```

Displayed in a browser, the code just shown creates a table that looks like the following:

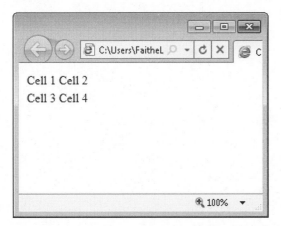

This table is not very interesting to look at in its default state. And because by default, HTML tables have no borders or shading, you can barely even tell it's a table at all. The text simply appears where it's supposed to appear according to the table's specification. (That's a big hint about how you will use tables for layout later in the chapter.)

The number of columns within a table is equal to the largest number of *<td>* tags in any given row. Watch what happens when I add another *<td>* tag to the second row. I'm also going to add a *border="1"* attribute in the *<table>* tag to make the table borders visible. so you can see what's going on more clearly. (You'll learn more about that attribute in Chapter 13, Formatting Tables.") The additions are shown in bold text in the following code:

```
<table border="1">
    <tr>
        <td>Cell 1</td>
        <td>Cell 2</td>
    </tr>
    <tr>
        <td>Cell 3</td>
        <td>Cell 4</td>
        <td>Cell 5</td>
    </tr>
</table>
```

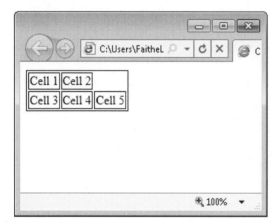

Notice that because the rows do not have the same number of cells, the browser inserts a blank space in the row that doesn't include the extra cell. In the section "Merging Table Cells" on page 220, you will learn how to merge multiple cells into a single cell.

In this exercise, you will create a simple table.

 SET UP Use the *products.htm* file in the practice file folder for this topic. This file is located in the Documents\Microsoft Press\HTML5 SBS\12Tables\CreatingTable folder. Open the *products* file in Microsoft Notepad and in Microsoft Internet Explorer.

1. In Notepad, in the empty space between the two consecutive *<hr>* tags, create the table, leaving a few blank lines between the opening and closing tags.

```
<table>

</table>
```

2. Within the table, create three rows. Indenting the lines as shown in the following code is optional but recommended.

```
<table>
    <tr>
    </tr>
    <tr>
    </tr>
    <tr>
    </tr>
</table>
```

3. Within the first row, create four columns.

```
<table>
    <tr>
        <td> </td>
        <td> </td>
        <td> </td>
        <td> </td>
    </tr>
    <tr>
    </tr>
    <tr>
    </tr>
</table>
```

4. Enter the text that will appear in the first row of the table, as follows:

```
<table>
    <tr>
        <td>Item #</td>
        <td>Name</td>
        <td>Price</td>
        <td>In Stock?</td>
    </tr>
    <tr>
    </tr>
    <tr>
    </tr>
</table>
```

Tip If you like, you can use *<th>* tags instead of *<td>* tags to indicate table headings. Some browsers automatically format table heading cells differently.

5. Save the file, and then refresh Internet Explorer.

Notice that the browser ignores the two empty rows.

6. In Notepad, enter a product name in each cell of the first empty row, as shown here:

```
<table>
   <tr>
       <td>Item #</td>
       <td>Name</td>
       <td>Price</td>
       <td>In Stock?</td>
   </tr>
   <tr>
       <td>CH384711</td>
       <td>Sampson & Company All-Natural Pesticide</td>
       <td>$14.99</td>
       <td>Yes</td>
   </tr>
   <tr>
   </tr>
</table>
```

7. Save the file, and then refresh Internet Explorer.

Notice that the columns have expanded to accommodate the longest entries.

 CLEAN UP Close the Notepad and Internet Explorer windows.

Specifying the Size of a Table

By default, a table sizes itself to accommodate all of its cells, and each cell's height and width changes to accommodate the largest entry in that row or column. The table structure expands or contracts as needed when you add or remove cells or content within cells.

With these default settings, a table can end up looking rather cramped, especially if you don't use borders between cells (which you'll learn more about in Chapter 13). In the table from the previous exercise, for example, some extra space would be welcome.

One way to add extra spacing in this instance would be to set the overall size of the table to 100 percent. This forces the table to expand horizontally to fill the available space in the browser window. To do this, add a width attribute to the opening *<table>* tag like this:

```
<table width=100%>
```

Alternatively, you can place the width specification in a style, like this:

```
<table style="width: 100%">
```

To apply the width specification to all tables, place it in a style sheet, as shown here:

```
table {width: 100%}
```

You don't need to specify 100 percent; you could also set the table's width to 50, 75, or any other percentage. You can do the same thing with table height, making it expand to fill the entire browser window vertically by using the following:

```
table (height: 100%)
```

The only drawback to specifying width and/or height by percentage is that you cannot be certain which size browser window the visitors to your site will be using. This example looks great in an 800 × 600 window, such as demonstrated here:

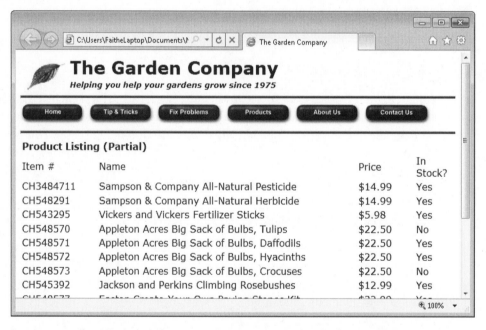

But in a smaller window, it becomes just as cramped as before, and the text wraps to multiple lines.

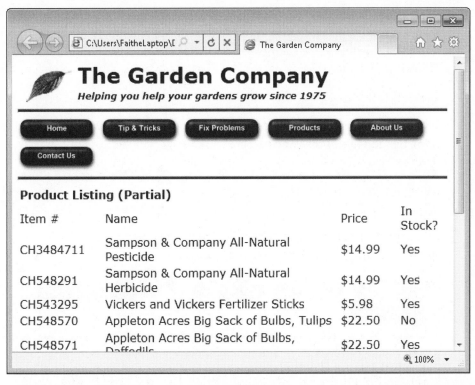

And in a larger window, the extra space between the columns becomes exaggerated.

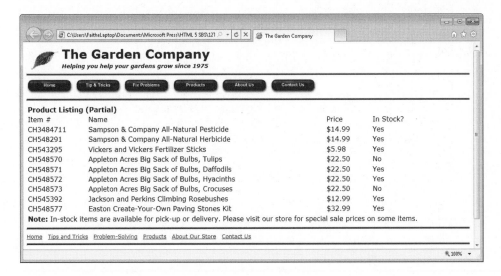

An alternative approach is to specify a number of pixels for the table's width. That way, the width the table requires in pixels does not change no matter what the size of the browser window. For example, to lock the table to a width of 750 pixels, use the following:

```
<table width="750px">
```

When a browser renders a fixed-width table in a smaller browser window, a horizontal scroll bar appears in the window.

Horizontal scroll bar

When displayed in a larger window, extra horizontal space appears to the right of the table (assuming the table is left-aligned) rather than being distributed throughout the table.

Although it is less common, there might also be cases where it is useful to set a specific table height, either in percentage or pixels. You do this by using the same method, except you specify height instead. For example, in a tag, use this:

```
<table height="400px">
```

To specify height in a style rule, use this:

```
table (height: 400px}
```

In this exercise, you will change a table's width using two different methods and check its appearance in various browser window sizes.

SET UP Use the *products.htm* file in the practice file folder for this topic. This file is located in the Documents\Microsoft Press\HTML5 SBS\12Tables\SpecifyingSize folder. Open the *products* file in Notepad and in Internet Explorer.

1. Modify the opening *<table>* tag to make the table exactly 700 pixels wide.

   ```
   <table width="700">
   ```

2. Save the file, and then refresh Internet Explorer. Experiment with different browser window sizes, and note how the table looks at each size.

3. Edit the *<table>* tag to make the table fill the width of the browser window.

   ```
   <table width=100%>
   ```

4. Save the file, and then refresh Internet Explorer. Experiment with different browser window sizes, and note how the table looks at each size.

5. Remove the width attribute from the table tag.

   ```
   <table>
   ```

6. Create a style rule in the *<style>* section that sets the default width for all tables to 100 percent of the browser window width.

   ```
   <style>
   table {width: 100%}
   </style>
   ```

7. Save the file, and then refresh Internet Explorer.

   It should not have changed from the last time you looked at it.

8. Add a height attribute to the *<table>* tag that sets the table height at exactly 500 pixels.

   ```
   <table height="500px">
   ```

9. Save the file, and then refresh Internet Explorer.

Extra space has been distributed vertically throughout the table.

 CLEAN UP Close the Notepad and Internet Explorer windows.

Specifying the Width of a Column

Setting the overall table size is useful, but for more control, you might prefer to set the width of each column separately. To set the width of a column to a certain minimum amount, specify a width in the *<td>* tag for any cell within that column. You can use the same method you used for the *<table>* tag in the preceding section, as shown in the following:

```
<td width="200px">
```

To specify the width of a column by using a style, use this:

```
<td style="width: 200px">
```

The traditional place to set the column width is in the first row of the table, but that is not a requirement; you can set a width for any cell in any row. The column as a whole will be as wide as the widest cell in that column.

In the following code, specific values are set for the column widths:

```
<table border="1">
   <tr>
      <td width="100px"> </td>
      <td width="400px"> </td>
      <td width="100px"> </td>
   </tr>
   <tr>
      <td> </td>
      <td> </td>
      <td> </td>
   </tr>
</table>
```

This code creates a table that looks like this:

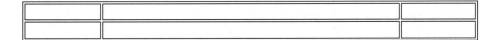

Tip The examples shown here use nonbreaking spaces (* *) as placeholders in empty cells. This is optional, but it makes an empty table appear as it will when you place content in the cells, which can be important when you are checking your work in a browser window as you build your page.

If you enter some text in one of the cells that exceeds the column's width, the browser wraps the text into multiple lines, as needed.

Wildflower seed assortments		

Note The text-wrapping behavior shown in the preceding example is not universal across all browsers. Some older versions of Internet Explorer, for example, will still expand the first column to fit all the text on one line. This illustrates the importance of checking your work in multiple browsers.

If you widen the browser window, the text remains wrapped because the column width is fixed.

You can also specify column width in percentages, for different wrapping and resizing behavior at different browser window widths. Suppose in the previous example that you specified 20 percent, 60 percent, and 20 percent for each of the three columns, respectively:

```
<table border="1">
   <tr>
      <td width="20%"> </td>
      <td width="60%"> </td>
      <td width="20%"> </td>
   </tr>
   <tr>
      <td> </td>
      <td> </td>
      <td> </td>
   </tr>
</table>
```

You would start out with a very small table, because the table is only as large as it needs to be to hold its content.

However, when you add text to a cell, the table expands. Keep in mind that the table expands proportionally; the first column will always be 20 percent of the width of the entire table, the second column 60 percent, and so on. The width of the browser window determines how much that first column can expand while still maintaining the proportion. Here's what the example table looks like in an 800 × 600 browser window, with sample text entered in the first cell, as in the previous example.

Wildflower seed assortments		

However, if you expand the browser window to, for example, 1024 × 768, the table cells stretch out to fill the available space, keeping their 20/60/20 percent proportions.

Wildflower seed assortments		

As you might guess, things can get complicated when you start combining overall table widths with individual cell widths. If a table doesn't turn out the way you expected, try removing all width specifications from the *<table>* and *<td>* tags and all width-related style rules from the style sheet, and then start over.

In this exercise, you will set specific widths for each column in a table.

SET UP Be sure to use the practice files provided specifically for this exercise, and not earlier versions. Use the *products.htm* file in the practice file folder for this topic. This file is located in the Documents\Microsoft Press\HTML5 SBS\12Tables\SettingWidth folder. Open the *products* file in Notepad and in Internet Explorer.

1. In Internet Explorer, examine the widths of the columns. Change the browser window to several different widths to see how the columns change.

2. In Notepad, set the width of the first column of the table to 100 pixels by using a *style* attribute.

    ```
    <tr>
        <td style="width: 100px">Item #</td>
        <td>Name</td>
        <td>Price</td>
        <td>In Stock?</td>
    </tr>
    ```

3. Set the width of the second column to 400 pixels.

    ```
    <tr>
        <td style="width: 100px">Item #</td>
        <td style="width: 400px">Name</td>
        <td>Price</td>
        <td>In Stock?</td>
    </tr>
    ```

4. Set the width of the third column to 75 pixels.

    ```
    <tr>
        <td style="width: 100px">Item #</td>
        <td style="width: 400px">Name</td>
        <td style="width: 75px">Price</td>
        <td>In Stock?</td>
    </tr>
    ```

    Note There is no need to set the width of the column farthest to the right at this point because its right edge is adjacent to blank space.

5. Save the file, and then refresh Internet Explorer. Experiment with various window widths in Internet Explorer to see how the table's column widths behave compared to step 1.

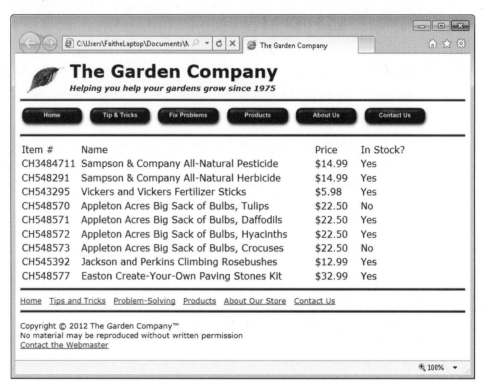

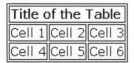 **CLEAN UP** Close the Notepad and Internet Explorer windows.

Merging Table Cells

As you have seen in the preceding sections, every cell in a given row must be the same height, and every cell in a given column must be the same width. You can't make individual cells different heights or widths, but you can *span* (merge) two or more adjacent cells so that one cell spans multiple rows and/or columns. This technique is useful for centering text across several columns.

It also comes in very handy when creating table-based page layouts, which you'll learn about on page 224.

To merge a cell into adjacent cells to its right, use the *colspan* attribute and specify the number of columns to be spanned, like this:

```
<td colspan="3">
```

To merge a cell into adjacent cells below it, use the *rowspan* attribute and specify the number of rows to be spanned, as shown in the following:

```
<td rowspan="2">
```

Using those two attributes, you can create sophisticated table layouts. For example, the following table has five columns and five rows, but some of the cells span multiple columns or rows:

```
<table border="1">
    <tr>
        <td colspan="2" rowspan="2">Survey Results</td>
        <td colspan="3">Age</td>
    </tr>
    <tr>
        <td>12 to 25</td>
        <td>26 to 40</td>
        <td>Over 40</td>
    </tr>
    <tr>
        <td rowspan="3">"What is your dream vacation destination?"</td>
        <td>Disneyworld</td>
        <td>25%</td>
        <td>50%</td>
        <td>25%</td>
    </tr>
    <tr>
        <td>Las Vegas</td>
        <td>25%</td>
        <td>50%</td>
        <td>25%</td>
    </tr>
    <tr>
        <td>Europe</td>
        <td>25%</td>
        <td>50%</td>
        <td>25%</td>
    </tr>
</table>
```

The preceding code creates a table that appears as follows:

Survey Results		Age		
		12 to 25	26 to 40	Over 40
"What is your dream vacation destination?"	Disneyworld	25%	50%	25%
	Las Vegas	25%	50%	25%
	Europe	25%	50%	25%

In this exercise, you will create two simple column spans.

SET UP Be sure to use the practice files provided specifically for this exercise, and not earlier versions. Use the *products.htm* file in the practice file folder for this topic. This file is located in the Documents\Microsoft Press\HTML5 SBS\12Tables\SpanningCells folder. Open the *products* file in Notepad and in Internet Explorer.

1. View *products.htm* in Internet Explorer. Notice that the table title wraps to multiple lines, and that the note at the bottom of the table does not span all columns.

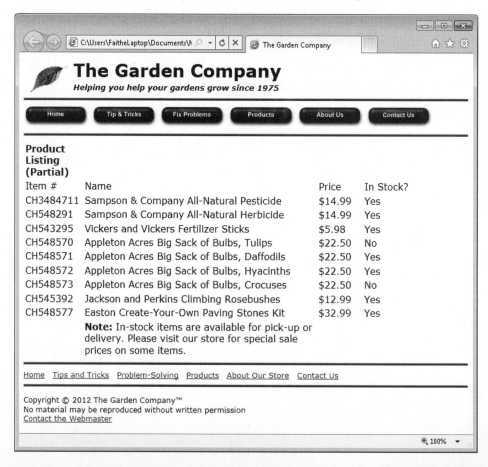

2. In Notepad, modify the table title to span all four columns.

```
<tr>
    <td colspan="4"><b>Product Listing (Partial)</b></td>
</tr>
```

3. In the last row of the table, move the cell containing the note to the first position.

```
<tr>
    <td><b>Note: </b>In-stock items are available for pick-up or delivery.
Please visit our store for special sale prices on some items.</td>
    <td></td>
    <td></td>
    <td></td>
</tr>
```

Note Step 3 is necessary because columns can be spanned only from left to right.

4. Format the note to span all four columns.

```
<tr>
    <td colspan="4"><b>Note: </b>In-stock items are available for pick-
up or delivery. Please visit our store for special sale prices on some
items.</td>
    <td></td>
    <td></td>
    <td></td>
</tr>
```

5. Save the file, and then refresh Internet Explorer.

 CLEAN UP Close the Notepad and Internet Explorer windows.

Using Tables for Page Layout

In addition to their value in laying out tabular data, tables are also useful in HTML for their page-structuring capabilities.

It is customary for a Web page to have a navigation bar at the top or on the left side. It is fairly easy to create a horizontal navigation bar with regular paragraphs, as you saw in Chapter 10, "Creating Navigational Aids," but to create a vertical navigation bar, you must somehow break the page into sections. One way to do that is by using divisions, as you learned in Chapter 11. Another way is to use a table.

When using a table for page layout, you might place your navigation hyperlinks in the column farthest to the left, and then place the body of your content in the other columns. The table cells act as containers into which you can put anything: paragraphs, lists, headings, graphics, and so on.

Some Web designers prefer to place everything in the table, and use row and column spans to merge cells where needed. Others place only certain content in a table, letting the rest of the text float around it.

The skills you have learned so far in this chapter will serve you well when creating table-based layouts. You can specify the exact widths of the columns by pixels or their relative width in percentages, and you can create row or column spans as needed.

In this exercise, you will convert a page with a horizontal navigation bar to one with a vertical bar by using a table.

SET UP Be sure to use the practice files provided specifically for this exercise, and not earlier versions. Use the *index.htm* file in the practice file folder for this topic. This file is located in the Documents\Microsoft Press\HTML5 SBS\12Tables\UsingTables folder. Open the *index* file in Notepad and in Internet Explorer.

1. View the *index* file in Internet Explorer. Note the navigation bar position.

2. In Notepad, insert opening *<table>* and *<tr>* tags after the first *<hr>* tag.

```
<body>
<a href="http://www.contoso.com" title="Home page">
<img src="images/leaf.gif" class="logo"></a>
<h1 class="pagetitle">The Garden Company</h1>
<h5 class="tagline"><i>Helping you help your gardens grow since 1975</i></
h5>
<hr>
<table>
<tr>
```

3. Enclose the top navigation bar in a *<td>* tag, and delete the *<hr>* below it.

```
<td>
<p style="margin:0px">
<a href="index.htm"><img src="images/btn_home.gif" style="border:none">
</a>
<a href="tips.htm"><img src="images/btn_tips.gif" style="border:none"></a>
<a href="problems.htm"><img src="images/btn_problem.gif" style=
"border:none"></a>
<a href="products.htm"><img src="images/btn_products.gif" style=
"border:none"></a>
<a href="about.htm"><img src="images/btn_about.gif" style="border:none">
</a>
<a href="contact.htm"><img src="images/btn_contact.gif"
style="border:none"></a></p>
</td>
```

4. Enclose the body of the document in a *<td>* tag, and then end the row and the table after it.

```
<td>
<p><img src="images/peaches.jpg" style="float: right; padding: 10px">
<b>Fruit trees are now in stock! </b>We have just received a large shipment
of peach, pear, apple, and plum trees with sturdy root systems and healthy
foliage, with prices as low as $29.99. Visit the <a href="products.htm">
Products</a> page for details.</p>

<p><b>New articles!</b> Check out these recently posted articles:
<li><a href="foliage.htm">Diagnosing Foliage Problems</a></li>
<li><a href="spray.htm">Spraying Techniques for Fruit Trees</a></li>
</ul>

<p><b>What does <i>that</i> mean?</b> Run into an unfamiliar gardening term?
Look it up in our <a href="glossary.htm" target="_blank">Glossary</a>.</p>
</td>
</tr>
</table>
```

5. Save the file, and then refresh Internet Explorer.

It looks alright, except the navigation bar area is too wide.

6. Format the first column to be exactly 150 pixels wide.

```
<table>
<tr>
<td style="width: 150px">
<p style="margin:0px">
<a href="index.htm"><img src="images/btn_home.gif" style="border:none"></a>
...
```

7. Save the file, and then refresh Internet Explorer. The navigation buttons are now set up vertically, one atop the other.

The Garden Company
Helping you help your gardens grow since 1975

Home

Tip & Tricks

Fix Problems

Products

About Us

Contact Us

Fruit trees are now in stock! We have just received a large shipment of peach, pear, apple, and plum trees with sturdy root systems and healthy foliage, with prices as low as $29.99. Visit the <u>Products</u> page for details.

New articles! Check out these recently posted articles:

- <u>Diagnosing Foliage Problems</u>
- <u>Spraying Techniques for Fruit Trees</u>

What does *that* mean? Run into an unfamiliar gardening term? Look it up in our <u>Glossary</u>.

<u>Home</u> <u>Tips and Tricks</u> <u>Problem-Solving</u> <u>Products</u> <u>About Our Store</u> <u>Contact Us</u>

Copyright © 2012 The Garden Company™
No material may be reproduced without written permission
<u>Contact the Webmaster</u>

CLEAN UP Close the Notepad and Internet Explorer windows.

Key Points

- To create a table, use the *<table>* tag. Enclose each row in a *<tr>* tag, and enclose each cell in each row in a *<td>* tag.

- You can specify table size in either pixels or as a percentage of the page width. Use the width attribute like this: *<table width="400">*.

- You can also set width by using a style rule like this: *<table style="width: 400">*.

- You can specify the width of each cell, either in percentages or pixels like this: *<td width="100">* or *<td style="width: 100">*.

- To merge (span) multiple cells, place the *colspan* or *rowspan* attribute in the cell at the top of or farthest to the left in the range to be spanned like this: *<td colspan="2">*.

- You can use tables as containers to facilitate page layout. You can place all or part of the body of a page in a table.

Chapter at a Glance

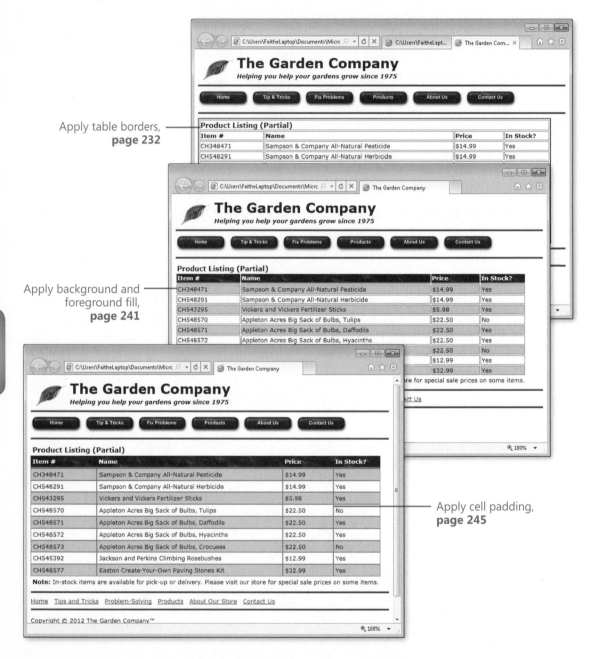

Apply table borders,
page 232

Apply background and
foreground fill,
page 241

Apply cell padding,
page 245

13 Formatting Tables

Chapter 12, "Creating Tables," explained how to create tables structurally; now it's time to learn how to make them more attractive. By default, a table is just a plain container—no border, no shading, and no text formatting. It's up to you to add all those things if you want them.

Not every table needs elaborate formatting. If you are using a table as a container for a page layout, as demonstrated in Chapter 12, you probably want the table to be as unobtrusive as possible. But even unobtrusive tables can benefit from some of the small improvements you'll learn about in this chapter, such as adjusting the amount of space between the border of a cell and its content. (That's called *padding*, as you might remember from Chapter 8, "Formatting Paragraphs by Using Style Sheets.")

In this chapter, you'll learn how to apply borders to table cells and how to fill their backgrounds with color or images. You'll learn how to fine-tune cell spacing and padding, and how to make the contents of a cell align a certain way vertically and horizontally.

See Also Do you need only a quick refresher on the topics in this chapter? See the Key Points at the end of this chapter.

Practice Files Before you can use the practice files provided for this chapter, you need to install them from the book's companion content page to their default locations. See "Using the Practice Files" in the beginning of this book for more information.

Applying Table Borders

Tables created using the default settings are pretty plain—in fact, they're invisible—so it can be difficult to distinguish where one cell ends and the next cell begins. To help with this problem, you can place borders around cells, either globally or selectively. You might also choose to fill (shade) certain cells to help them stand out. For example, the spacing in the following table makes it difficult for a reader to follow a line across the page.

You could make it easier to read by applying borders as shown in the image that follows.

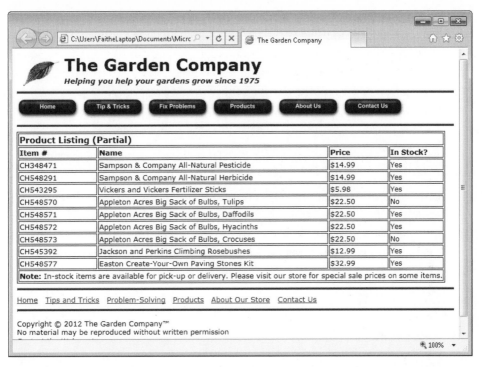

Tip If you don't like the double lines between each cell, set the cell spacing to 0. You'll learn how to do that in "Changing Cell Padding, Spacing, and Alignment," on page 245.

You can apply borders to a table either by adding attributes to the *<table>* tag or with styles, either applied to the individual table or placed in an internal or external cascading style sheet. This chapter shows both methods, but the style method is the more modern and reliable one, because it produces consistent results across all browsers.

Applying Borders by Using Attributes

By default, a table has no border. To add a one-pixel border around both the table as a whole and around each individual cell, you can add this attribute to the *<table>* tag, as shown in the following code:

```
<table border="1">
```

As shown in the following examples, increasing the number increases the width of the outer border around the whole table, but not the inner borders:

You may recall from Chapter 12 that the *border="1"* attribute is a quick way to see the borders of a table for the purposes of learning or debugging.

Unfortunately, different browsers display the *border* attribute differently. The above examples show tables rendered in Internet Explorer; borders render similarly in Google Chrome. Netscape and Firefox, however, render the border using two shades of gray for the outer border. Here's what a *border="10"* attribute looks like in Firefox:

Note You can apply a beveled border in any browser, without worrying about incompatibility, by using style-based formatting (use *border-style:outset*). Style-based formatting is covered in the next section of this chapter.

The *border* attribute applies a border to all sides of all cells. If you do not want the border on some of the sides, you can use the *frame* and/or *rules* attributes. The *frame* attribute specifies which sides of the outer frame of the table will display the border. The valid values are:

- *above*   Top border only
- *below*   Bottom border only
- *border*   All four sides
- *box*   All four sides
- *hsides*   Top and bottom only (stands for horizontal sides)
- *vsides*   Left and right only (stands for vertical sides)
- *lhs*   Left side only (stands for left-hand side)
- *rhs*   Right side only (stands for right-hand side)
- *void*   No outer border

The *rules* attribute does the same thing for the inner lines of the table (the cell borders). The valid values are:

- *all*   All inner lines
- *cols*   Only vertical inner lines
- *rows*   Only horizontal inner lines
- *none*   No inner lines
- *groups*   Lines around defined groups, if any (such as column groups, which you'll learn about later in this chapter)

For example, if you want only vertical borders in your table, around both the table as a whole and around each of the cells, apply these attributes to the *<table>* tag:

```
<table border="1" frame="vsides" rules="cols">
```

Applying Borders by Using Styles

You can also apply borders by using cascading style sheets (CSS), which is the most flexibile and consistent method. You should choose the CSS method in most cases, especially on sites that you expect to be active for many years to come, because the older methods of formatting tables may be deprecated in the future.

In Chapter 8, you learned about style-based borders for paragraphs. You use them the same way for the *<table>* and *<td>* tags. To review:

- The *border-width* attribute controls the thickness of the border. Specify a value in pixels.
- The *border-color* attribute controls the color of the border. Specify a color by name, hexadecimal number, or RGB value.
- The *border-style* attribute controls the line style. Choose among solid, dotted, dashed, double, groove, ridge, inset, outset, or none.
- To set all three attributes at once, use the *border* attribute and then place the settings after it in this order: *width, color, style*.
- To format the border sides individually, replace the border attribute with the *border-top, border-bottom, border-left,* or *border-right* attribute.

You can apply these attributes either to the entire table (by using the *<table>* tag or a style rule) or to individual cells (by using the *<td>* tags). You can apply them to individual instances within the opening tags themselves, you can create rules in the *<style>* area that govern all instances within a document, or you can create rules in the external style sheet that govern all documents that use it.

For example, the following code applies a black dotted border around the outside of a table and a silver grooved border around one specific cell:

```
<table style="border-style: dotted; border-color: black">
   <tr>
      <td style="border-style: groove; border-color: silver">Cell 1</td>
      <td>Cell 2</td>
   </tr>
   <tr>
      <td>Cell 3</td>
      <td>Cell 4</td>
   </tr>
</table>
```

To format all tables or all cells the same way, define the attributes in an embedded style sheet, like this:

```
<style>
table {border-style: dotted; border-color: black}
td {border-style: groove; border-color: silver}
</style>
```

This code produces a result that looks as follows:

As always, you can override the style rule with a `style` attribute placed specifically within an individual tag. For example, to make the first cell borderless, modify its *<td>* tag like this:

```
<table>
   <tr>
      <td style="border-style: none">Cell 1</td>
      <td>Cell 2</td>
   </tr>
   <tr>
      <td>Cell 3</td>
      <td>Cell 4</td>
   </tr>
</table>
```

This code produces a result that looks like this:

In this exercise, you will add default table border settings to an external style sheet, and then you will override those settings for an individual instance within a document.

 SET UP Use the *default.css* and *products.htm* files in the practice file folder for this topic. These files are located in the Documents\Microsoft Press\HTML5 SBS\13FmtTables\ApplyingBorders folder. Open the *default.css* file in Microsoft Notepad, and open the *products.htm* file in Internet Explorer.

1. Add the following style rules to the *default.css* style sheet:

```
table {border-style: outset; border-color: gray; border-width: 2px}
td {border-style: solid; border-color: gray; border-width: 1px}
```

2. Save and close *default.css*, and then refresh Internet Explorer.

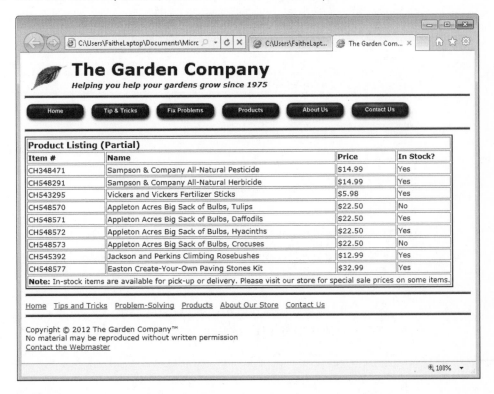

3. Open *products.htm* in Notepad, and remove the outer border from all sides of the table.

```
<table style="border-style: none">
```

4. Save the file, and then refresh Internet Explorer.

   Each cell has a border around it, but there is no overall border surrounding the table.

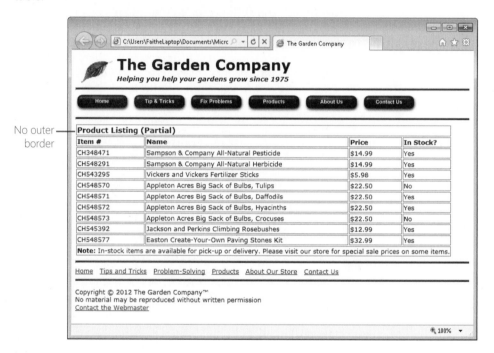

No outer border

5. Remove the border from the top row. (There is only one cell in this row because it is spanned.)

```
<table style="border-style: none">
   <tr class="tabletitle">
       <td colspan="4" style="border-style: none"><b>Product Listing
(Partial)</b></td>
   </tr>
```

6. Save the file, and then refresh Internet Explorer.

   The top cell now appears to be floating above the rest of the table, borderless.

Border removed from first row

7. In the row containing the column headings, make the bottom border three pixels thick.

```
<tr class="tablehead">
    <td style="width: 100px; border-bottom-width: 3px">Item #</td>
    <td style="width: 300px; border-bottom-width: 3px">Name</td>
    <td style="width: 75px; border-bottom-width: 3px">Price</td>
    <td style="border-bottom-width: 3px">In Stock?</td>
</tr>
```

Note You can't apply the *style="border-bottom-width"* attribute to a *<tr>* tag because technically a row has no borders; it only has cells, which in turn have borders. Therefore, you must apply the border setting separately to each cell in the row.

8. Save the file, and then refresh Internet Explorer.

Thicker border below heading row

9. Remove the borders from all sides of the cells in the row containing the column headings. (Hint: type the attributes once, and then copy and paste.)

```
<tr class="tablehead">
    <td style="width: 100px; border-bottom-width: 3px; border-top-style:
none; border-left-style: none; border-right-style: none">Item #</td>
    <td style="width: 300px; border-bottom-width: 3px; border-top-style:
none; border-left-style: none; border-right-style: none ">Name</td>
    <td style="width: 75px; border-bottom-width: 3px; border-top-style:
none; border-left-style: none; border-right-style: none ">Price</td>
    <td style="border-bottom-width: 3px; border-top-style: none;
border-left-style: none; border-right-style: none ">In Stock?</td>
</tr>
```

10. Remove the border from the bottom row of the table. (There is only one cell because it is spanned.)

```
<tr class="tablebody">
    <td colspan="4" style="border-style: none"><b>Note: </b>In-stock items
    are available for pick-up or delivery. Please visit our store for
    special sale prices on some items.</td>
</tr>
```

11. Save the file, and then refresh Internet Explorer.

Top, left, and right borders removed from this row

Border removed from last row

 CLEAN UP Close the Notepad and Internet Explorer windows.

Applying Background and Foreground Fills

Each table, row, and cell is its own distinct area, and each can have its own background. For example, you might want to apply a different color background to a heading row to make it stand out, or change the color of every other line in a listing to help visitors track a line across the table, as shown in the following example.

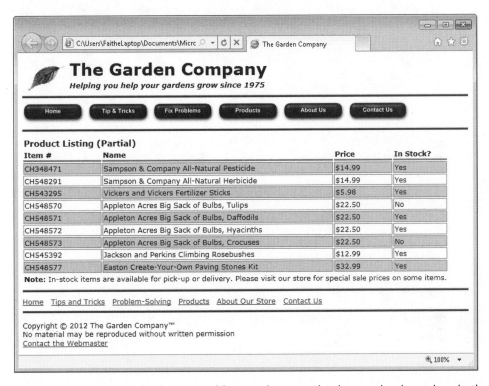

To apply a background color to a table, use the same *background-color* style rule that you use for documents. For example, to make a certain row orange, use the following:

```
<tr style="background-color: orange">
```

The table background can also be a picture, just like a document background. Apply the *background-image* attribute to any portion of a table. For example, to apply it to the entire table, use this:

```
<table style="background-image: url(images/leaf.gif)>
```

If the image is smaller than the allotted space, it will be tiled, just as when you apply an image to a page background.

Product Listing (Partial)

Item #	Name	Price	In Stock
CH348471	Sampson & Company All-Natural Pesticide	$14.99	Yes
CH548291	Sampson & Company All-Natural Herbicide	$14.99	Yes
CH543291	Vickers and Vickers Fertilizer Sticks	$5.98	Yes
CH	Appleton Acres Big Sack of Bulbs, Tulips	$22.50	No
CH648571	Appleton Acres Big Sack of Bulbs, Daffodils	$22.50	Yes
CH548572	Appleton Acres Big Sack of Bulbs, Hyacinths	$22.50	Yes
CH54	Appleton Acres Big Sack of Bulbs, Crocuses	$22.50	No
CH	Carson and Perkins Climbing Rose Bushes	$12	Yes
CH548577	Easton Create-Your-Own Paving Stones Kit	$32.99	Yes

Note: In-stock items are available for pick-up or delivery. Please visit our store for special sale prices on some items.

Note If you apply both a background color and a background image to the same cell(s), the more specific application takes precedence. For example, if you apply a background color to the table as a whole, and then apply a different color to an individual cell, the different color will appear in that cell.

The foreground of an element is its text, as you learned in Chapter 4, "Using Lists and Backgrounds." You can set the color of any table element like this:

```
<table style="color: blue">
```

In this exercise, you will apply background and foreground colors to a table and use an image as a background.

 SET UP Use the *products.htm* file in the practice file folder for this topic. This file is located in the Documents\Microsoft Press\HTML5 SBS\13FmtTables\ApplyingBackground folder. Open the *products* file in Notepad and in Internet Explorer.

1. Add a style to the second row of the table (*Sampson & Company All-Natural Pesticide*) that sets the background color to pale green.

```
<tr class="tablebody" style="background-color:palegreen">
    <td>CH348471</td>
    <td>Sampson & Company All-Natural Pesticide</td>
    <td>$14.99</td>
    <td>Yes</td>
</tr>
```

2. Copy the edited *<tr>* tag from the second table row and insert it into every other row (the fourth, sixth, eighth, and tenth rows).

```
<tr class="tablebody" style="background-color:palegreen">
    <td>CH543295</td>
    <td>Vickers and Vickers Fertilizer Sticks</td>
    <td>$5.98</td>
    <td>Yes</td>
</tr>
<tr class="tablebody" style="background-color:palegreen">
    <td>CH548571</td>
    <td>Appleton Acres Big Sack of Bulbs, Daffodils</td>
    <td>$22.50</td>
    <td>Yes</td>
</tr>
<tr class="tablebody" style="background-color:palegreen">
    <td>CH548573</td>
    <td>Appleton Acres Big Sack of Bulbs, Crocuses</td>
    <td>$22.50</td>
    <td>No</td>
</tr>
<tr class="tablebody" style="background-color:palegreen">
    <td>CH548577</td>
    <td>Easton Create-Your-Own Paving Stones Kit</td>
    <td>$32.99</td>
    <td>Yes</td>
</tr>
```

3. Save the file, and then refresh Internet Explorer.

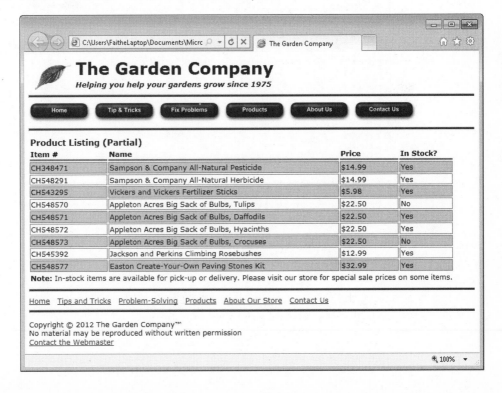

4. In Notepad, in the row containing the column headings, add a style rule that sets the background to the file *greenbk.jpg* (in the images folder) and sets the foreground (text) color to white.

```
<tr class="tablehead" style="background-image: url(images/greenbk.jpg);
color: white">
    <td style="width: 100px; border-bottom-width: 3px; border-top-style:
none; border-left-style: none; border-right-style: none">Item #</td>
    <td style="width: 300px; border-bottom-width: 3px; border-top-style:
none; border-left-style: none; border-right-style: none ">Name</td>
    <td style="width: 75px; border-bottom-width: 3px; border-top-style:
none; border-left-style: none; border-right-style: none ">Price</td>
    <td style="border-bottom-width: 3px; border-top-style: none;
border-left-style: none; border-right-style: none">In Stock?</td>
</tr>
```

5. Save the file and refresh Internet Explorer.

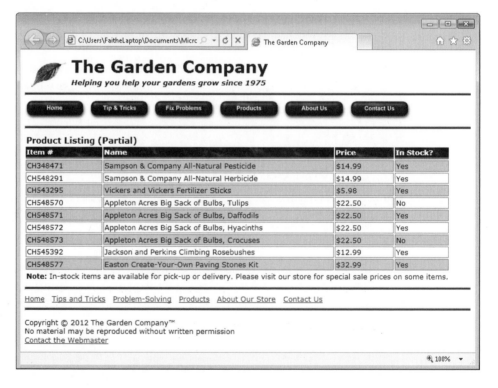

 CLEAN UP Close the Notepad and Internet Explorer windows.

Changing Cell Padding, Spacing, and Alignment

Cell padding, cell spacing, and cell alignment are three different ways you can control how cell content appears on a page. You learned about these features in earlier chapters, but let's briefly review them.

- Padding refers to the amount of space between an element's content and its outer edge. For a table cell, padding refers to space between the cell border and the text or graphic within it.

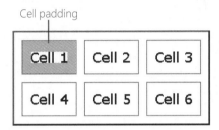

- Spacing refers to the amount of space between the outside of an element and the adjacent element. For a table cell, spacing refers to the space between the border of one cell and the border of the adjacent cell.

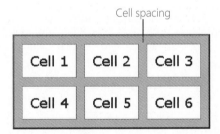

- Alignment refers to the placement of the content within its allotted area, either vertically or horizontally. For normal paragraphs (not in a table), alignment refers only to horizontal placement between the margins. For a table cell, however, there are separate settings for vertical and horizontal alignment.

Top Left	Top Center	Top Right
Middle Left	Middle Center	Middle Right
Bottom Left	Bottom Center	Bottom Right

Setting Cell Padding

To set the padding for the entire table, use the *cellpadding* attribute in the *<table>* tag. (The *cellpadding* attribute does not work with individual row and cell tags.)

```
<table cellpadding="4px">
```

To set the padding for an individual cell, use the *padding* attribute in a style, as you did in Chapter 8 for a paragraph.

```
<td style="padding: 4px">
```

To set padding in a style sheet:

```
td {padding: 4px}
```

Note You can't apply padding to a row, because technically a row has no cells to be padded. The *<tr>* tag is just a container for cells, and only *<td>* tagged cells (or an entire table) can have padding.

Setting Cell Spacing

The default table border looks like a double line, but this effect is just a combination of the border around the table as a whole and the border around each cell. The double effect is created by the spacing between the cells.

To make the borders a single solid line between one cell and another, set the cell spacing to zero:

```
<table cellpadding="10px" cellspacing="0px">
```

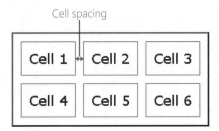

Cell spacing

Setting Horizontal and Vertical Alignment

A cell's content has two alignments: vertical (top, middle, or bottom) and horizontal (left, center, right, or justify). You can set these with attributes or with styles. To set alignment with attributes, use the *align* attribute to specify the horizontal alignment and the *valign* attribute to specify the vertical alignment, as shown in the following:

```
<td align="center" valign="middle">
```

You can also set alignment with a style by using *text-align* to specify the horizontal alignment and *vertical-align* to specify the vertical alignment, like this:

```
<td style="text-align: center; vertical-align: middle">
```

These can be applied to the entire table, to individual rows, or to individual cells. (Yes, alignment works with rows, unlike spacing and padding.)

In this exercise, you will adjust the padding, spacing, and alignment of a table.

SET UP Use the *products.htm* file in the practice file folder for this topic. This file is located in the Documents\Microsoft Press\HTML5 SBS\13FmtTables\ ChangingPadding folder. Open the *products* file in Notepad and in Internet Explorer.

1. Set the padding for the entire table to **4px**.

   ```
   <table style="border-style: none" cellpadding="4px">
   ```

2. Set the cell spacing for the entire table to **0px**.

   ```
   <table style="border-style: none" cellpadding="4px" cellspacing="0px">
   ```

3. Save the file, and then refresh Internet Explorer.

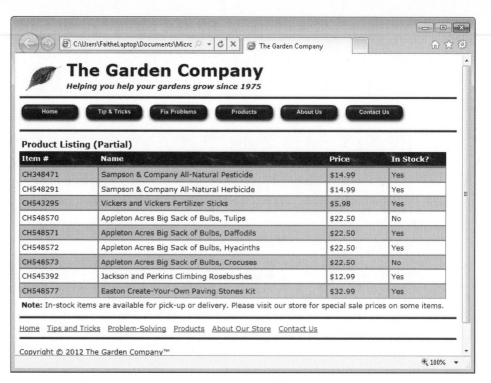

Note Notice that wherever two bordered cells touch, the border appears double thick. You can change that by removing the border from one side of each of those cells. For example, you could remove the right and bottom border on a cell like this:

```
<td style="border-right-style: none; border-bottom-style: none">
```

Alternatively, you could simply increase the table's outer border thickness so that it matches the thickness of the inner borders.

 CLEAN UP Close the Notepad and Internet Explorer windows.

Key Points

- To apply a simple default border to a table, include the *border="1"* attribute in the table's opening tag. A value greater than 1 increases the table border but not the cell borders.

- The *frame* attribute specifies which sides of the table frame display the border; the *rules* attribute specifies which sides of the cell borders display the border.

- For maximum flexibility, specify borders by using style sheets. Border style attributes in tables are the same as border style attributes around paragraphs: *border-width*, *border-color*, and *border-style*.

- To format one side of a border individually, specify the side in your attribute: *border-top-width*, *border-bottom-style*, and so on.

- You can apply a background color by using the *style="background-color: color"* attribute for the whole table or for an individual row or cell. To set the text color (foreground color), use the *color* attribute.

- Padding is the amount of space between the border of the cell and its contents. Set it by using the *cellpadding* attribute in the *<table>* tag. For an individual cell, set the padding by using a style, like this: *<td style="padding: 4px">*.

- Spacing is the amount of space between the outside of an element and an adjacent element. Set it by using the *cellspacing* attribute in the *<table>* tag.

- Alignment is the placement of the content within the cell. For vertical alignment, use the *valign* attribute; for horizontal alignment, use *align*. To align using a style, use *text-align* for horizontal or *vertical-align* for vertical.

Chapter at a Glance

Create a basic form,
page 252

Create check boxes
and option buttons,
page 259

Create menus,
page 262

14 Creating User Forms

In this chapter, you will learn how to

✔ Create a basic form.

✔ Create check boxes and option buttons.

✔ Create lists.

✔ Understand CGI and other advanced tools.

Gathering feedback from your Web site's visitors can be a valuable way of assessing your site's success, and it can help you build a customer or subscriber database. For example, a business could collect the addresses of people who are interested in receiving product samples, e-mail newsletters, or notifications of special offers.

To receive feedback, you can set up an e-mail hyperlink, as you did in Chapter 5, "Creating Hyperlinks and Anchors," but an e-mail message is not structured, and respondents are given no guidance as to the type of information you want to collect. When you need specific information, such as complete mailing addresses, it is helpful to provide visitors with a form to complete. You can use HTML to create user input forms that can send their results to you in an e-mail message, or you can store the data in a file on your server.

In this chapter, you will learn how to create several types of user input forms. You'll set them up to deliver their results to you in an e-mail message because that's the simplest method—and the most convenient for a low-traffic Web site. You'll learn how to create forms with text boxes, option buttons, check boxes, and drop-down lists. You'll also learn about some of the new HTML5 form controls, such as date boxes. At the end of this chapter, you'll find some information and Web resources that can help you create even more advanced forms by using Common Gateway Interface (CGI) scripting and third-party utilities and services.

Caution Many Web design professionals strongly recommend against using e-mail to deliver Web form results. Not only is e-mail not secure, but Web forms do not interface very well with some e-mail programs and some older browsers (such as Internet Explorer 3.0). If a visitor's e-mail program or browser does not support Web form submittal, the form won't work, but the visitor won't know until he clicks the Submit button, at which point the form will simply be cleared or a blank message window will open. However, nearly all of the other alternatives to e-mail submission require either programming knowledge or going through an external service. In this chapter, you'll test your forms by using e-mail, but use caution when relying on them for your real-world sites. Be sure to read the section, "Understanding CGI and Other Advanced Tools," at the end of this chapter for alternatives.

See Also Do you need only a quick refresher on the topics in this chapter? See the Key Points at the end of this chapter.

Practice Files Before you can use the practice files provided for this chapter, you need to install them from the book's companion content page to their default locations. See "Using the Practice Files" in the beginning of this book for more information.

Creating a Basic Form

You can place a form anywhere in the body of an HTML document. Some people like to use a table to organize form elements; others create form fields within ordinary paragraphs. A form is enclosed in a two-sided *<form>* tag:

```
<form method="post">
...
</form>
```

The *method* attribute specifies what will happen when the form is submitted. Almost all forms use the *method="post"* attribute, meaning that the data users enter into the form will be collected and either delivered (by e-mail) or sent to the server, where server-side code can retrieve it and perform tasks such as storing it (in a database).

Within the opening *<form>* tag, you specify an *action* attribute. This is typically either an e-mail address to which to send information, or the URL of a script that will run when the user submits the form. For an e-mail delivery, the *action* attribute might look like this:

```
<form action="mailto:edward@contoso.com" enctype="text/plain">
```

Note The *enctype* attribute specifies how the results will be encoded. An encoding type of *text/plain* is required when sending result by using e-mail; otherwise, the results might be unreadable.

To send the form contents to a CGI script, you include the URL for the appropriate CGI script stored on your server, as shown here:

```
<form action="http://www.contoso.com/cgi-bin/feedback.pl">
```

You place the various tags that create form controls between the opening and closing *<form>* tags. Form controls available include text boxes, buttons, check boxes, lists, and/ or command buttons. A *command button* is a button that executes a function, such as submitting the form or resetting it.

Creating a Text Box

The most basic type of control is a text box. Users can enter data such as names, addresses, phone numbers, and comments into text boxes. There are two types of text boxes: regular text boxes (single line) and text areas (multi-line). In the following figure, the top four fields are single-line text boxes, while the Comments box is a multi-line text area.

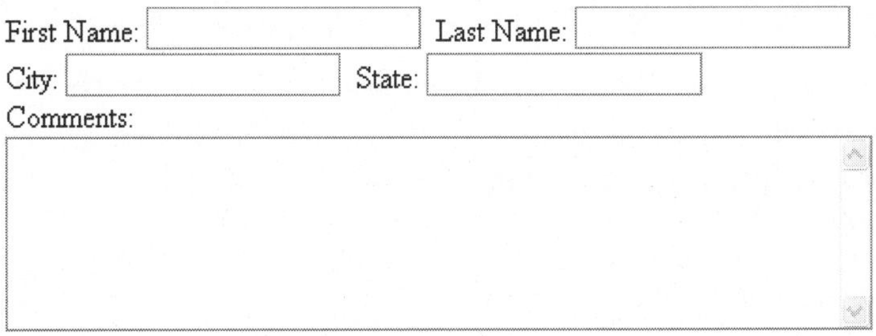

First Name: [   ]   Last Name: [   ]
City: [   ]   State: [   ]
Comments:
[   ]

You create a regular text box using a single-sided *<input>* tag with a *type="text"* attribute, as shown in the following:

```
<input type="text">
```

Note Remember, if you are writing XHTML-compliant code, you must place a space and a forward slash / at the end of single-sided tags, like this: *<input type="text" />*. That's not necessary if you are creating HTML code, so you won't see it in the examples presented in this book.

Each control within a form must have a unique name, expressed with the *name* attribute. For example, to name a particular text box *firstname*, use the following:

```
<input type="text" name="firstname">
```

You can specify a width for the text box with the *size* attribute. The default width is 20 pixels.

```
<input type="text" name="phone" size="30">
```

You can also specify a maximum length for the text string that users enter into the text box. This is different from the size of the text box. If the specified maximum length is greater than the text box width, the text scrolls horizontally as the user types. When users reach the specified maximum number of characters, the text box does not accept any more input. Use the *maxlength* attribute like this:

```
<input type="text" name="phone" size="30" maxlength="100">
```

In HTML5, you can require users to fill out a field before they will be able to submit the form (applies to HTML5-compliant browsers only). To mark a field as required, add the *required* attribute to its tag, like this:

```
<input type="text" name="phone" size="30" maxlength="100" required>
```

Special Field Types for E-Mail and Web Addresses

Two new *input* field types in HTML5 support e-mail addresses and Web addresses. Use the attribute *type="email"* instead of *type="text"* to define a field designed to collect e-mail addresses. If a browser doesn't support HTML5, the field defaults to a text type, so you don't risk anything by using it.

```
<input type="email" name="email-address">
```

The same goes for Web addresses (also known as uniform resource locators, or URLs). There is a special *type* attribute in HTML5 for them, as shown here:

```
<input type="URL" name="website">
```

In most browsers, you won't notice any difference. One exception is in the Apple iPhone browser, in which a special version of the onscreen keyboard pops up when the user selects an e-mail or Web field. This special keyboard provides dedicated keys for the most common symbols used for typing e-mail addresses and URLs. Other browsers might eventually implement special treatment for these field types, too.

Creating a Text Area

You create a multi-line text area by using a two-sided *<textarea>* tag containing a *rows* attribute that specifies the number of lines of text that the box should accommodate, such as shown in the following example:

```
<textarea name="comments" rows="5"></textarea>
```

You can also include a *columns* attribute that specifies how many characters (each character represents a single column) wide the text area will be. The default is 40 characters.

```
<textarea name="comments" rows="5" cols="60"></textarea>
```

The *columns* attribute affects only the size of the box, not the maximum number of characters that can be entered. You can use the *maxlength* attribute to limit the number of characters a user can enter.

Creating a Submit or Clear Button

You will need to include a Submit button on the form so visitors can send the information to you. *Submit* refers to the button's function, not the wording that appears on the button face. The default button text is *Submit*, but you can use a *value* attribute to display different text on the button. For example, to make the word *Send* appear on the button face, set up the *value* attribute, as shown here:

```
<input type="submit" value="Send">
```

You can also include a Reset button on the form, which allows the user to clear all the fields. Again, use the *value* attribute to change the text on the button.

```
<input type="reset" value="Clear">
```

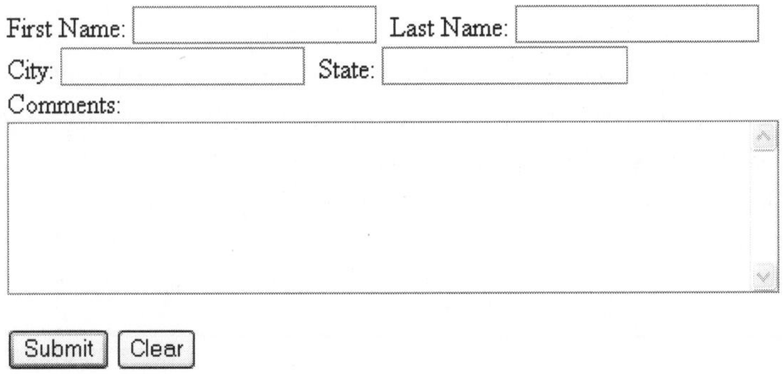

First Name: [   ] Last Name: [   ]
City: [   ] State: [   ]
Comments:
[   ]

[Submit] [Clear]

Many Web designers find it useful to place form fields in tables to make it easier to align the fields. For example, as shown in the following image, you could place field labels in one column and the actual fields themselves in another. You'll see this type of design in the next exercise.

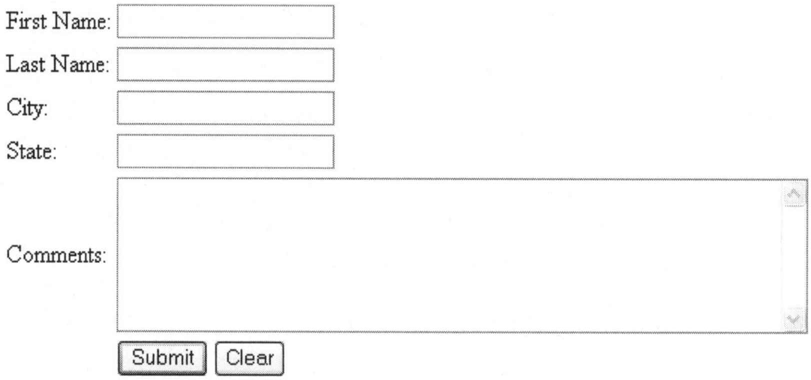

First Name: [   ]
Last Name: [   ]
City: [   ]
State: [   ]

Comments: [   ]

[Submit] [Clear]

Adding Default or Placeholder Text

By default, text boxes and text areas are blank when the form loads. You can optionally place either default or placeholder text in them.

- Default text is regular text that is submitted with the form results as if the user had actually typed it in.

- Placeholder text is "phantom" text that appears as a prompt within the text box but disappears when the user types something else there. If the user chooses to leave that text box blank, nothing is submitted.

Most browsers support the use of default text, even if they do not support HTML5. For a text box, add a *value* attribute to the tag that specifies the default text, as shown here:

```
<input type="text" name="country" value="United States of America">
```

For a text area, you should place default text between the opening and closing *<textarea>* tags, like this:

```
<textarea name="comments" rows="5">Great job! Keep up the good work.</textarea>
```

Placeholder text displays only in HTML5-compliant browsers. To use placeholder text, add the *placeholder* attribute, like this:

```
<input type="text" name="country" placeholder="Enter your country here">
```

In this exercise, you will create a simple form with text boxes and text areas in a table.

 SET UP Use the *signup.htm* file in the practice file folder for this topic. This file is located in the Documents\Microsoft Press\HTML5 SBS\14Forms\CreatingForms folder. Open the *signup* file in Microsoft Notepad and Microsoft Internet Explorer.

1. Immediately following the opening *<table>* tag, create an opening *<form>* tag that sends results to your own e-mail address. Substitute your address for *youremail*.

   ```
   <form method="post" enctype="text/plain" action="mailto:youremail">
   ```

2. In the empty *<td>* tag following *Name:*, create a single-line text box.

   ```
   <tr>
   <colgroup align="right" valign="top">
       <td>Name:</td>
       <td><input type="text" name="name"></td>
   </tr>
   ```

3. In the empty *<td>* tag following *E-mail address:*, create a single-line text box with a type of *email* and a maximum length of 100 characters.

   ```
   <tr>
       <td>E-mail address:</td>
       <td><input type="email" name="email" maxlength="100"></td>
   </tr>
   ```

4. Add a placeholder for the email field of *Enter your e-mail address*.

   ```
   <tr>
       <td>E-mail address:</td>
       <td><input type="email" name="email" size="30" maxlength="100"
       placeholder="Enter your e-mail address"></td>
   ```

5. In the empty *<td>* tag following *Comments:*, create a six-line text area with a width of 50 characters.

   ```
   <tr>
       <td>Comments:</td>
       <td><textarea name="comments" rows="6" cols="50"></textarea></td>
   </tr>
   ```

6. Add a *placeholder* attribute for the *comments* field of *Enter comments here*.

   ```
   <tr>
       <td>Comments:</td>
       <td><textarea name="comments" rows="6" cols="50" placeholder="Enter
       comments here"></textarea></td>
   </tr>
   ```

7. Save the file, and then refresh Internet Explorer to check your work.

8. Add another row at the bottom of the table, immediately before the closing *</colgroup>* tag. Leave the first cell empty, and in the second cell, place **Submit** and **Reset** buttons, separated by a nonbreaking space:

```
<tr>
   <td></td>
   <td><input type="submit" value="Submit"> 
   <input type="reset" value="Clear"></td>
</tr>
```

9. Save the file, and then refresh Internet Explorer to check your work.

Sign Up for E-Mail Specials

Name:

E-mail address:

Comments:

Submit   Clear

10. In Internet Explorer, enter some text into each field on the form (it doesn't matter what you enter.), and then click the **Submit** button.

Note Depending on your browser and e-mail program settings, you might see a warning message. Respond to these by clicking Yes or OK to allow the browser to send the message.

11. Check your e-mail inbox for the form results.

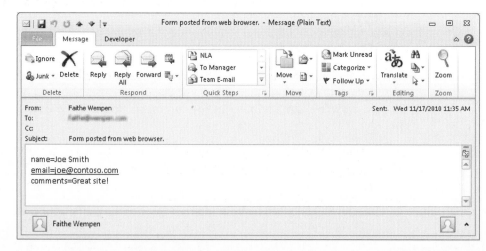

Note The speed at which mail servers deliver messages can vary. The results might arrive almost immediately or take an hour or more.

 CLEAN UP Close the Notepad and Internet Explorer windows.

Creating Check Boxes and Option Buttons

When the valid responses to a particular prompt will always be one of a few simple options, such as gender or employment status, you will get more consistent and easier-to-evaluate results by using *check boxes* and *option buttons* rather than text boxes.

For example, suppose you are asking site visitors a yes/no question such as, "Are you interested in receiving our catalog by mail?" If you provide a text box, people might answer the question in any number of ways: *y, n, Y, N, yes, no, Yes, No, YES, NO, maybe, Sure, No Thanks*, and so on. Tabulating such results would be tedious because a human would need to evaluate each one. But by providing a check box, you remove any doubt: a check mark means yes; the lack of a check mark means no.

You use *check boxes* for single binary (yes/no) questions. A form might contain multiple check boxes, but each one is a separate decision for the person filling out the form.

What topics would you like to read about?
Home repair ☑
Gardening ☑
Child care ☐

To create a check box, use the *type="checkbox"* attribute with the *<input>* tag, such as in the following:

```
<input type="checkbox" name="repair">
```

By default, the results of the form will show a value of *On* when the check box has been selected. For the check box just shown, the results would appear like this:

repair=on

You can change that default by specifying a *value* attribute. For example, you could report the word *Yes* for the check box, as shown here:

```
<input type="checkbox" name="repair" value="Yes">
```

By default, check boxes appear unselected; users must click each check box to select it. In some cases, however, it might be advantageous to have a check box preselected. For example, to encourage people to sign up for your newsletter, you could select the Newsletter check box by default, so that users must click it to clear it. To do this, add the *checked="checked"* attribute, as in the following tag:

```
<input type="checkbox" name="newsletter" checked="checked">
```

Use *option buttons* (also called *radio buttons*) to present a group of mutually-exclusive options. When you select an option button, all the other option buttons in the group are cleared.

When will you be buying a new or used car?

Immediately	◉
Within 6 months	○
Within 1 year	○
Not sure	○
Do not plan to purchase	○

To create a group of option buttons, choose a name for the group. You will specify the same name in the *name* attribute for each individual button. Use the *value* attribute (which will be different for each button in the set) to specify the value that will be reported for the group in the form results.

For example, suppose you want users to choose among three membership categories: Gold, Silver, and Bronze. Because you make the most money on a Gold membership, you want to make it the default choice.

```
<p><input type="radio" name="category" value="gold" checked="checked"> Gold<br>
<input type="radio" name="category" value="silver"> Silver<br>
<input type="radio" name="category" value="bronze"> Bronze</p>
```

Each button is followed by text describing that option (Gold, Silver, Bronze). This is just ordinary text.

◉ Gold
○ Silver
○ Bronze

Note The space before the text is inserted by default to prevent the option buttons from running into the text. You don't need to add any space yourself.

When the form results are returned, this button group will report its name and the selected value like this:

```
category=gold
```

In this exercise, you will enhance a form by adding a group of option buttons and a check box.

 SET UP Use the *signup.htm* file in the practice file folder for this topic. This file is located in the Documents\Microsoft Press\HTML5 SBS\14Forms\CreatingButtons folder. Open the *signup* file in Notepad and Internet Explorer.

1. In the cell after the one that contains *Level of gardening expertise:*, create a set of option buttons that allow the user to choose among Beginner, Intermediate, Expert, or Professional.

```
<tr>
    <td>Level of gardening expertise:</td>
    <td>
    <input type="radio" name="level" value="Beginner">Beginner<br>
    <input type="radio" name="level" value="Intermediate">Intermediate<br>
    <input type="radio" name="level" value="Expert">Expert<br>
    <input type="radio" name="level" value="Pro">Professional<br>
    </td>
</tr>
```

2. Save the file, and then refresh Internet Explorer to see the results.

3. Insert a check box to the left of the *Yes, I would also like...* text, and set its default value to **checked**.

```
<tr>
    <td></td>
    <td><input type="checkbox" name="partner" value="Yes"
checked="checked">Yes, I would also like to receive coupons and offers from
other gardening-related companies.</td>
    </tr>
```

4. Change the *mailto* address in the opening *<form>* tag to your own e-mail address.

5. Save the file, and then refresh Internet Explorer to see the results.

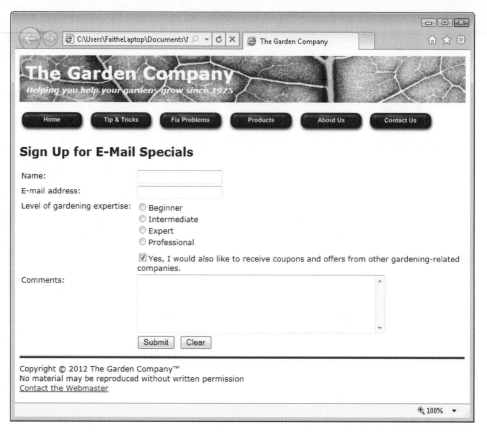

6. Fill out the form (use any text you like, and select any of the option buttons), and then click **Submit** to send it to yourself.

✖ **CLEAN UP** Close the Notepad and Internet Explorer windows.

Creating Lists

Check boxes are good for yes/no questions, and option buttons are appropriate when there are a few options to choose from, but what if you have a dozen or more choices? Option buttons for that many choices can take up a lot of space onscreen and can overwhelm a Web visitor.

For situations involving many options, consider a *list*, also called a *menu*. A list can contain as many options as needed, yet it takes up very little space on the form.

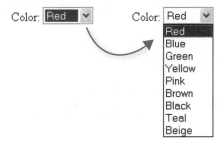

To create a list, start with a two-sided *<select>* tag. Within it, place each option in its own *<option>* tag. Place the text that you want to appear on the list between the opening and closing *<option>* tags. For example, to create the list just shown, do the following:

```
<p>Color: <select name="colors" size="1">
<option>Red</option>
<option>Blue</option>
<option>Green</option>
<option>Yellow</option>
<option>Pink</option>
<option>Brown</option>
<option>Black</option>
<option>Teal</option>
<option>Beige</option>
</select></p>
```

Note By default, the form results will report the text of the selected option. If you want to make the form report something different, include it in a *value* attribute in the option's opening tag.

A list can be any height you like. In the preceding code, the *size* attribute is set to 1, which creates a drop-down list. If you set the *size* attribute to a larger value, the element renders as a list box instead. If there are more items in the list than will fit in the viewing space, a scroll bar appears automatically at the right side of the box. For example, you might change the opening *<select>* tag in the preceding code to this:

```
<p>Color: <select name="colors" size="5">
```

The result would be a list like this.

If the list's choices fall into categories, you might want to break them up into sections.

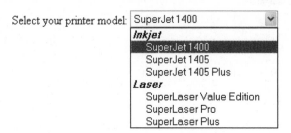

To format a list as shown in the previous example, surround the groups of options with an *<optiongroup>* tag. Include a *label* attribute that specifies the heading text for each option group. Here's the code for the preceding example:

```
<p>Select your printer model:
<select name="printers" size="1">
    <optgroup label="Inkjet">
        <option>SuperJet 1400</option>
        <option>SuperJet 1405</option>
        <option>SuperJet 1405 Plus</option>
    </optgroup>
    <optgroup label="Laser">
        <option>SuperLaser Value Edition</option>
        <option>SuperLaser Pro</option>
        <option>SuperLaser Plus</option>
    </optgroup>
</select></p>
```

In this exercise, you will add a drop-down list to a form.

 SET UP Use the *signup.htm* and *states.txt* files in the practice file folder for this topic. These files are located in the Documents\Microsoft Press\HTML5 SBS\14Forms\ CreatingLists folder. Open the *signup* file in Notepad and Internet Explorer.

1. In Notepad, replace the *<input>* tag for the text box that follows *State:* with an empty *<select>* tag.

```
<tr>
    <td>State:</td>
    <td>
    <select name="state">

    </select>
    </td>
</tr>
<tr>
```

Note Because it would be time-consuming to type *<option>* tags for all 50 states, I have created them for you.

2. In a separate Notepad window, open the *states* text file.

3. Press **Ctrl+A** to select the entire content of the file, and then press **Ctrl+C** to copy it to the Clipboard.

4. In the *signup* file, click between the opening and closing *<select>* tags. Press **Ctrl+V** to paste the options for each state into the file.

5. Save the file, and then refresh Internet Explorer. Click the down arrow to the right of the **State** box to ensure the drop-down list appears.

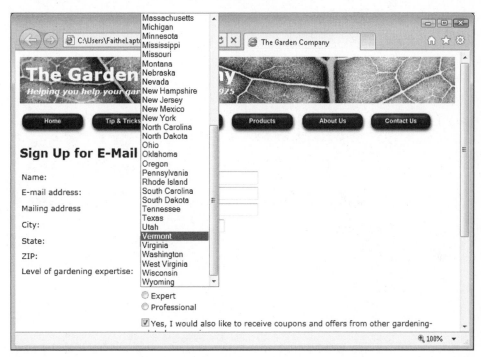

6. Enclose the 50 states in an *<optgroup>* tag with a label of *States*.

```
<optgroup label="States">
  <option>Alabama</option>
...
  <option>Wyoming</option>
</optgroup>
```

7. After the closing tag of the States option group, add a Territories option group that contains entries for American Samoa, Guam, Northern Mariana Islands, Puerto Rico, and the U.S. Virgin Islands.

```
...
    <option>Wyoming</option>
</optgroup>
<optgroup label="Territories">
    <option>American Samoa</option>
    <option>Guam</option>
    <option>Northern Mariana Islands</option>
    <option>Puerto Rico</option>
    <option>U.S. Virgin Islands</option>
</optgroup>
</select>
```

8. Save the file, and then refresh Internet Explorer. Scroll to the bottom of the **State** drop-down list to see the changes.

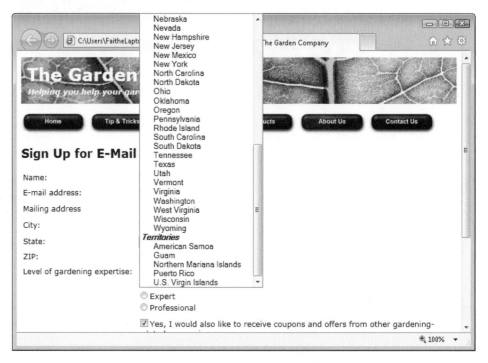

 CLEAN UP Close the Notepad and Internet Explorer windows.

Additional Input Types in HTML5

HTML5 provides several other field types that can add that extra bit of polish to your forms. If the user's browser doesn't support them, it renders and treats them as text fields, so you can use them freely without worrying about backward compatibility.

Spin boxes are used to increment numeric values.

Copies: 1

The preceding spin box was created by using the following code:

```
<input type="number" name="copies" min="0"max="100" step="1" value="1">
```

The *min* and *max* attributes control the minimum and maximum values, respectively. The *step* attribute specifies how much the value increments or decrements when you click the up or down arrow buttons. The *value* attribute specifies the default value.

A *slider* is a sliding bar that you can drag from side to side. Its type is *range*, and its attributes are nearly identical to those for a spin box.

Copies: ▯━━━━━━━━━

```
<input type="range" name="copies" min="1"max="4" step="1" value="1">
```

A *date picker* pops up a calendar on which the user can click and select a date. Use the *date* type to get a date picker in HTML5-compliant browsers, as follows:

```
<input type="date">
```

For a standard date, use *type="date"*. This enables the user to select a specific date from a calendar. You can also use any of the following types for other date and time-related selections:

- *Type="month"* selects an entire month
- *Type="week"* selects an entire week
- *Type="time"* selects a time only (no date)
- *Type="datetime"* select both a date and a time
- *Type="datetime-local"* selects both a date and time using the user's local time zone

Understanding CGI and Other Advanced Tools

As you have seen, directing form results to an e-mail address is a quick, no-hassle way of collecting information, provided the visitor's Web browser and e-mail program support it. As the volume of messages increases, however, organizing all the information you receive can become a challenge. You need to copy the information from the form results into a database, or at least print out a copy of the e-mail messages. When you start receiving hundreds of form submissions a day, that responsibility can become overwhelming.

As an alternative, you can rely on a server-based script or application to handle the form results. A Common Gateway Interface (CGI) script written in a programming language such as Perl is one common, low-cost possibility. You reference the script in your *<form>* tag's *action* attribute. (The server on which you host your site must allow CGI scripts (some don't, for security reasons.)

Important One drawback of using CGI scripts is lack of security. Unless you put security measures in place, the collected data resides in a file on the server, which is a potential security risk. For this reason, you shouldn't use a CGI script to collect sensitive information such as credit card or Social Security numbers unless you also implement security measures that prevent the data from being compromised. Most commercial sites use a secure server for that; you can partner with a company that offers secure form processing, including credit card processing, for a monthly fee.

There are hundreds of Web sites that offer free CGI scripts that you can modify in a text editor (such as Notepad) to meet your needs. To do this, you must know a little something about programming, which is beyond the scope of this book. However, if you're interested in learning about Perl and CGI scripting, or you are looking for a service that will host your CGI script, see one of these Web sites:

- Comprehensive Perl Archive Network: *www.cpan.org*
- Matt's Script Archive: *www.scriptarchive.com*
- The CGI Resource Index: *cgi.resourceindex.com*
- BigNoseBird.Com: *www.bignosebird.com*

As your Web site becomes more sophisticated, you also might want to include a public bulletin board area where people can post and read comments, or a guest book where people can leave public comments. You can't create one of those by using only HTML, but you can integrate add-on components into your site that will do the job. There are many free and low-cost sources of programming code for a message board, both in CGI (mentioned previously) and other languages. For example, check out the phpBB open-source bulletin board package at *www.phpbb.com* (your server must support PHP). There are also many services that will host your bulletin board on their server, such as ProBoards (*www.proboards.com*). You place a link to the message board hosting site on your Web page; to your visitors, it seems like the message board is part of your site.

Key Points

- To create a form, use a two-sided *<form>* tag. Within it, place one or more *<input>* tags that define the form fields.

- In the opening *<form>* tag, place a *method="post"* attribute and an *action* attribute that describes how the form should be processed. The most common attribute is *action="mailto:address"* where *address* is a valid e-mail address. If you are collecting form results by using e-mail, include an *enctype="text/plain"* attribute.

- To create a text box, use *<input type="text" name="fieldname">*, where *fieldname* is the unique name you assign to the text box. Optional additional attributes include *size* and *maxlength*.

- For Web and e-mail collection, you can optionally use the *URL* and *email* input types, respectively. These work only in HTML5-compliant browsers.

- To create a multi-line text box (a text area), use a two-sided *<textarea>* tag with a *name* attribute and a number of rows and columns. For example, *<textarea name="comments" rows="5" columns="40"></textarea>*.

- To create a Submit button, use an *<input>* tag with a *type="submit"* attribute. If you want to change the button text, use the *value* attribute. For example, *<input type="submit" value="Send">*. Use *type="reset"* to create a Reset button that clears the form.

- A check box is a one-sided, standalone element. Use an *<input>* tag with a *type="checkbox"* attribute.

- An option button operates in a group with other option buttons; only one in a group can be selected at a time. Use a one-sided *<input>* tag with a *type="radio"* attribute. For each option, use a common *name* attribute and a unique attribute.

- To create a list, use a two-sided *<select>* tag, and within it, include two-sided *<option>* tags for each list item.

- Use a *size="1"* attribute with the *<select>* tag to create a drop-down list, or specify a higher number to create a list box with a scroll bar.

- To create category headings on a list, use a two-sided *<optgroup>* tag with a label for the text that should appear. For example, *<optgroup label="Inkjet">*.

- HTML5 offers several other input types for special cases, such as spin boxes (*type="number"*), sliders (*type="range"*), and date pickers (*type="date"*).

- To process form input on a server, use a Common Gateway Interface (CGI) script or a third-party program.

Chapter at a Glance

Play a video,
page 279

15 Incorporating Sound and Video

In this chapter, you will learn how to

✔ Understand the purpose and scope of the new *<audio>* and *<video>* tags in HTML5.

✔ Play multimedia types and choose formats and codecs.

✔ Use the *<video>* tag.

✔ Use the *<audio>* tag.

Playing video and audio on the Web is a bit more difficult than other Web-related tasks. This stems from the multitude of formats that are available from competing vendors and open source groups. These formats have varying degrees of support in the popular modern Web browsers; often they have no support at all in older browsers. Together, these factors make it difficult to deliver audio and video that's consistently playable for all of your visitors.

The addition of the *<video>* and *<audio>* tags in HTML5 makes the process of delivering and playing video and audio more straightforward. Playing multimedia will get easier over time as newer browsers support the tags and people upgrade their older browsers. However, for the foreseeable future, it will still be necessary to encode your multimedia files into multiple formats.

See Also Do you need only a quick refresher on the topics in this chapter? See the Key Points section at the end of this chapter.

> **Practice Files** Before you can use the practice files provided for this chapter, you need to install them from the book's companion content page to their default locations. See "Using the Practice Files" in the beginning of this book for more information.

What's New with Audio and Video in HTML5?

Traditionally, developers and designers have most commonly set up pages to play video and audio on the Web using Adobe Flash. Sites such as YouTube (*http://www.youtube. com*) embed video inside of a Flash file. This requires that the end user has the Adobe Flash player installed.

The HTML5 specification introduces an alternative to that: a standard tag, *<video>*, which enables the playing of video content. However, the *<video>* tag still requires a video file and also requires end users to have an appropriate player installed on their computers.

For audio clips, the traditional delivery method has been to use the *<object>* or *<embed>* tag to embed a clip on a page. HTML5 provides the *<audio>* tag to do this instead.

As of this writing, the *<audio>* and *<video>* tags have limited support in Web browsers. Adding to the complexity is the need to support multiple formats for video, depending on what your visitor's browser can play.

This chapter shows you how to take advantage of the new *<audio>* and *<video>* tags and helps to sort out the difficulties surrounding video compatibility. Before going further, you should understand that at the time of this writing, support for these two new tags is limited to the following browsers:

- Internet Explorer 9+
- Firefox 3.5+
- Safari 3+
- Chrome 3+
- Opera 10.5+
- iPhone 1+
- Android 2+

Browsers that don't support these tags ignore them, but if you want to deliver your audio or video to a full range of browsers—new and old, you'll need to be able to do it without the use of these tags. This chapter shows both the old and new methods.

HTML Multimedia Basics

Before getting into the details of creating multimedia-rich Web pages, you should have a basic understanding of how HTML5—and previous versions of HTML—present audio and video clips.

The most common method of placing multimedia content on a Web page is to *embed* an audio or video clip in the page so that it plays within the page itself when the visitor clicks a button. For this to work, visitors to your site must be using a Web browser that supports the type of sound or video file you're providing, or they must download and install a plug-in (a helper program) to add support for that file to their browser. If your audience uses Microsoft Internet Explorer version 5.5 and higher, you can use the *<object>* tag for this; otherwise you use the *<embed>* tag. Or, if your audience uses an HTML5-compliant browser, you can use the new *<audio>* and *<video>* tags for this.

As an alternative, you can *link* to an audio or video clip so that it plays in an external application (such as Microsoft Windows Media Player) when the visitor clicks its hyperlink. For this to work, the visitor must have an external application that supports the type of sound or video file you're providing, or they must download and install a separate program. This technique works the same in all browsers, though, which is a plus. Use the *<a>* tag for the link, just like with any other hyperlink. For example:

```
<a href="mysong.mp3">Playing my song!</a>
```

This chapter focuses mainly on the embedding type of multimedia presentation.

Multimedia Formats and Containers

Discussion of multimedia on the Web must begin with an understanding of the different formats. When people talk about video files, they're usually talking about files with an .avi, .mp4, or .mkv extension. These extensions are simply indicators of the container format for the video file itself; they don't indicate the format in which the video was encoded.

There are several common container formats, including Ogg (.ogv), Flash Video (.flv or .f4v), the aforementioned Audio Video Interleave (.avi), MPEG-4 Part 14 (.mp4), Matroska (.mkv), and many others. See *http://en.wikipedia.org/wiki/Container_format_%28digital%29* for an overview of container formats.

Additionally, video files almost always contain audio tracks. The container file includes both the video and audio components.

There is also a new format, called WebM, which is similar to Matroska. WebM is an open-source video container format that will likely grow in popularity due in part to its support by Google. WebM is meant to be used exclusively with the VP8 video codec and the Vorbis audio codec (more on codecs in the next section).

Codecs: Decoding the Video and Audio

When a producer (the person or organization making the audio or video available) encodes multimedia, they choose the format in which to encode the file. The person who views that video or listens to the audio must have the appropriate decoding software installed on their computer to play the file. This decoding software is called a *codec*.

You'll see the word codec in this chapter and in other publications about video and audio. The word itself is shorthand for encode/decode (or decode/encode depending on whom you ask). The codec refers to the style in which the video or audio file was encoded or formatted. To decode a video or audio file means that the computer uses an algorithm to decipher the encoded video or audio into a human-consumable form.

Now throw in the Web browser. The browser, such as Internet Explorer, either needs to have built-in support for a format or needs to have a plug-in available to recognize that it can play the audio or video file. Luckily, all of the common formats and codecs today are either supported natively or are readily available in some form of plug-in installer for the popular Web browsers. As newer browsers that support HTML5 appear, the use of specific third-party plug-ins—at least for video and audio—will (hopefully) become a thing of the past.

Just as there are numerous container formats, there are also several common video encoding formats. Some of the most popular ones include H.264, VP8, DivX, Theora, and several others. If you plan to do much video work on the Web, you'll likely need to account for several different formats and containers to reach the widest possible audience.

As with video, playing audio through a computer or hand-held mobile devices (such as SmartPhones) requires a codec to read the file and play it back. Two popular formats are MPEG-4 Audio Layer 3, which you might recognize as MP3, and AAC, frequently used by Apple. Other formats include Vorbis, which is frequently used in an Ogg container.

Many of the video formats support *profiles*, which are essentially the parameters used when the video is encoded. For example, a high profile H.264 video provides higher quality but at the cost of a much larger file size—too large for general use on the Web. For now, it's sufficient to know that different profiles exist, and different profiles are appropriate for different applications.

Which Format to Choose?

If all of this sounds complex, it is. Not only is it tough to choose among the multiple formats, but whatever your choice, there's no guarantee that your visitors will be able to play that format anyway. At a high level, audio is easier than video, so for all intents and purposes, your energy will be put into working with video formats.

So how do you choose which format to use? The answer is that you don't choose one format; you choose three or four. The ultimate goal is to make the video available to the widest possible audience. With that in mind, you will need to be able to convert a source video file to several formats to ensure that visitors can play it.

Table 15-1 shows the three primary containers that you'll use, not including Flash.

TABLE 15-1 Common Video Formats for the Web

Container	Video Codec	Audio Codec
Ogg	Theora	Vorbis
mp4	H.264	AAC
WebM	VP8	Vorbis

As of this writing, Microsoft Internet Explorer 9 supports the *<video>* tag, but it only supports the H.264 video format. Previous versions of Internet Explorer don't support the *<video>* tag, but don't worry; you'll see how to work around that restriction a bit later in this chapter.

Mozilla Firefox versions 3.5 and later support the WebM and Ogg containers. Safari supports H.264 video and AAC audio in an mp4 container. Opera supports WebM and Ogg containers as well. The Ogg container will almost certainly contain Theora video and Vorbis audio.

File Size and Quality

The word "size" has two meanings for a video clip: the file size and the display size (the number of pixels vertically and horizontally). As you might expect, these two factors are related—the larger the clip's display window, the larger the file size. A clip on a Web page need not fill the entire monitor; a window of two to three inches is usually sufficient.

The display size is not the only determinant of the file size, however. Some file formats are smaller than others because they use varying degrees of compression to decrease their file sizes. A video clip is compressed using a certain compression *algorithm*, which is a set of math formulas used to remove excess space in the clip for storage. To play a compressed clip, the computer playing it must possess an appropriate codec.

Note A compression algorithm works by identifying repeated characters or patterns in the data file and substituting more compact codes for them. For example, an algorithm might change 00000000000000000000 to something like 20*0.

Further, video clips vary according to the number of frames per second (fps); more frames per second means smoother playback and larger file size. A VHS videotape records at 30 fps, but for Web use, a frame rate of 15 fps works well because it results in a much smaller file size. You can set the number of frames per second when you record the video clip, or use a third-party program to decrease the frames per second of a pre-recorded clip.

When a sound clip is digitized (converted to digital format), a series of sound "snapshots" are taken per second. These snapshots are called *samples*. Higher *sampling rates* (the number of samples per second) yield higher sound reproduction accuracy, but at the cost of larger file sizes. Sampling rates for audio clips are measured in kilohertz—for example, 11 KHz, 22K Hz, or 44 KHz.

Note "Kilo" means thousand; an 11 KHz clip contains approximately 11,000 samples per second.

Sound clips also have varying *sample resolutions*, which are the number of bits used to describe each sample. Common sample resolutions are 8-bit, 16-bit, and 32-bit. The more bits that are sampled, the larger the file will be.

Sound clips can be recorded in either mono or stereo, referring to the number of audio channels in the recording. Mono uses a single channel, which is duplicated in each speaker. Stereo uses two channels, with one channel playing back in each of two speakers. Stereo clips are approximately double the file size of mono ones.

When recording audio clips, you can usually choose between various sampling rates and resolutions. Here are some of the most common combinations of settings:

Settings	Quality
8 KHz, 8-bit, mono	Telephone quality
22 MHz, 16-bit, stereo	Radio quality
44 KHz, 16-bit, stereo	CD quality

Encoding Video

Now that you have a high-level view of video and audio playback on the Web, you might be wondering how you encode your favorite vacation videos into three formats (four if you count Flash). The clips provided for the exercises in this chapter are ready to go, but you will need to prepare your own video clips on your own.

Just as playback is complex, so too is encoding. People frequently employ a combination of software to encode and convert videos between formats. For example, software called Handbrake is popular for converting video to H.264 and AAC format for playback on Apple devices, and is also useful for converting video for the Web.

Converting to an Ogg Theora video with Vorbis audio can be accomplished using several different software packages including ffmpeg2theora, VLC media player, Firefogg (a plug-in for Firefox), and others. Firefogg, ffmpeg, and several others can also convert to WebM format.

Tip If you're using Firefox (or want to encode video), a simple and effective way to do so is to use VLC. Be prepared to wait, though. Converting videos between formats can be a slow process. I used VLC for all the conversions made while writing this chapter.

With the goal of making video on your site widely available, you'll typically encode your videos into each of these three formats as well as Flash. Using those four formats makes the video natively available in new browsers with built-in support for the new *<video>* and *<audio>* tags but still makes Flash available for visitors with older browsers.

Embedding Video Clips

So far, you've seen a lot of background material for something that seems like it should be easy! And to think we've only scratched the surface. This section shows how to use the *<video>* tag to place video on a page as well as how to fall back to Flash video if necessary.

Introducing the <video> Tag

At a basic level, the *<video>* tag looks like this:

```
<video src="myvideo.ogv"></video>
```

There are several attributes and different ways to use the *<video>* tag that make it more configurable for your needs and the needs of your audience. Several attributes are helpful, including:

- *autoplay*
- *controls*
- *height*
- *loop*
- *preload*
- *width*

Not surprisingly, you use the *width* and *height* attributes to set the width and the height of the video display area on the page, as shown in the following example:

```
<video src="myvideo.ogv" width="320" height="240"></video>
```

The *controls* attribute determines whether a default set of playback controls should be visible within the browser. This can be helpful and I recommend using it. In fact, if you don't use the controls attribute, the visitor has no way to replay the video without reloading the entire page. How annoying! Here's an example of the *controls* attribute:

```
<video src="myvideo.ogv" controls></video>
```

The *preload* attribute tells the browser to begin downloading the video immediately when the element is encountered. If the video is the central theme of the page, and it's likely that all (or most) visitors will want to watch the video, then it's a good idea to use the preload option. However, if the video element is a small part of the page and visitors aren't likely to watch it, then preloading the video is just a waste of bandwidth. Here's the preload attribute in action:

```
<video src="myvideo.ogv" preload></video>
```

The *loop* attribute tells the browser to restart the video immediately when it's finished playing, as shown here:

```
<video src="myvideo.ogv" loop></video>
```

Finally, the *autoplay* attribute makes the video automatically play when the page is loaded. For most purposes, this is generally a bad idea from a usability standpoint. Most users will want control over the video; they'll play it when their attention is focused and they're ready to consume the video element. And even with the *autoplay* attribute enabled, your visitors might have that option disabled in their browsers. For that reason, along with the usability problem, I recommend not using the *autoplay* attribute with one notable exception: if you don't include the *controls* attribute, then you need to include *autoplay*; otherwise, the video won't play and visitors will have no way to start it. Here's an example of the *autoplay* attribute:

```
<video src="myvideo.ogv" autoplay></video>
```

Putting it together, a real-world video element looks like this:

```
<video src="myvideo.ogv" width="320" height="240" controls></video>
```

The preceding examples all work well if your visitors have a browser such as Firefox 3.5 or later or Opera 10.5 or later. However, what if a visitor has Internet Explorer? In that case, you'll need to encode the video so that it can be played in Internet Explorer. The *<video>*

tag enables more than one source (via the source element) which you can capitalize on by including links to multiple versions of a video. You can also add a *type* attribute to tell the browser a bit more about the video file to which you're linking. For example, a *<video>* tag that includes the Ogg container video in the preceding example as well as an H.264 video in an mp4 container and a WebM container video would look like this:

```
<video width="320" height="240" controls>
    <source src="myvideo.mp4" type="video/mp4">
    <source src="myvideo.ogv" type="video/ogg">
    <source src="myvideo.webm" type="video/webm">
</video>
```

Additionally, an optional codec portion of the type attribute can also indicate to the browser which codec the audio and video portions of the file use. The use of the codec option is beyond the scope of this book.

With those two options you now have Internet Explorer 9 and Safari covered (thanks to the mp4 container); Firefox and Chrome covered (thanks to the Ogg container); and other browsers covered too (thanks to the WebM container).

The <embed> Tag: Your Fallback Plan

But what happens when someone visits your site with an older browser that doesn't support HTML5? In this case, they won't be able to view video through the *<video>* tag. Luckily, older browsers will simply ignore the video tag so its mere presence won't cause errors. However, you still need to find a way for those visitors to view the video.

You'll find that most users of Internet Explorer also have Adobe Flash installed. With that in mind, you can also include a Flash version of the video on your page. You can include an extra element with the help of the *<embed>* tag. Adobe Flash can play H.264 encoded video with AAC audio; therefore, you don't need to convert your video to yet another format. Here's an example:

```
<embed src="myvideo.mp4" type="application/x-shockwave-flash"
    width="320" height="240" allowscriptaccess="always"
    allowfullscreen="true">
```

Placing a Video Clip on a Web Page

Now that you've got a handle on the theory, it's time to put it into practice with an exercise.

In this exercise, you'll add a video to an HTML page as an embedded clip with the *<video>* tag, and provide an alternative copy as a downloadable link with the *<a>* tag. You'll also practice embedding the clip with the *<embed>* tag.

SET UP Use the *winter.html, myvideo.mp4, myvideo.wehm, and myvideo.ogv* files in the practice file folder for this topic. These files are located in the Documents\ Microsoft Press\HTML5 SBS\15Video\AddVideo.

1. Open the *winter.html* file in Notepad and in Internet Explorer 9 (or some other HTML5-compliant browser).

2. In the *#main* division, immediately before its closing *</div>* tag, enter the code for inserting video.

```
<p>Watch the following video to learn how to prune and cover a rose bush
for winter.</p>
<video width="320" height="240" autoplay controls>
<source src="myvideo.mp4">
<source src="myvideo.webm">
<source src="myvideo.ogv">
</video>
</div>
```

3. Refresh Internet Explorer to view the clip on the page.

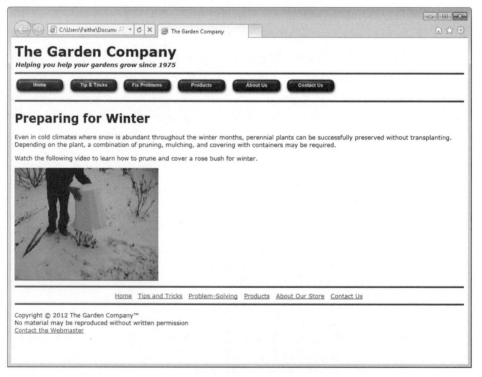

You should see the video and it should start playing automatically. If it doesn't, you might not be using an HTML5-compliant browser.

4. Return to Notepad. Immediately before the closing *</video>* tag, add an *<embed>* tag to play the clip via Flash.

```
<p>Watch the following video to learn how to prune and cover a rose bush
for winter.</p>
<video width="320" height="240" autoplay controls>
<source src="myvideo.mp4">
<source src="myvideo.webm">
<source src="myvideo.ogv">
<embed src="myvideo.mp4" type="application/x-shockwave-flash"
    width="320" height="240" allowscriptaccess="always"
    allowfullscreen="true">

</video>
</div>
```

5. Enter the following after the *<embed>* tag:

```
<p>Click here to download a high-resolution version of the clip in AVI
format.</p>
```

6. Make the words *Click here* into a hyperlink that points to the file *myvideo.avi*.

```
<p><a href="myvideo.avi">Click here</a> to download a high-resolution
version of the clip in AVI format.</p>
```

7. Save your work in Notepad, and then refresh the page in Internet Explorer to see the changes.

Note If a security warning appears in the browser window, you might need to click a button to allow the Flash content to play.

 CLEAN UP Close the Notepad and Internet Explorer windows.

Incorporating Audio on a Web Page

The good news is that by working your way through the video information in this chapter, you've already learned nearly all the background that you need to play audio on a Web page. The bad news is that the same format and encoding problems that plague video on the Web also apply to audio, except that the audio problems are a bit worse. This section examines the *<audio>* tag and its alternatives.

Playing Audio with the <audio> Tag

You might be thinking that playing audio on a Web page would be easier than video, but for the most part, it's not. You still need to provide for different browsers and encode your audio into different formats. In addition, for the most part, your visitors will still need special plug-ins to play audio. With that said, the *<audio>* tag is new to HTML5 and, assuming that the browser manufacturers can come to some type of agreement (and that's about as possible as me winning the lottery), playing audio on the Web should become easier.

Like the *<video>* tag, the *<audio>* tag supports multiple sources. With no common format, you'll need to encode the audio multiple times to try to get the audio out to the widest possible audience. Also like the *<video>* tag, the *<audio>* tag supports attributes such as *controls*, *autoplay*, *loop*, and *preload*. Therefore, the syntax for the *<audio>* tag is essentially the same as the syntax for the *<video>* tag.

Tip There are numerous applications that convert audio between formats. As with the video conversions, I used VLC to convert the audio when writing this chapter. VLC is available at *http://www.videolan.org/vlc/*.

I've had good success when using the MP3 and Ogg Vorbis formats simultaneously. You'll find support for at least one of these two formats in Firefox, Chrome, Safari, Opera, and Internet Explorer 9. Again, as with video, you'll need to embed your audio stream into a Flash object so older versions of Internet Explorer can use it.

Here's an example that shows the *<audio>* tag with two files, which are called with the help of the *<source>* element that you saw earlier in the video section of this chapter:

```
<audio controls>
    <source src="myaudio.mp3"></source>
    <source src="myaudio.ogg"></source>
</audio>
```

Playing Audio in Older Browsers

As with video, playing audio in older browsers requires the *<embed>* tag. When used with audio, you'll typically use two attributes, *src* and *autostart*; *src* configures the source of the audio, and *autostart* controls whether the audio clip should play automatically upon page load. Adding the *<embed>* tag to the previous example results in this HTML:

```
<audio autoplay loop>
<source src="myaudio.mp3">
<source src="myaudio.ogg">
<embed src="myaudio.mp3">
</audio>
```

By default, content included with *<embed>* will be automatically played. If you don't want this, then add the *autostart="false"* attribute tag, like so:

```
<embed src="myaudio.mp3" autostart="false">
```

Note Even when using *<embed>* to include audio, the visitor must still have software capable of playing the type of file being sent.

One other attribute commonly used with *<embed>* is the *loop* attribute. The *loop* attribute, when set to *true* or *infinite*, restarts the audio clip when it completes. It can also be set to *false* to indicate that the audio clip should play only once. However, the default is to play the audio clip only once; therefore, omitting the *loop* attribute is the same as setting it to *false*.

Placing an Audio Clip on a Web Page

Now you get to practice placing an audio clip. In this exercise, you'll add an audio file to an HTML5 page.

SET UP Use the *index.html, myaudio.mp3*, and *myaudio.ogg*.files in the practice file folder for this topic. These files are located in the Documents\Microsoft Press\HTML5 SBS\15Video\AddAudio.

1. Open the *audio.html* file contained in the source code for the book.

2. Immediately above the closing *</div>* tag for the *#main* division, add the codes for the audio clip.

```
<audio autoplay loop>
<source src="myaudio.mp3">
<source src="myaudio.ogg">
</audio>

</div>

</p>
```

2. Before the closing *</audio>* tag, add an *<embed>* tag that will play the clip in a non–HTML5-compliant browser.

```
<audio autoplay loop>
<source src="myaudio.mp3">
<source src="myaudio.ogg">
<embed src="myaudio.mp3">

</audio>

</div>
```

3. Open Internet Explorer 9 or later and view the page.

The audio should start playing automatically, looping back to the beginning when it completes.

 CLEAN UP Close the Notepad and Internet Explorer windows.

Key Points

- Incorporating sound and video is accomplished by providing video and audio files in multiple formats to ensure that your visitors can view the multimedia no matter what browser they're using.

- It's important to understand the different containers and codecs available for video and audio and how those are supported across your visitor's browsers.

- HTML5 introduces the *<video>* and *<audio>* tags, which enable multimedia to be included in Web pages.

- Older browsers don't support the *<audio>* and *<video>* tags, so it's important to provide video in legacy formats such as Flash to enable visitors who use these browswer to view the content as well.

- Use the *<embed>* tag to include audio and video content in a format that non–HTML5-compliant browsers can interpret.

Chapter at a Glance

Add JavaScript code, **page 289**

Your first JavaScript page.

Use Canvas elements on a page, **page 303**

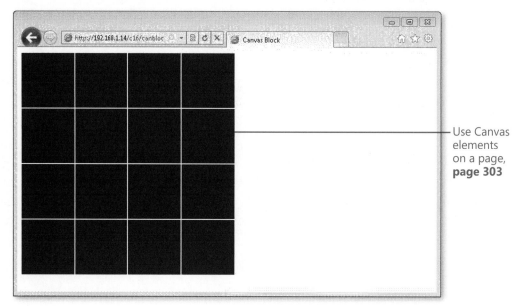

16 Including JavaScript and External Content

In this chapter, you will learn how to

✔ Use the Canvas element.

✔ Use JavaScript to enhance your Web page.

✔ Handle Web page events with JavaScript and jQuery.

✔ Use the HTML5 *<canvas>* tag.

✔ Include external content in Web pages.

This chapter examines how you can use JavaScript to enhance the functionality of your Web pages. This chapter also discusses the new HTML5 *<canvas>* tag and other HTML tags for including external content within your Web page. If you already know at least some JavaScript, and you're familiar with jQuery, you can skip to the section titled "Using the HTML5 <canvas> Tag" on page 303. However, if you skip ahead and get a bit lost, jump back to the JavaScript section to get up to speed quickly.

See Also Do you need only a quick refresher on the topics in this chapter? See the Key Points section at the end of this chapter.

> **Practice Files** Before you can use the practice files provided for this chapter, you need to install them from the book's companion content page to their default locations. See "Using the Practice Files" in the beginning of this book for more information.

Introducing the Canvas

One of the most exciting elements added in HTML5 (and there are many) is the canvas element. The canvas element enables advanced graphics and interactions in ways that previously you could only achieve by using slow, plug-in–laden pages. The canvas element is a free-form area where you can use images, drawn graphics, animation, and text to enhance the user experience on a Web page.

You add a canvas element to a Web page with the aptly titled *<canvas>* tag. Like other HTML tags, the *<canvas>* tag accepts attributes, the most basic of which are the pixel height and width of the canvas on the page. The code to create a 200 × 200 pixel canvas looks like this:

```
<canvas width="200" height="200"></canvas>
```

Here's the syntax for an entire page with the 200 × 200 canvas inside:

```
<!DOCTYPE HTML>
<html>
<head>
<meta http-equiv="Content-Type" content="text/html; charset=utf-8">
<title>Canvas</title>
</head>
<body>
<canvas width="200" height="200"></canvas>
</body>
</html>
```

This HTML creates a canvas on the page that is ready for content. But wait! What advantage does a canvas element provide on a page? How do you make a cool animated clock or menu or other widget? Alas, therein lies the problem. When simply included in a page like the one shown, a *<canvas>* tag doesn't do anything. In fact, it's just blank; go ahead and load that code into a canvas-compatible browser (Internet Explorer 9, Firefox 1.5 or newer, Safari, and so on). The page is blank.

So, how might you get the canvas to do something? The answer lies in the programming language that all modern browsers understand: JavaScript. You bring the canvas element to life with JavaScript; everything within the canvas is drawn, animated, and destroyed with JavaScript.

You might not know much, if anything, about JavaScript. However, the information in this chapter will give you an introduction. After learning a bit about JavaScript you'll be able to make the canvas element do some fun and interesting things!

JavaScript, Briefly

JavaScript is not Java; it bears no relation to the Java programming language, the drink, or the country. JavaScript is a programming language that is used primarily to provide additional functionality to Web pages and applications, and it's used heavily in the "Web 2.0" paradigm of highly interactive Web sites.

While this chapter won't show you how to build the next Microsoft Bing Maps interface, it does explore JavaScript basics, with the goal of introducing you to the language and what it can do. Be aware that this is simply an introduction; learning JavaScript to add complex functionality and building a JavaScript-based application for your Web site is beyond the scope of this chapter.

Just as HTML is codified through standards, JavaScript is also based on a standard called the ECMA-262 specification. The latest version of the specification, version 5, was released in 2009. Unfortunately, different Web browsers implement the ECMA-262 specification differently—which means that JavaScript programmers must take care to work around the quirks and differences in the various browser implementations.

One approach to provide JavaScript that works the same way across all popular browsers is to use a library or framework. One popular framework, jQuery, enables rapid development and use of JavaScript without the need for you to learn the intricacies and nuances involved for the different Web browsers. jQuery also simplifies many common JavaScript tasks for Web developers.

Including JavaScript on Your Web Page

To use JavaScript on your page, you include a *<script>* tag. Specifically, the opening tag you use is as follows:

```
<script type="text/javascript">
```

And the closing tag is this:

```
</script>
```

The magic happens between the opening and closing tags, which is where you place the JavaScript code. The *<script>* tag also frequently includes a *src* attribute that specifies that the page should include an external JavaScript file. For example, if you had a file containing JavaScript code called "myjavascript.js", you could include it like this:

```
<script type="text/javascript" src="myjavascript.js"></script>
```

Note that you still need to include the closing *</script>* tag when you're including an external JavaScript file, as in the example just shown.

Your First JavaScript Web Page

In the following exercise, you'll see how to use JavaScript within your Web page.

SET UP Open Notepad.

1. In Notepad, type the following:

```
<!DOCTYPE HTML>
<html>
<head>
<meta http-equiv="Content-Type" content="text/html; charset=utf-8">
<title>JavaScript 101</title>
</head>
<body>
<div id="contentDiv">Your first JavaScript page.</div>
</body>
</html>
```

2. Add some JavaScript to the page, placing it just before the closing *</body>* tag, as shown here:

```
<!DOCTYPE HTML>
<html>
<head>
<meta http-equiv="Content-Type" content="text/html; charset=utf-8">
<title>JavaScript 101</title>
</head>
<body>
<div id="contentDiv">Your first JavaScript page.</div>
<script type="text/javascript">
    alert("hello world");
</script>
</body>
</html>
```

3. Save the file in Notepad as **javascript01.html**.

4. View the page within a Web browser. You should receive an alert such as this:

 CLEAN UP Close Internet Explorer. Leave the *Javascript01.html* file open in Notepad for the next exercise.

The example shown in the preceding exercise placed the *<script>* tags and the JavaScript code within the *<body>* tag. You can also place *<script>* tags and related code within the *<head>* block.

JavaScript includes methods for choosing or selecting elements on a page. For example, the JavaScript method *getElementById()* selects an element on a Web page based on its *id* attribute. JavaScript includes other similar methods as well, such as *getElementsbyTag Name()* which returns all the elements of a certain tag type, such as all the *<div>* ele-ments on a page.

In the following exercise, you will retrieve the element that has an *id* attribute of *contentDiv* (as you saw in the previous exercise) and change its background color to a shade of gray.

SET UP Use the *Javascript01.html* file that you created in the previous exercise. Open the file in Notepad, if it is not already open.

1. Delete the following line from the code:

   ```
   alert("hello world");
   ```

2. Between the *<script>* and *</script>* tags, place the following:

   ```
   <script type="text/javascript">
           var divContent = document.getElementById("contentDiv");
           divContent.style.backgroundColor = "#abacab";
   </script>
   ```

3. Save your work in Notepad.

4. Open the file in Internet Explorer to test it. Instead of a Hello World dialog box, the text on the page appears with a gray background:

CLEAN UP Close Internet Explorer. Leave the *Javascript01.html* file open in Notepad for the next exercise.

In this example, the code retrieves the element identified in the page with the *id* of *contentDiv* by using the *getElementById* method. It places that element into a variable called *divContent* and uses that variable with another JavaScript function, *style()*, to change the div element's *backgroundColor* property value to *#abacab*.

Keeping JavaScript Away from the Browser

As you develop Web sites, you will inevitably encounter visitors who have JavaScript disabled in their Web browsers or who haven't installed the latest versions of their Web browsers. There are numerous reasons why a visitor might not have JavaScript enabled, including accessibility reasons, and personal preference. For example, many people use the NoScript add-on to Mozilla Firefox, which disables JavaScript automatically.

Whatever the reason, you need to first assume that JavaScript is not available—using the approach that JavaScript acts only as an enhancement to usability. Or put another way, you want to make sure that JavaScript fails gracefully so that your site still functions without JavaScript enabled.

One approach to check whether JavaScript is enabled is to use the *<noscript>* tag. Using *<noscript>*, you can provide content if the browser doesn't support or use JavaScript. Insert the *<noscript>* tags within your page and place HTML between them. If a visitor to your site doesn't have JavaScript enabled, they'll see the content within the *<noscript>* tags. See *http://www.w3.org/TR/html4/interact/scripts.html* for more information on *<noscript>*.

Now that you've programmed your first JavaScript-enabled Web page and seen a bit more about JavaScript in use on a page, it's time to move on to bigger and better things. What else can JavaScript do on a page? One need only look at such sites as Microsoft's Bing Maps (*http://www.bing.com/Maps/*) to get an idea. But just about any modern Web interface uses JavaScript in one form or another.

JavaScript Events and jQuery

Most modern Web sites use JavaScript to dynamically respond to mouse actions on a Web page and change elements of that page based on those movements or on other user input. Doing this requires "event handling" which is a somewhat advanced concept—or at least one that requires JavaScript programming beyond what you've seen in the first few pages of this chapter!

To introduce event handling at this very early stage in your JavaScript adventure, I need the help of an additional tool, called jQuery. jQuery is an open source JavaScript file that not only removes the need for developers to handle many of the cross-browser incompatibilities but also simplifies much more advanced programming than would normally be available to novice JavaScript programmers. The jQuery JavaScript framework is an excellent tool for both working with JavaScript events and for all-around general JavaScript programming.

Obtaining jQuery

You can download jQuery from *http://jquery.com*. jQuery is a single file, and you should place it in the document root, or main folder, of your Web site (or wherever you place JavaScript files in your environment). jQuery comes in two forms, a development version and a production version. The production version is "minified," meaning that it's been optimized for speed (the download size is smaller), but that makes it very hard to use. The development version is not minified, so you can read the code more easily.

Note For almost all production uses of jQuery, you'll want to obtain and deploy the minified version.

As of this writing, jQuery was at version 1.4.4. That version's downloaded file is called "jquery-1.4.4.min.js." You include this file in your Web page just like any other external JavaScript file, using the *<script>* tag, as you've already seen in this chapter:

```
<script type="text/javascript" src="jquery-1.4.4.min.js"></script>
```

Note The version of jQuery will likely be different by the time you read this, so the *<script>* tag example you've just seen would need to point to the version of jQuery that you download.

Here's a completed example page (although it doesn't *do* anything) that includes jQuery:

```
<!DOCTYPE html>
<head>
<script type="text/javascript" src="jquery-1.4.4.min.js"></script>
<title>Including jQuery</title>
</head>
<body>
</body>
</html>
```

It's also possible to use jQuery hosted on a Content Delivery Network (CDN). With the CDN-based jQuery, you can simply point the *<script>* tag toward the URL of the library on the external CDN. Doing so looks like this:

```
<script type="text/javascript"
        src="http://code.jquery.com/jquery-1.4.4.min.js"></script>
```

However, as just noted, it's recommended to host the file yourself for production purposes on live sites rather than relying on the CDN. There's nothing worse than having your Web site up and operational but reliant on a CDN-based library Web site that is down. For the purposes of this chapter though, it's perfectly acceptable to use the CDN-based version rather than downloading jQuery yourself. Most of the examples in this chapter assume that you have downloaded jQuery locally and adjusted the version number to fit the version that you downloaded. If you'd like to use the CDN-based version see *http://docs.jquery.com/Downloading_jQuery#CDN_Hosted_jQuery* for the current URL.

Getting Ready for jQuery

Imagine this problem: You've written some JavaScript and included it just before the closing *</body>* tag as shown earlier in the chapter. One of the things that your JavaScript does is change an image on the page. The problem is that your image hasn't loaded, so now the JavaScript runtime can't find it, and the page loads incorrectly.

The root cause of this all-too-common problem is that browsers execute JavaScript as they encounter scripts on the page. So even though the JavaScript is at the bottom of the page, the browser may not have loaded the entire page prior to running the JavaScript. In other words, the document isn't ready by the time the JavaScript runs, so chaos ensues.

A workaround for this problem is to use an *onload* or *load* event on the page, but even that is fraught with danger, not to mention it's bad practice. Luckily, jQuery includes a function called *.ready()* which executes only after the page has been loaded by the browser and is ready for JavaScript code to be run. The *.ready()* function is a simple way to execute JavaScript while safely knowing that all elements of the page have been loaded and are ready to use. jQuery code begins with a dollar sign and parentheses, as you'll see in the upcoming example.

Using the *.ready()* function is easy. The following code shows an example of the *.ready()* function in action.

```
<!DOCTYPE html>
<html>
<head>
<title>Document Ready</title>
<script type="text/javascript" src="jquery-1.4.4.min.js"></script>
</head>
<body>
<script type="text/javascript">
$(document).ready(alert('Hello Again'));
</script>
</body>
</html>
```

When viewed in a browser, you'll receive an alert like this:

The code shown above includes the jQuery library, and then it uses both the *.ready()* function and some other JavaScript to show an alert. This is an important point about jQuery: you use it to help write JavaScript. jQuery is *not* JavaScript; instead, it's a tool that you use to help perform common JavaScript tasks and sometimes to simplify tasks that are difficult to perform using JavaScript alone.

Note There are also other frameworks available to assist you with JavaScript coding, including MooTools, the Yahoo! User Interface (YUI) library, prototypeJS, and others. I chose jQuery for the examples in this book because it's popular and also because it's included with some Microsoft products as well.

You've now seen how to get jQuery, how to include it in a Web page, and how to run JavaScript code with the help of jQuery's *.ready()* function. The next item on the agenda is selecting elements.

Selecting Elements with jQuery

jQuery has its own syntax for selecting elements such as *<p>*, *<img>*, *<div>*, and so on. The jQuery selector syntax replaces the *getElementById* example that you saw earlier in the chapter. Recall that the example HTML code included a *<div>* element with an *id* attribute of *contentDiv*, as shown here:

```
<div id="contentDiv">Your first JavaScript page.</div>
```

jQuery makes it easy to select that element using jQuery, using this syntax:

```
$("#contentDiv")
```

Alternatively, you could select all the *<div>* elements with this syntax:

```
$("div")
```

You can also select elements by their cascading style sheet (CSS) class with a dot prefix, similar to that used in the CSS file itself:

```
$(".className")
```

jQuery provides several other ways to select elements, including hierarchical functions by which you can select the children of an element; a way to select every other element except a specified element; an element's parent elements; and many other selectors. See *http://api.jquery.com/category/selectors* for information on all the available selectors in jQuery.

What can you do with a selected element? The answers are virtually limitless. For instance, recall that in an example in an earlier chapter you changed the background color of the *<div>* to gray using JavaScript. Here's how you would do the same thing using jQuery:

```
$("#contentDiv").css("backgroundColor","#abacab");
```

Here's a bonus example using the jQuery *fadeOut()* function:

```
<!DOCTYPE HTML>
<html>
<head>
<meta http-equiv="Content-Type" content="text/html; charset=utf-8">
<title>jQuery 101</title>
<script type="text/javascript" src="jquery-1.4.4.min.js"></script>
</head>
<body>
<div id="contentDiv">Your second JavaScript page.</div>
<script type="text/javascript">
    $("#contentDiv").css("backgroundColor", "#abacab");
    $("#contentDiv").fadeOut();
</script>
</body>
</html>
```

Viewing this page in a browser will result in the *contentDiv* fading out after a certain default (and short) time period. If you find that time period too short, you can specify the duration, as well. Time is measured in milliseconds for this (and most other) functions in jQuery, so every second is 1000 milliseconds. Therefore, to set the fade-out duration to 5 seconds, you would write:

```
$("#contentDiv").fadeOut(5000);
```

See Also The *.fadeOut()* function accepts other arguments as well. See *http://api.jquery.com/fadeOut/* for more information on how to use this function.

You've now seen how to download jQuery, connect it to your page, and use it to select elements. And you just looked at a bonus example of a built-in function in jQuery called *.fadeOut()*. This leads to a more generalized discussion of functions in jQuery and Java Script. I promise that we'll get to the cool stuff soon.

Calling Functions with JavaScript

Functions are groupings of code that perform a task. Here's a function:

```
function doSomething() {
    alert("Hello World");
}
```

That's it, that's all there is to functions. Well, almost. But there's no reason to clutter the discussion of functions when a simple example will suffice. The *.fadeOut()* example gave you a glimpse at another important part of a function: a function *argument*. A function argument is a value that is passed to the function that determines how or what the function should do as it carries out its designed task. The *.fadeOut()* function uses the duration argument (passed as 5000 in the example at the end of the preceding section) to set the length of time that the function waits before it fades the element out.

For example, here's a *showAlert()* function that accepts a single argument called *alertText*, and then shows it in an alert dialog box:

```
function showAlert(alertText) {
    alert(alertText);
}
```

Calling or invoking the function looks like this:

```
showAlert("Showing an alert is fun and easy.");
```

One other important aspect of functions is that they can return a value. Typically, the return value would be the result of whatever the function accomplishes, although the return value can be whatever you'd like it to be. For now, you'll work on a typical example, where the return value is the logical result of the function. In this next example, the function adds two numbers and returns the result.

```
function addTwo(num1, num2) {
    var result = num1 + num2;
    return result;
}
```

You call the function the same way as in the previous example, but this time, the function returns a value that you want to capture so that you can use it later, as shown here:

```
var getSum = addTwo(2,5);
```

With this code, the sum of the two numbers, 2 and 5, would be placed into the variable *getSum*, which you could then use later in the program.

You'll frequently use functions and pass arguments into functions, especially when working with event handling in JavaScript and jQuery. A JavaScript program of minimal complexity and size will typically use functions, as well.

With all this background knowledge now complete, it's time to look at working with events in JavaScript and jQuery. Events are actions like mouse clicks, keystrokes, and entering text into a form.

Responding to Events with jQuery and JavaScript

Responding to events with JavaScript is a complex process that involves working with multiple event models exposed by different Web browsers and multiple versions of the Document Object Model (DOM) to try to get the correct code to execute at the correct time. Therefore, rather than spend the next 30 pages on an in-depth discussion of event handling, I'll shortcut the learning curve to show you how to handle events with jQuery.

jQuery includes several event-related functions such as *.click()* for responding to mouse clicks, *.submit()* for responding to a form submission, *.hover()* to respond when a mouse cursor hovers over an element, and several others. In fact, the *.ready()* function that you saw earlier is an event handler. See *http://api.jquery.com/category/events* for more information on event handlers, including a list of the available jQuery handler functions.

Earlier in the chapter, you saw the *.fadeOut()* function in use. That function ran when the page loaded (or more accurately, when the browser encountered the JavaScript). To make the *<div>* element fade out when a user clicks it with the mouse, you need to attach a click event handler to that *<div>* element. In jQuery, you do this with the help of the *.click()* function, which looks like the following example (I've highlighted the relevant code in bold):

```
<!DOCTYPE HTML>
<html>
  <head>
   <meta http-equiv="Content-Type" content="text/html; charset=utf-8">
   <title>jQuery 101</title>
   <script type="text/javascript" src="jquery-1.4.4.min.js"></script>
  </head>
```

```
<body>
  <div id="contentDiv">Your second JavaScript page.</div>
  <script type="text/javascript">
    $("#contentDiv").css("backgroundColor", "#abacab");
    $("#contentDiv").click(function() {
          $(this).fadeOut(5000);
    });
  </script>
</body>
</html>
```

Note that the *.click()* function is attached directly to the *<div>* that has the *id* of *content-Div*. The *.click()* function itself calls another function (an anonymous function, enclosed in curly brackets) which calls the *.fadeOut()* function. You'll notice that there's a new part here, the *$(this)* identifier. The *$(this)* identifier refers to the item that raised the event, so in the example shown, *$(this)* refers to the *contentDiv* element. You could also write it like this:

```
$("#contentDiv").click(function() {
      $("#contentDiv").fadeOut(5000);
});
```

When you load this page in a Web browser you'll see a screen like the one shown below. When you click within the *<div>* element, the entire *<div>* will slowly fade out.

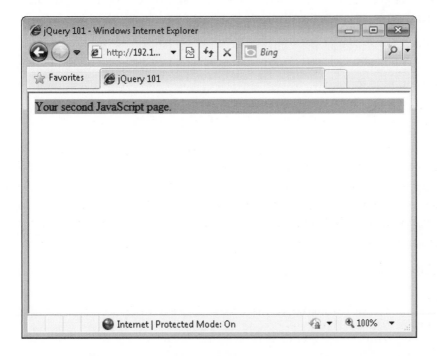

Validating a Web Form with jQuery and JavaScript

One typical use of JavaScript is to validate a Web form, or more appropriately, pre-validate a Web form. When a Web form is submitted, it is sent to a server-based program which can then do something useful with the data, such as complete an order, or store the data in a database. However, using JavaScript for validation provides no security for the server-based program.

Don't Substitute JavaScript Validation for Server-Side Validation

There is no guarantee that the visitor to your Web page has JavaScript enabled in their browser. Therefore, you cannot rely on JavaScript as the sole means to verify that the user has entered properly formatted data. More than one Web site has been hacked because the programmer relied solely on JavaScript to validate and verify the contents of user input from a Web form.

All data must be verified at the server or within the server code. No amount of JavaScript validation, trying to require JavaScript, or other tricks will ensure that the data is safe. Always verify data at the server. When used as a means to validate form data, JavaScript is to be used only to enhance the user experience by providing early feedback on known invalid data. JavaScript is never—and should never be—used to truly test whether the data is valid.

With that in mind, here's a simple form and some JavaScript/jQuery code to validate the text box on the form:

```
<!DOCTYPE HTML>
<html>
<head>
<meta http-equiv="Content-Type" content="text/html; charset=utf-8">
<title>jQuery 101</title>
<script type="text/javascript" src="jquery-1.4.4.min.js"></script>
</head>
<body>
<form id="myForm" name="myForm" action="#" method="post">
<p>Answer: <input id="firstName" type="text" name="firstname"></p>
<p><input type="submit" name="formSubmit" value="Check Form"></p>
</form>
<script type="text/javascript">
    $("#myForm").submit(function() {
        if ($("#firstName").val() == "Yes") {
            alert("Form entered correctly");
        } else {
            alert("Form not correct");
            return false;
        }
```

```
    });
</script>
</body>
</html>
```

The code introduces a few new concepts, namely the *if* conditional. In this case, the code uses the *if* conditional to test whether the value entered by the user matches what you're expecting from the text field on the form. The jQuery *.val()* function in the preceding code is also new here. The *.val()* function obtains the value of whatever has been entered into the text box (or whatever element has been selected). Finally, when the text box is not filled in correctly, there's a *return false;* statement. In this context, *return false;* indicates that processing of the Web form should not continue, and the form should not be submitted.

When submitted with a value of *Yes* in the text box, the code displays an alert and continues with form submission. If the user enters anything else and submits the form, the validation code displays an alert indicating that the form wasn't filled in correctly, and halts form submission to the server by returning *false*.

A more complex yet more user-friendly approach for handling errors is to change the background color on the form field that was filled in incorrectly. Obviously, for the one field form in this example, it's clear which field is incorrect. But on a more complex form, it may not be as obvious which field contains an incorrect value. Here's the code to change the background color:

```
$("#myForm").submit(function() {
    if ($("#firstName").val() == "Yes") {
        alert("Form entered correctly");
    } else {
        $("#firstName").css("backgroundColor","red");
        return false;
    }
});
```

This code changes the *backgroundColor* of the form element identified by the *id first Name* to red when filled in incorrectly. However, best practice dictates not changing CSS style information within JavaScript code. It's much better to add and remove CSS styles from elements. Doing so makes troubleshooting easier and results in cleaner code all around.

jQuery has functions to add and remove CSS classes from elements: the aptly titled *.addClass()* and *.removeClass()* functions. On form validation pages, I'll typically create a CSS error class that sets the background color to a red (or a reddish color that attracts attention).

The CSS style might look like this:

```
.errorField {
    background-color: red;
}
```

Then within the code, rather than changing the actual CSS background color, I'll apply the error class with the help of the *.addClass()* function, as shown in the following:

```
$("#firstName").addClass("errorClass");
```

The full page, including JavaScript code and CSS style information, is shown in the following code:

```
<!DOCTYPE HTML>
<html>
<head>
<meta http-equiv="Content-Type" content="text/html; charset=utf-8">
<title>jQuery 101</title>
<script type="text/javascript" src="jquery-1.4.4.min.js"></script>
<style type="text/css">
    .errorClass {
        background-color: red;
    }
</style>
</head>
<body>
<form id="myForm" name="myForm" action="#" method="post">
<p>Answer: <input id="firstName" type="text" name="firstname"></p>
<p><input type="submit" name="formSubmit" value="Check Form"></p>
</form>
<script type="text/javascript">
    $(document).ready(function() {
        $("#myForm").submit(function() {
            if ($("#firstName").val() == "Yes") {
                $("#firstName").removeClass("errorClass");
                alert("Form entered correctly");
            } else {
                $("#firstName").addClass("errorClass");
                return false;
            }
        });
    });  //end document ready function
</script>
</body>
</html>
```

Notice that the JavaScript code is wrapped within the *.ready()* function. While this is not strictly necessary here, I wanted to illustrate how you can use *.ready()*. Also, you'll note that upon form submission, the code uses the *.removeClass()* function to remove the *errorClass* class from the form element. In practice, you could move that *.removeClass()*

call to any number of other places in the code, including within the main *.ready()* function call, or within the *.submit()* function.

There is much, much more to error handling, jQuery, and JavaScript than can be shown in one short chapter, but with this basic knowledge in hand, you can now explore why the HTML5 *<canvas>* tag is so important.

Note If you'd like to learn more about JavaScript and jQuery, the book, *JavaScript Step by Step*, provides greater detail with regard to everything you've seen in this chapter. Additionally, the jQuery home page at *http://www.jquery.com* is an excellent resource for learning about jQuery and all that it can do.

Using the HTML5 <canvas> Tag

New in HTML5 is a tag called *<canvas>*, which provides a space on which you can draw graphics, run animations, and much more within a Web page. However, the *<canvas>* tag, by itself, doesn't do anything. Instead, the *<canvas>* tag relies on JavaScript to draw the graphics it can contain. So you can see that it's no coincidence that you've spent so much time learning about JavaScript in this chapter!

The *<canvas>* tag is one of the easiest tags in HTML5. You simply tell the browser how large you want the canvas area to be, and it creates the container accordingly. For example, The following example shows a 250 × 250 pixel *<canvas>*:

```
<canvas width="250" height="250" id="myCanvas"></canvas>
```

Unfortunately, as of this writing, many browsers don't support the *<canvas>* element; therefore, you'll need to provide alternative content for browsers that aren't ready for canvas-based graphics yet. You can provide this alternative content by placing it between the opening and closing *<canvas>* tags, like this:

```
<canvas width="250" height="250" id="myCanvas">
    <p>Alternate content goes here</p>
</canvas>
```

Browsers that don't understand the *<canvas>* tag will ignore it and display the contents of the HTML found within it; in this case, a *<p>* tag.

You use JavaScript to draw on the canvas, so it's lucky that you just learned so much about the language!

To draw on the canvas you need to specify the coordinates at which you'd like to begin. Canvas coordinates use a grid system, like the one shown in the following image:

In the grid shown above, the coordinates 0,0 represent the top-most and left-most cell in the grid and the numbers increase as you move both to the right and down. The cells themselves represent pixels on the screen. The points along the horizontal axis on the grid are called *x coordinates* while points along the vertical axis are called *y coordinates*.

You draw using combinations of lines and primitive shapes. For example, you can create rectangles of various forms using functions such as *fillRect* to draw a filled-in rectangle and *strokeRect* to draw an outlined rectangle. Both of these functions accept x and y coordinates to determine where they should begin drawing, along with a width and height specification. The code to draw a 50 × 100-pixel rectangle beginning at x coordinate 10 and y coordinate 20 looks like this:

```
fillRect(10,20,50,100)
```

Before you start drawing though, you need a canvas. Additionally, you need to call the *getContext()* function for the canvas as well. You'll see examples of how to do this in the following code example, which shows an entire page that uses the *<canvas>* tag to draw this rectangle.

Important The following examples require the use of the jQuery library. The examples show the use of the CDN-based version of jQuery. You can use the version that you downloaded based on the previous examples in this chapter as well. If you're using a local version of jQuery, place it into the same folder as these code examples. For more information on how to download jQuery, see the section, "Obtaining jQuery," on page 293.

```html
<!DOCTYPE HTML>
<html>
<head>
<meta http-equiv="Content-Type" content="text/html; charset=utf-8">
<title>Canvas</title>
<script type="text/javascript"
        src="http://code.jquery.com/jquery-1.4.4.min.js"></script>
</head>
<body>
<canvas width="250" height="250" id="myCanvas">
    <p>Alternate content goes here</p>
</canvas>
<script type="text/javascript">
    $(document).ready(function() {
        var canvas = document.getElementById("myCanvas");
        if (canvas.getContext) {
            var canvasContext = canvas.getContext("2d");
            canvasContext.fillStyle = "blue";
            canvasContext.fillRect(10,20,50,100);
        } else {
            // You could do something else here
            // because the browser doesn't support
            // the canvas element.
        }
    });
</script>
</body>
</html>
```

This code creates a *<canvas>* element (and provides alternative content for non-HTML5 browsers). The bulk of the page consists of the JavaScript code to draw the rectangle, as shown here:

```javascript
var canvas = document.getElementById("myCanvas");
if (canvas.getContext) {
    var canvasContext = canvas.getContext("2d");
    canvasContext.fillStyle = "blue";
    canvasContext.fillRect(10,20,50,100);
} else {
    // You could do something else here
    // because the browser doesn't support
    // the canvas element.
}
```

This code retrieves the element with the id *myCanvas*, and places that into a JavaScript variable called *canvas*. Next, the code tests to see if the *getContext()* function is available. If this function isn't available, then the browser almost certainly doesn't support the *<canvas>* element. Therefore, attempting to use *getContext()* would result in a JavaScript error.

If, however, the *getContext()* function is available, then the code continues by calling *getContext()*, setting the *fillStyle* to blue, and drawing the rectangle.

Viewing this page in a *<canvas>*-compatible browser such as Mozilla Firefox results in a page with a blue rectangle, like the one shown here:

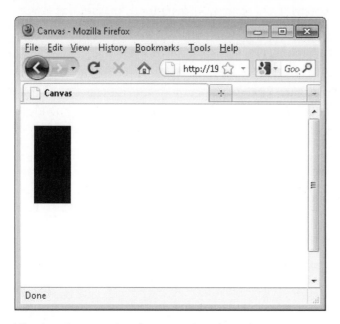

Viewing the page in a browser that doesn't support *<canvas>* results in the alternative content being displayed.

Here's another example. This example resizes the rectangle dynamically using JavaScript, based on where you clicked within the canvas area:

```
var canvas = document.getElementById("myCanvas");
if (canvas.getContext) {
    var canvasContext = canvas.getContext("2d");
    canvasContext.fillStyle = "blue";
    canvasContext.fillRect(0,0,50,100);
    $("#myCanvas").click(function(f) {
        var x = f.pageX - this.offsetLeft;
        var y = f.pageY - this.offsetTop;
        canvasContext.clearRect(0,0,250,250);
        canvasContext.fillRect(0,0,x,y)
    });
} else {
    // You could do something else here
    // because the browser doesn't support
    // the canvas element.
}
```

This example adds a *.click()* function thanks to jQuery. The *.click()* function examines where the mouse click occurred within the canvas element. It then clears the canvas and draws a new rectangle at the point where the mouse was clicked. This example begins to show the interactivity that's possible with the canvas element.

Finally, here's the fun example that I promised. Building on the previous example, the code shown here creates a larger canvas on a page, and then builds a number of blocks on the page. As you click each block, the code removes that block. Load this example into a canvas-compatible browser (or run it from Javascript02.html provided in the _Solutions folder for this chapter) and see how fast you can clear all the blocks!

Important If you jumped ahead to the fun example, then you'll need to use the jQuery library for the example shown here, which uses a CDN-based jQuery. Feel free to use your local copy of jQuery if you have one downloaded, or refer to the "Obtaining jQuery" section on page 293 for assistance on downloading jQuery.

```
<!DOCTYPE HTML>
<html>
<head>
<meta http-equiv="Content-Type" content="text/html; charset=utf-8">
<title>Canvas Block</title>
<script type="text/javascript"
        src="http://code.jquery.com/jquery-1.4.4.min.js"></script>
</head>
<body>
<canvas width="400" height="400" id="myCanvas">
        <p>Alternate content goes here</p>
</canvas>
<script type="text/javascript">
        $(document).ready(function() {
                var canvas = document.getElementById("myCanvas");
                if (canvas.getContext) {
                        var canvasContext = canvas.getContext("2d");
                        canvasContext.fillStyle = "blue";
                        var numBlocks = 4;
                        var canWidth = $("#myCanvas").attr("width");
                        var canHeight = $("#myCanvas").attr("height");
                        var blockWidth = (canWidth/numBlocks) - 2;
                        var blockHeight = (canHeight/numBlocks) - 2;
                        var offsetX = 0;
                        var offsetY = 0;
                        var colCount = 0;
                        var numTotal = numBlocks * numBlocks;
```

```
                    for (i = 0; i < numTotal; i++) {
                            canvasContext.fillRect(offsetX,offsetY,
                                    blockWidth,blockHeight);
                            offsetX = offsetX + blockWidth + 2;
                            colCount++;
                            if (colCount == numBlocks) {
                                    colCount = 0;
                                    offsetY = offsetY + blockHeight + 2;
                                    offsetX = 0;
                            }
                    }
                    $("#myCanvas").click(function(f) {
                            var x = f.pageX - this.offsetLeft;
                            var y = f.pageY - this.offsetTop;
                            var xBlock = Math.floor((x / blockWidth));
                            var yBlock = Math.floor((y / blockHeight));
                            var xSpan = 0, ySpan = 0;
                            if (xBlock > 0) {
                                    xSpan = xBlock * 2;
                            }
                            if (yBlock > 0) {
                                    ySpan = yBlock * 2;
                            }
                            var xPos = (blockWidth * xBlock) + xSpan;
                            var yPos = (blockHeight * yBlock) + ySpan;
                            canvasContext.clearRect(xPos,yPos,blockWidth,
                                    blockHeight);
                    });
            } else {
                    // You could do something else here
                    // because the browser doesn't support
                    // the canvas element.
            }
    });
</script>
</body>
</html>
```

Here's what this application initially looks like:

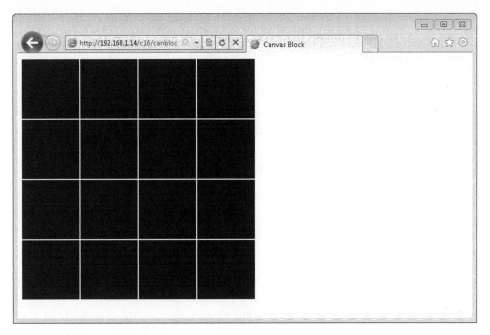

If you become bored with a 4 by 4 grid, change the number of blocks by changing this line in the code, as follows:

```
var numBlocks = 4;
```

The code in the example will dynamically change the grid to match the number of blocks you specify by setting the *numBlocks* variable. Although this example uses several Java-Script elements that are beyond the scope of this book, it is a good introduction to the interactivity possible with even a basic canvas application.

The *<canvas>* element will grow in popularity and usage over the next several years, but it will be quite some time before all browsers will support it. For example, even though Internet Explorer 9 will support the canvas element, the older versions of Internet Explorer will linger for years to come. However, If you'd like to learn more about the *<canvas>* element, including seeing additional (and much more full-featured) examples and a tutorial, visit *https://developer.mozilla.org/en/HTML/Canvas*.

Including External Content in Web Pages

HTML5 introduced the *<eventsource>* tag which enables you to push external server content to a Web page. The model is called "push" in contrast to the traditional "pull" model that is used on the Web, where the Web browser always requests information from the server. Like the *<canvas>* element, as of this writing the *<eventsource>* tag is not widely supported in Web browsers; therefore, it's of limited use for practical Web programming until new browsers appear and are widely adopted. For more information on *<eventsource>*, see *http://www.whatwg.org/specs/web-apps/current-work/*.

Another method for including external data (and multimedia in this case) is the *<embed>* tag. Unlike *<eventsource>*, the *<embed>* tag has wide support across browsers. Even though *<embed>* wasn't formalized in the HTML specification until version 5, people have been using the tag for years due to its cross-browser compatibility.

The *<embed>* tag is frequently used to insert elements such as Flash or background audio on a Web page. The *<embed>* tag uses several attributes, such as *src* to define the resource to embed, *type* to define the type of content being embedded, and *height* and *width* to set the height and width of the element, respectively.

Using *<embed>* to embed an MP3 file is as simple as this:

```
<embed src="myfile.mp3"></embed>
```

Just as when including any multimedia or other objects in a page, playback is dependent on the client. While my browser supports playing an MP3 audio file, there's no guarantee that another visitor will be able to do so. Therefore, I recommend using *<embed>* only when absolutely necessary.

Key Points

- JavaScript is an important language on the Web and provides for much of the behavioral elements on Web sites.

- JavaScript can be included on any Web page and has specific syntax for accessing the Canvas element within a page.

- jQuery is a JavaScript library that enables rapid development of previously difficult or time-consuming JavaScript tasks.

- The Canvas element was introduced in HTML5 and provides an area for advanced graphics and animation. The Canvas element is programmed using JavaScript.

- There are other ways to include external content within Web pages, including the new *<eventsource>* tag introduced in HTML5 and the *<embed>* tag as well.

Part 4

Other Ways to Create HTML Code

Chapter at a Glance

Create a new
Web site, **page 320**

Create a page
using a CSS
template,
page 325

Insert graphics,
page 328

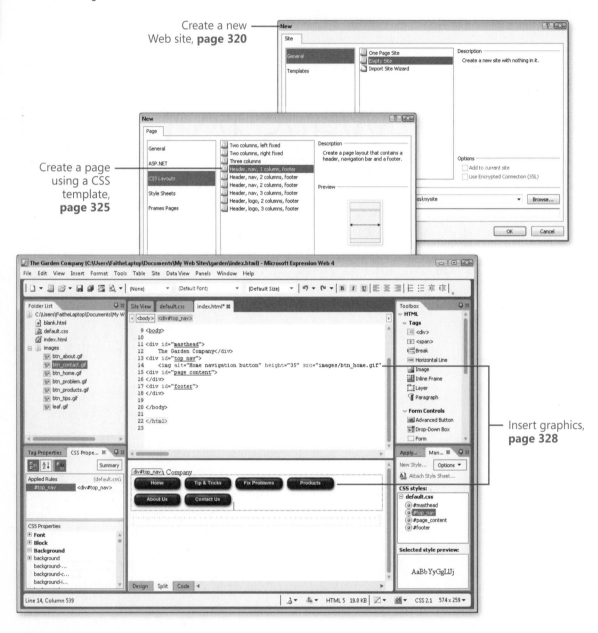

17 HTML and Microsoft Expression Web

In this chapter, you will learn how to

✔ Use the Expression Web interface.

✔ Create a new Web site.

✔ Create a new page using a CSS template.

✔ Insert text and graphics.

✔ Apply text and page formatting.

✔ Insert hyperlinks.

Throughout this book, you've been building your HTML knowledge by working directly with the code in Notepad. That's the best way to understand what is really going on in a Web page.

However, after you achieve basic HTML proficiency, you might decide that using a Web development application such as Microsoft Expression Web makes sense for your situation. Web development software can dramatically cut down on the amount of typing that you need to do, and you gain the ability to both edit and preview your pages within a single application.

In this chapter, you will learn the basics of Microsoft Expression Web, which is one possible application that you might choose for HTML editing. Expression Web is a simple graphical Web design application, sold in retail stores and online. You'll learn how to create a basic Web site using Expression Web, how to create a page that uses a CSS-based layout, and how to place and format text and graphics on the pages of your Web site.

This chapter uses Expression Web 4 for its examples, which was the most recent version available at the time of this writing. Expression Web 4 provides only very limited support for HTML5, but you can manually type in any HTML5 tags as needed.

See Also Do you need only a quick refresher on the topics in this chapter? See the Key Points section at the end of this chapter.

> **Practice Files** Before you can use the practice files provided for this chapter, you need to install them from the book's companion content to their default locations. See the section "Using the Practice Files" in the beginning of this book for more information.

Exploring the Expression Web Interface

You can purchase Expression Web either as a standalone product or as a part of the Microsoft Expression Studio suite, along with several other development tools. After installing Expression Web on your PC, you can run it from the Start menu, the same as any other application.

When you open Expression Web, you'll see a five-pane interface. The large pane in the center is where you will create your Web pages; the four smaller panes along the sides provide access to tools and lists.

Folder List pane shows the pages in the active Web site

Toolbox contains tags you can drag into the document

Properties pane enables you to add attributes and properties to code

Styles pane enables you to create and manage CSS

In this exercise, you will open a Web page in Expression Web and view it in several ways.

SET UP Use the *index.htm* file in the practice file folder for this topic. This file is in the Documents\Microsoft Press\HTML5 SBS\17Expression\ViewingPage folder.

1. In the **Start** menu, click Microsoft Expression Web.

2. Select **File | Open**.

3. Navigate to the folder containing the files for this lesson. Double-click the ViewingPage folder, and then double-click the file **index.htm**.

   The file opens in Expression Web.

4. At the bottom of the editing page, click the **Code** tab.

   The page appears as HTML code. When in Code View, you see the actual HTML tags, as if you were working in Notepad; however, Expression Web understands the syntax of HTML elements, so it colors tags, attributes, and content differently to simplify reading the code.

Click here for Code view

5. Click the **Design** tab.

The code disappears, and the page now appears in what-you-see-is-what-you-get (WYSIWYG) mode, which is similar to previewing it in a Web browser window.

If the pane is not as wide as the page, content
may wrap differently when previewed here

Click here for Design view

6. Click the **Split** tab.

This view provides the best of both worlds. The top half of the screen shows the Code View, and the bottom half shows the Design View.

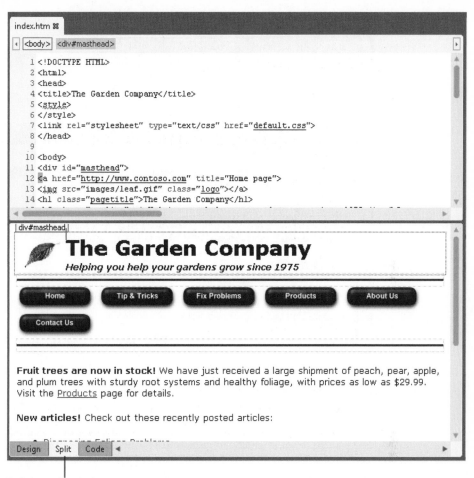

Click here for Split view

7. In the lower (Design) pane, click somewhere in the tagline *Helping your gardens grow since 1975* located under the title.

Notice that the code for that text is highlighted in the upper (Code) pane.

8. In the Design pane, change *1975* to **1976**. The date also changes in the upper pane.

9. In the Code pane, change *1976* back to **1975**. The date also changes in the lower pane.

10. In the Code pane, in the bar across the top, click *<div#mastead>*.

The code panel highlights the entire Masthead section in the code.

Click here...

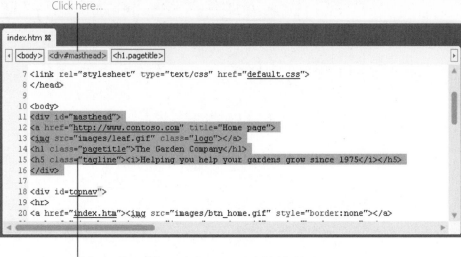

```
index.htm ✖

◄  <body>   <div#masthead>   <h1.pagetitle>                              ►

      7 <link rel="stylesheet" type="text/css" href="default.css">
      8 </head>
      9
     10 <body>
     11 <div id="masthead">
     12 <a href="http://www.contoso.com" title="Home page">
     13 <img src="images/leaf.gif" class="logo"></a>
     14 <h1 class="pagetitle">The Garden Company</h1>
     15 <h5 class="tagline"><i>Helping you help your gardens grow since 1975</i></h5>
     16 </div>
     17
     18 <div id=topnav>
     19 <hr>
     20 <a href="index.htm"><img src="images/btn_home.gif" style="border:none"></a>
```

...and the section of the code it represents is highlighted

11. In the lower pane, click in the first body paragraph (the one beginning with *Fruit trees are now in stock!*).

A border appears around the text, with a small *p* tab at the top, indicating that it is a paragraph that uses the *<p>* tag.

Tab shows the tag assigned to the paragraph

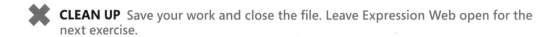

Fruit trees are now in stock! We have just received a large shipment of peach, pear, apple, and plum trees with sturdy root systems and healthy foliage, with prices as low as $29.99. Visit the Products page for details.

❌ **CLEAN UP** Save your work and close the file. Leave Expression Web open for the next exercise.

Creating Web Sites and Web Pages

A Web site, in Expression Web lingo, is a folder that contains all the files you need for a set of interconnected Web pages. That folder might reside locally on your own hard disk or remotely on a server. In most cases, you will want to develop the site locally and then upload it to the server when it is ready to be published. (It is called a Web site even if it is not technically on the Web yet.)

To work with Web sites, use the Site menu in Expression Web. From there you can create a new site or open an existing one. You can also import content from other sites, and manage the publishing settings for a site.

After you have your site established, you can then create new pages or import existing pages into your site.

In this exercise, you will start a new Web site and add a new blank page to it.

 SET UP Start in Expression Web.

1. Click **Site | New Site**.

   The New dialog box opens.

2. Click **Empty Site**.

   This creates a site without any pages in it; you'll add the pages later.

3. In the **Location** box, delete the *mysite* portion at the end of the current path and type **\\garden** in its place.

   Note You can optionally change the entire path to a different location if you have somewhere else that you prefer to store the examples for this book.

4. In the **Name** box, type **Garden**.

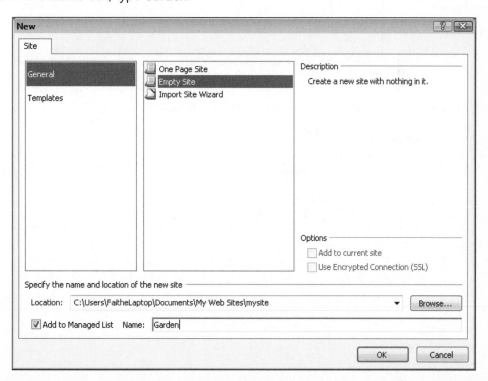

5. Click the **OK** button.

Expression Web creates the site, including a new folder in the chosen location. The folder appears in the Folder List pane in the upper-left corner of the Expression Web window.

6. Click **File | New | HTML**.

A new Web page document opens. As you can see in the Code pane, Expression Web fills in all the basic tags for you automatically. However, notice that the document type is not HTML5, but an earlier type: XHTML Transitional. To use Expression Web for HTML5-compliant code, you must change the document type.

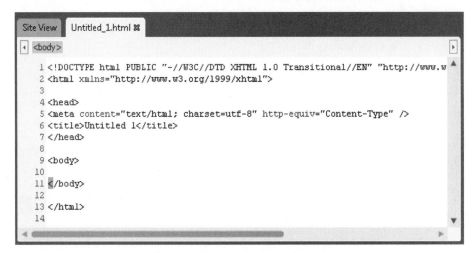

```
1 <!DOCTYPE html PUBLIC "-//W3C//DTD XHTML 1.0 Transitional//EN" "http://www.w
2 <html xmlns="http://www.w3.org/1999/xhtml">
3
4 <head>
5 <meta content="text/html; charset=utf-8" http-equiv="Content-Type" />
6 <title>Untitled 1</title>
7 </head>
8
9 <body>
10
11 </body>
12
13 </html>
14
```

7. Click the **X** on the **Untitled-1.html** tab to close the unsaved new page. If prompted, do not save your changes.

8. Click **File | New | Page**.

The New dialog box opens.

9. Click the **Page Editor Options** hyperlink.

The Page Editor Options dialog box opens.

10. Open the **Document Type Declaration** drop-down list, and then click **HTML5**.

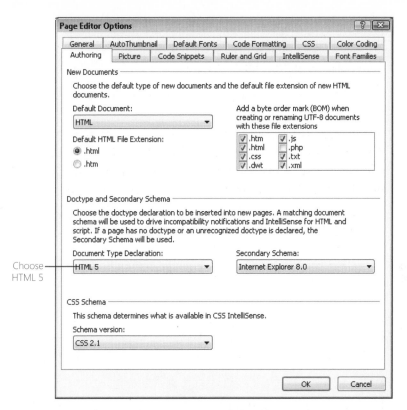

Choose HTML 5

11. Click **OK** to close the **Page Editor Options** dialog box.

12. In the **New** dialog box, ensure that **HTML** is selected on the **General** list, and then click **OK**.

Once again, Expression Web creates a new page, but this time with HTML5 as its type.

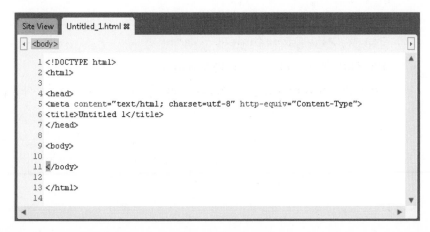

13. Click **File | Save**.

The Save As dialog box opens.

14. In the **File Name** box, type **blank**.

Note Expression Web defaults to an .html extension, not .htm, so be sure that you type the extension along with the file name change.

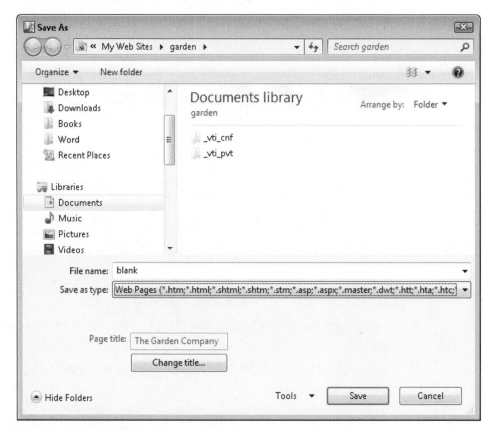

15. Click the **Change Title** button. Type **The Garden Company**, and then click **OK**.

The new page title appears in the Page Title box.

16. Click **Save** to save the page.

17. Click the **X** on the **blank.html** tab. If prompted to save changes, click Yes.

Expression Web closes and saves the page. The page now appears in the Folders List pane (in the upper left corner of the Expression Web window). Leave the Web site open for the next exercise.

CLEAN UP Leave the page and the Web site open in Expression Web for the next exercise.

Create a Page by Using a CSS Template

When creating a new page, you can start with a blank layout (as you just saw) or you can choose one of the templates that come with Expression Web. These templates use CSS layouts, like those that you learned how to create manually in Chapter 11, "Creating Division-Based Layouts."

In this exercise, you will create a Web page using one of the CSS templates that ship with Expression Web.

SET UP Start in Expression Web, with the Web site still open from the previous exercise.

1. Click **File | New | Page**.

   The New dialog box opens.

2. Click **CSS Layouts**.

3. Click the layout titled **Header, nav, 1 column, footer**.

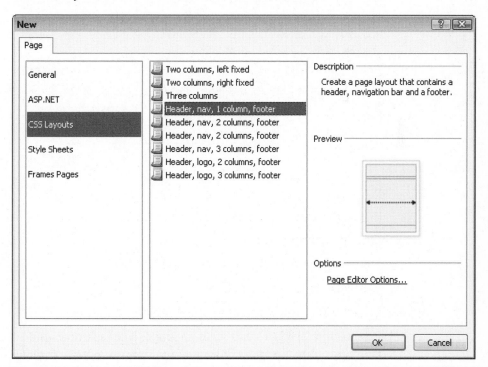

4. Click the **OK** button.

Expression Web creates your new page. Two separate tabs appear at the top of the editing pane: one for the new untitled HTML document, and one for the untitled external cascading style sheet.

Note Even though you previously set the Page Editor Options to use the HTML5 document type, the layout does not use HTML5, but instead uses XHTML 1.0 Transitional. That's because the template that Expression Web uses is pre-created with that document type.

5. In the Code pane, edit the document type tag so it contains the following:

```
<!DOCTYPE html>
```

6. Click **File | Properties**. In the **Page Properties** dialog box, in the **Title** box, type **The Garden Company**.

7. Click **OK**.

Notice that in the Code pane, the title appears as follows:

```
<title>The Garden Company</title>
```

Tip The method you just used to set the page title is an alternative to specifying a page title when you save your work, as you did in the previous exercise.

Note Notice that there are four divisions in the document, and that each one is represented both in the code and in the Design pane.

8. In the Design pane, click in the uppermost box.

A div#masthead tab appears above it. Look in the Code pane, and notice that the insertion point there is in the *<div id="masthead">* tag area.

9. Type **The Garden Company**.

The text appears in both the Design and the Code pane.

Tip The border around the division in the Design pane is on-screen only; it will not appear when the page is viewed in a Web browser.

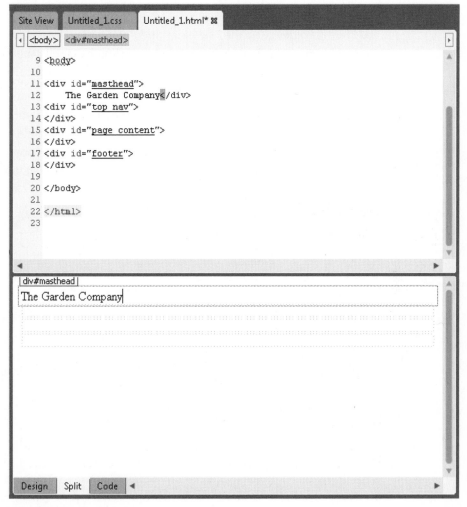

10. Click **File | Save**.

The Save As dialog box opens.

11. In the **File name** box, type **index**.

12. Click **Save**.

A separate Save As dialog box appears for the CSS file.

13. In the **File name** box, type **default**.

14. Click **Save**.

Notice the following:

- In the Code pane, notice the <link> tag referencing default.css. Expression Web linked and applied the style sheet without you having to do any manual coding.

- In the Folder List pane, the index and default files appear. The icon for the index.html file appears as a house, indicating it is the home page for the Web site. Expression Web shows it that way because of its name; index is the standard name given to the main page.

- In the Styles pane (lower-right corner), the #Masthead style is selected because that's the currently selected division. The red circle next to it indicates that it's a uniquely named division, as does the number sign (#) preceding its name. Other types of document sections and tags display different colored circles.

 CLEAN UP Leave the page and the Web site open in Expression Web for the next exercise.

Insert Graphics

When you insert a graphic image on a page, Expression Web automatically creates the *<a>* tag needed to reference it and makes sure that the graphic's location is appropriately referenced. That can be a big time-saver compared to manual coding when you have a lot of graphics.

Import an Images Folder

As in the examples in earlier chapters, you will probably want to create a special folder (such as "images") within your main Web site folder to store the images you're using for the site. One easy way to do this is to copy an existing images folder into the Web site in Expression Web. You'll learn how to do that in the following exercise.

In this exercise, you will copy the Images folder from the data files for this lesson into the Web site that you have created in Expression Web.

 SET UP Start in Windows Explorer. Expression Web should also be open, with the Web site still open from the previous exercise.

1. In Windows Explorer, navigate to the folder for this lesson (17Expression).
2. Select the **Images** folder and press **Ctrl+C** to copy it.
3. Switch to Expression Web and click in the **Folder List** pane.
4. Press **Ctrl+V** to paste the folder.

   The folder and all its images are now accessible from the Folder List pane.
5. Click the **+** (plus character) next to the folder.

   The folder expands to list all the graphics available.

 CLEAN UP Leave the page and the Web site open in Expression Web for the next exercise.

Place Images on a Page

After you have added images to a Web site, you can easily drag them into the Web page layout wherever you want them.

In this exercise, you will insert graphics on a Web page.

 SET UP Start in Expression Web, with the Web site still open from the previous exercise.

1. Drag the **btn_home.gif** button from the **Folder List** pane into the **#topnav** division in the Design pane (the second division from the top).

   An Accessibility Properties dialog box opens.

2. In the **Alternate Text** box, type **Home navigation button**.

3. Click the **OK** button.

4. Repeat steps 1–3 for the following buttons, in the order shown, placing each new button to the right of the previous one. You can assign alternate text as appropriate for the button's name. Depending on the width of the Expression Web window, the buttons might wrap to a second row.

   - Btn_tips.gif
   - Btn_problem.gif
   - Btn_products.gif
   - Btn_about.gif
   - Btn_contact.gif

Drag each button
from here...

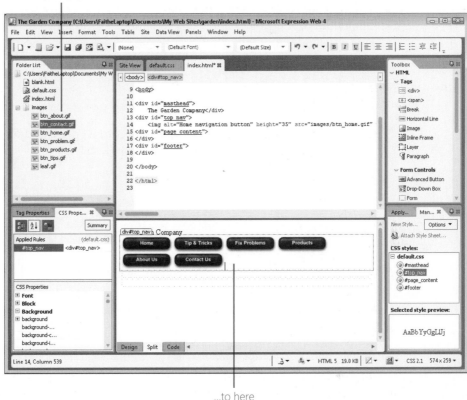

...to here

 CLEAN UP Leave the page and the Web site open in Expression Web for the next exercise.

Add a Background Image to a Division

You can also add graphics as background images to divisions, as you learned in Chapter 6, "Introduction to Style Sheets." To do so, select the division, and then work in the Properties pane (lower-left corner) to define the CSS style for that division.

In the following exercise, you will apply a background image to a division.

SET UP Start in Expression Web, with the Web site still open from the previous exercise.

1. Click in the Masthead division in the Design pane.

2. In the Properties pane (lower-left), click the **CSS Properties** tab if it is not already selected.

3. Scroll down through the properties and find the **Background** category. If it is not already expanded, click the **+** (plus character) to expand it.

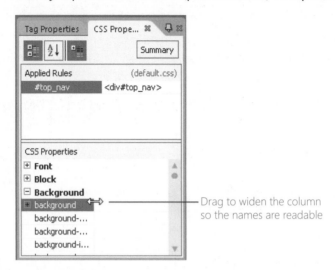

Drag to widen the column so the names are readable

4. Click the **background-image** property.

   A Build button (...) appears to its right.

5. Click the **Build** button.

   A Select File dialog box appears.

6. Browse to the exercise files for this lesson, open the **Images** folder, select the file **leaf-green.jpg**, and then click **Open**.

   The image appears as the background for the Masthead division.

Note The Masthead division is not very tall, and that's okay for now. We'll fix that later.

7. Above the Code pane, click the **default.css** tab to switch the view to the associated CSS file. In that view, notice the following:

- The tab appears as default.css*. The asterisk means that there are unsaved changes to the file.

- The code that places the background image in the Masthead division is in the CSS file, not in the HTML document itself. Division-level formatting is placed in the external style sheet by default, if present.

```
Site View   default.css* ✖   index.html*

 1 /* CSS layout */
 2 #masthead {
 3     background-image: url('../../Microsoft Press/HTML 5 SBS/17Expression/ima(
 4 }
 5 #top_nav {
 6 }
 7 #page_content {
 8 }
 9 #footer {
10 }
```

✖ **CLEAN UP** Leave the page and the Web site open in Expression Web for the next exercise.

Formatting Text

As you know from earlier chapters, there are many ways to format text. Here's a quick review:

- You can use direct formatting, in which an individual block of text receives certain formatting. For example, you might make a word bold in a paragraph by using the <b> tag, as follows:

```
This is a <b>great</b>party.
```

- You can create a span, and then apply formatting to the text within the span, such as shown here:

```
<p>This is a <span style="font-size: 13px">great</span> party.
```

- You can place a style in the opening tag for a certain paragraph or other block of text. For example, you might specify a certain color for a paragraph's text, as shown in the following:

```
<p style="color: green">This is a great party.</p>
```

● You can create a style that refers to the tag used for that text block. For example, you could create a style for the <p> tag that formats all list items a certain way. This style can be placed in either an internal or external style sheet, such as this:

```
p {font-family: "Verdana", "Arial", sans-serif; font-size: 13px}
```

● You can define formatting for a new class in a style sheet, as in the following:

```
.tangent {font-family: "Verdana", "Arial", sans-serif; font-size: 13px}
```

● And then you can assign the class to certain tags within the document, like this:

```
<p class="tangent">This is a great party.</p>
```

When you apply formatting in Expression Web, the application chooses an appropriate formatting method based on its internal rules. These rules take into consideration the type of formatting being applied and the size of the block to which it is being applied. If you don't like the method that Expression Web selects, you can edit the code manually.

In this exercise, you will apply text formatting in several ways, resulting in several types of tags and attributes being created in the code.

 SET UP Start in Expression Web, with the Web site still open from the previous exercise.

1. In the Page Content division, in the Design pane, type the following text:

   ```
   Fruit trees are now in stock! We have just received a large shipment of
   peach, pear, apple, and plum trees with sturdy root systems and healthy
   foliage, with prices as low as $29.99.
   ```

2. In the Code pane, enclose the paragraph you just typed in <p> and </p> tags.

   ```
   <p>Fruit trees are now in stock! We have just received a large shipment of
   peach, pear, apple, and plum trees with sturdy root systems and healthy
   foliage, with prices as low as $29.99.</p>
   ```

   Note When you type <p> in the Code pane, Expression Web automatically adds a </p> tag following it. Cut this </p> tag (Ctrl+X is one way) and then paste it (Ctrl+V) at the end of the paragraph.

3. Select the sentence *Fruit trees are now in stock!*, and then click **B** (the bold button) on the toolbar, or press **Ctrl+B**.

   The selected text is enclosed in a *<strong></strong>* tag pair.

   ```
   <p><strong>Fruit trees are now in stock!</strong> We have just received a
   large shipment of peach, pear, apple, and plum trees with sturdy root sys-
   tems and healthy foliage, with prices as low as $29.99.</p>
   ```

4. In the Styles pane (lower-right), on the **Manage Styles** tab, click **#page_content** to select that division.

5. In the Properties pane (lower-left), click the **CSS Properties** tab, and then click **+** (plus character) next to **Font** to expand that category.

6. Click in the box to the right of the **Font-Family** property. A drop-down arrow appears. Click that arrow to open a menu, and then choose the item named **Arial, Helvetica, sans serif**.

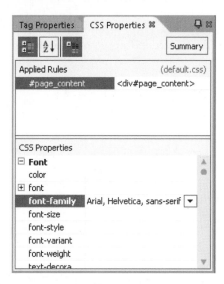

7. Click the **default.css** tab at the top of the Code pane to view the CSS.

Notice that a style rule has been created for the *#page_content* division:

```
#page_content {
        font-family: Arial, Helvetica, sans-serif;
}
```

8. Press **Ctrl**+**Z** to undo the last action.

Expression Web removes the style rule for that division.

9. Click back to the **index.html** tab.

10. In the Styles pane (bottom-right), click **New Style**.

The New Style dialog box opens.

11. Open the **Selector** drop-down list, and then click **p**.

12. Open the **Define In** drop-down list, and then click **Existing Style Sheet**.

13. In the URL box, type **default.css**.

Note This places the new style in default.css rather than in an internal style sheet, which is the default.

14. On the **Category** list, make sure **Font** is selected.

15. Open the **Font-Family** drop-down list, and then click **Arial, Helvetica, sans-serif**.

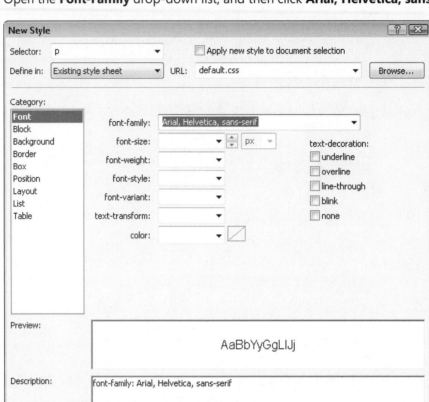

16. Click the **default.css** tab and confirm that the new style rule for paragraphs appears there, as shown in the following:

```
p {

        font-family: Arial, Helvetica, sans-serif;

}
```

Note The p style appears in the Styles pane with a blue circle next to it. The blue circle indicates that it is a style applied to one of the standard HTML tags.

17. In the Styles pane, right-click the **p** style, and then click **Modify Style**.

The Modify Style dialog box opens. It is just like the New Style dialog box you saw earlier.

18. In the **Font-Size** text box, type **13**.

19. Click **OK** to apply the change, and then click the **index.html** tab to see the results of the change.

20. In the #Masthead division, select *The Garden Company*.

21. On the toolbar, open the **Font** drop-down list and select the **Arial, Helvetica, sans-serif** item.

22. Open the **Font Size** drop-down list and select **xx-large**.

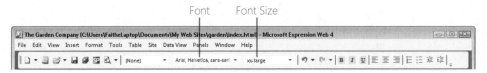

23. Click the down arrow adjacent to the **Font Color** to open its drop-down list.

If the Expression Web window is not wide enough to see that button on the toolbar, click the down arrow at the right end of the toolbar to see the additional buttons, and then click it from there.

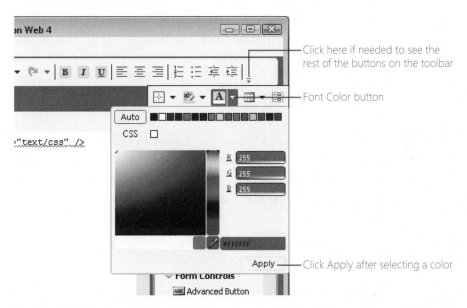

Look in the Code pane. You'll see that a new class has been created, called *auto-style1*, and applied to that text:

```
<div id="masthead" class="auto-style1">

     The Garden Company</div>
```

Look in the *<head>* section of the code. Notice that a *<style>* tag has been inserted, creating an internal CSS style sheet for the document:

```
<style>
.auto-style1 {
        font-family: Arial, Helvetica, sans-serif;
        font-size: xx-large;
        color: #FFFFFF;
}
</style>
```

Tip If you want to avoid using an internal style sheet, you can select the style (*.auto-style1 {font-family: Arial, Helvetica, sans-serif;}*) and then cut and paste it over to the default.css style sheet. Some Web designers prefer to keep all styles in one place. This way, they don't need to be concerned about where a particular style is stored.

24. Press **Ctrl+S** to save *index.html*.

A Save Embedded Files dialog box opens, prompting you to also save the associated style sheet.

25. Click **OK** to save both files.

 CLEAN UP Leave the page and the Web site open in Expression Web for the next exercise.

Formatting a Division

As you just saw, one way to format text is to apply certain formatting to the division that contains the text. You can also format divisions in other ways, such as specifying certain positions, margins, or padding for them. Making changes such as these is easy in Expression Web; you can resize and reposition a division by simply dragging elements in the Design pane.

In this exercise, you will apply text formatting in several ways, resulting in several types of tags and attributes being created in the code.

 SET UP Start in Expression Web, with the Web site still open from the previous exercise.

1. At the bottom of the editing pane, click **Design** to display the page in Design view only (not split).

2. Click in the Masthead division to select it.

3. Position the mouse pointer over the bottom of the Masthead division.

White square selection handles appear around the division.

4. Drag the center-bottom selection handle downward to increase the height of the Masthead to 70 pixels in total (a ScreenTip pops up as you drag showing the current measurement).

Drag the bottom border

5. In the Properties pane (bottom-left), make sure #*Masthead* is selected at the top.

6. Open the **Box** category, and then click in the **padding-top** property.

7. Open the drop-down list for the property and click **Pick Length**.

The Length dialog box opens.

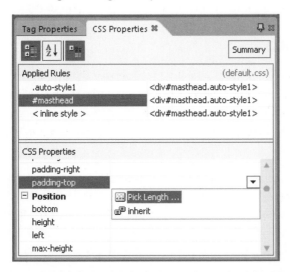

8. In the **Length** dialog box, type **16**, and then click **OK**. Expression Web adds 16 pixels of padding to the top of the *masthead* division.

9. Repeat steps 6–8 for the **padding-left** property and add 16 pixels of padding to the left side.

10. View the *default.css* file in the Code pane to see what Expression Web added to the style definition for the division.

```
#masthead {
        background-image: url('../../Microsoft Press/HTML5 SBS/17Expression/
images/leaf-green.jpg');
        padding-top: 16px;
        padding-left: 16px;
}
```

11. Press **Ctrl+S** to save *index.html*.

    A Save Embedded Files dialog box opens, prompting you to also save the associated style sheet.

12. Click **OK** to save both files.

 CLEAN UP Leave the page and the Web site open in Expression Web for the next exercise.

Inserting Hyperlinks

Expression Web provides an easier way of inserting hyperlinks than typing them manually. You can either use the Insert | Hyperlink command or press **Ctrl+K** to open the Insert Hyperlink dialog box, and then type the specifications for the hyperlink you want. Alternatively, you can right-click a button or a block of selected text and choose Hyperlink, which opens the same dialog box.

In the dialog box, you can choose from any of these hyperlink types:

- **Existing File or Web Page**   This is the standard type of hyperlink that inserts a reference to another page or file. You would use this for the navigation buttons on a site, for example.

- **Place in This Document**   This type of hyperlink is for an anchor point within the current document.

  Tip Review Chapter 5, "Creating Hyperlinks and Anchors," if you need a refresher on anchor points and how they work.

- **Create New Document**   This hyperlink type generates a new document of the type you specify. This type is not frequently used.

- **E-Mail Address**   This type inserts a hyperlink that opens the default e-mail application and begins composing a message.

In this exercise, you will add text hyperlinks and navigation buttons.

 SET UP Start in Expression Web, with the Web site still open from the previous exercise.

1. Switch the main editing window back to Split view if it is not already there.

2. In the Design pane, click the **Tips & Tricks** button to select it.

3. Choose **Insert | Hyperlink**.

   The Insert Hyperlink dialog box opens.

4. In the **Address** box, type **tips.htm**.

   Note The tips.htm file is not in your Web site yet, but that's okay. You can create hyperlinks that refer to files you will add later.

5. Click the **ScreenTip** button. Type **Tips Page**, and then click **OK**.

6. Click **OK**.

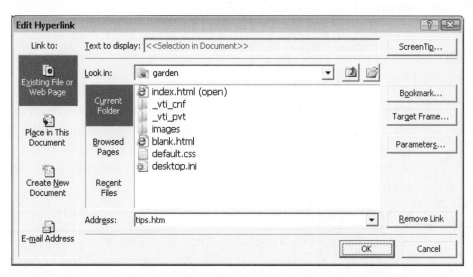

7. In the Code pane, check the code that has been added for the hyperlink.

```
<img alt="Home navigation button" height="35" src="images/btn_home.gif"
width="114"><a href="tips.htm" title="Tips Page"><img alt="Tips and Tricks
navigation button" height="35" src="images/btn_tips.gif" width="114"
class="auto-style2"></a><img alt="Problem navigation button" height="35"
src="images/btn_problem.gif" width="114"><img alt="Products navigation but-
ton" height="35" src="images/btn_products.gif" width="114"><img alt="About
navigation button" height="35" src="images/btn_about.gif" width="114"><img
alt="Contact navigation button" height="35" src="images/btn_contact.gif"
width="114"></div>
```

Tip You should recognize these tags from Chapter 6; the *<a>* tag is the hyperlink itself, and it contains the title attribute with the ScreenTip text. The *<img>* tag shows the button. It is contained within the double-sided *<a>* tag.

8. In the Code pane, click to move the insertion point into the footer division and type **<p>**.

   Expression Web places a closing *</p>* tag there automatically.

   ```
   <div id="footer"><p></p>
       </div>
   ```

9. Inside the *<p>* tag, type the following:

   ```
   <p>Site Map | Contact Us | Legal Information</p>
   ```

10. Click **Insert | Hyperlink**.

    The Insert Hyperlink dialog box opens.

11. Click **E-Mail Address**.

12. In the **E-mail Address** box, type **alice@contoso.com**.

13. In the **Subject** box, type **Question about site**.

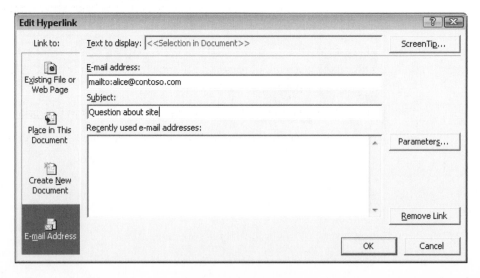

14. Click **OK**.

    The hyperlink is applied to the text, which appears underlined in the Design pane.

15. Look at the code in the Code pane to see the hyperlink that was created.

    ```
    <a href="mailto:alice@contoso.com?subject=Question about site">Contact Us</a>
    ```

✖ **CLEAN UP** Save your changes to all files and close Expression Web.

Key Points

- Expression Web is an application for creating Web pages in a graphical, what-you-see-is-what-you-get interface.

- The Expression Web interface can show your page in Design view, in Code view, or in Split view (which shows half of each).

- To work with Web sites, use the Site menu. From there you can create a new site or open an existing ones.

- When creating a new page, use the Page Editor Options dialog box to specify that you want to create HTML5-compliant code.

- Expression Web includes many CSS templates for creating page layouts. Choose File | New | Page and click CSS Layouts.

- To insert graphics, drag them from the Folder List pane onto the page in Design view.

- To add a background to a division, set its Background property in the CSS Properties pane to include a reference to a graphic file.

- You can format text directly using Expression Web's toolbar buttons. The code for the formatting is placed either in the individual tags or in the CSS, depending on the type of formatting.

- You can change a division's size by dragging its border in Design view.

- Use the Insert | Hyperlink command to insert hyperlinks.

Part 5

Appendixes

A Designing for Usability

Although there is a certain amount of artistic freedom when creating a Web site, there are also well-established "best practices" among professional Web designers. Have you ever visited a Web page that was hard to navigate, difficult to understand, or just plain ugly? A good Web designer can look at these pages and offer suggestions for improvement.

In this guide, you'll learn some techniques for making your Web site as usable as possible. By making your Web site easy and fun for your visitors to navigate, you increase the time people will spend at your site and the number of times they will return.

Note Want a laugh or two along with your learning? Visit "Vincent Flanders's Web Pages That Suck" at *http://www.webpagesthatsuck.com*. This site contains hundreds of examples of what not to do on your site!

Understanding Usability

Usability refers to the experience visitors have when they view your Web site. It includes these qualities, summarized from *Usability.gov* (a U.S. Government guide to Web usability):

- **Ease of learning.**   How quickly do people understand how the site navigation works? Can people who have never before seen the interface learn it well enough to find their way around without a steep learning curve?

- **Ease of use.**   After people have figured out how to navigate the site, how easy is it for them to actually find the information they need? A highly usable site puts information at the visitors' fingertips, with flexible and powerful searching and browsing tools.

- **Memorability.**   How much will a typical repeat visitor remember about your site? A highly usable site sticks in visitors' minds.

- **Error handling.**   How often do visitors make mistakes in navigating your site, and how easy is it for them to get back on track? A highly usable site provides helpful error messages when problems occur, complete with hyperlinks that help users do what they intended.

- **Subjective satisfaction.**   How much do people enjoy visiting your site? A highly usable site is just fun to explore.

Tip For more in-depth exploration of these usability issues, see *http://www.usability.gov/basics*.

Usability is extremely important in generating loyal, repeat visitors to your site. An advertising campaign can drive visitors to your site initially, but if the site is not easy to use, most of them will never return. According to Web site design expert Jakob Nielson:

> *Studies of user behavior on the Web find a low tolerance for difficult designs or slow sites. People don't want to wait. And they don't want to learn how to use a home page. There's no such thing as a training class or a manual for a Web site. People have to be able to grasp the functioning of the site immediately after scanning the home page—for a few seconds at most.*

Planning for Usability

Usability planning should begin before you create the first page of your Web site because your answers to key questions about purpose and audience will shape the overall organization and layout of your site.

First of all, why do you want a Web site? What do you hope to achieve with it? A Web site designed for selling products online will probably look very different from one that is mostly for sharing information. Clarifying your goals before you begin designing your site makes it easier to define and create the site you want. For example, the goal of The Garden Company (the gardening store featured in the examples in this book) was to provide gardening resources and information to its customers. Although the company did plan on including some information about its inventory, the main idea was to educate people.

Try to make your goals specific and tie them to your business or organization's objectives. The Garden Company's goals might have been, for example, to reduce phone calls from customers needing help with gardening problems, to make visitors feel more confident about investing in gardening as a hobby, and to encourage customers to think about the products that could make gardening more enjoyable.

Next, what audience are you targeting? "Everyone" is a poor answer to that question. You can't please everyone, and if you try, you'll end up pleasing no one. The Garden Company, for example, might be specifically interested in people who live near one of its brick-and-mortar stores. With that audience in mind, the company might want to provide local maps showing their stores' locations, directions from major highways, and printable coupons. Think about the characteristics of the people you are targeting and what they are looking for in a Web site. For example, The Garden Company's customers might turn to the Web site to get information about a specific problem they are having; making troubleshooting information easy to find would attract customers and keep them interested in the site.

Sketching the Site Organization

The next step is to sketch out a chart showing how users will access content, starting with your home page (start page) at the top. Any pages that will be directly accessible from the home page will appear at the first level, and pages that are subordinate to those will appear at lower levels.

Here are some tips for planning the site organization:

- Decide what links will be in the navigation bar. Arrange the links in order of importance from top to bottom (or left to right). The home page should always be the topmost or leftmost link on the navigation bar.

- Decide what content you will deliver on each page. Eliminate any pages that visitors won't want or that don't deliver information that supports your business or organization's goal for the site.

- Plan ways to reduce the number of clicks the average user needs to make. One way to do this is to put a direct link on the home page to the most popular content.

Designing a Consistent Page Template

For ease of navigation, the entire site should have a consistent layout, with common elements such as the navigation bar and the page title in the same place on each page. The simplest way to accomplish this is to create a template page and then base all other pages upon it. Your template page can use tables, frames, or divisions for layout.

Here are some tips for the layout of your template page:

- Place a masthead across the top of the page, containing your organization's logo and name.

- Place the navigation bar at the right, left, or top of the page. Left and top bars are the most common, but many usability experts say that a navigation bar at the right is actually more intuitive for a visitor to use.

- If you have a very information-rich site, consider having multiple navigation bars—one at the top of the page to include the overall main categories, and one at the left or right with a longer list of subcategories.

- Make the navigation bar stand out somehow. It can be a different color, have a different background, or be surrounded by a box, for example.

- Place a text-only navigation bar at the bottom of the page so people do not need to scroll back up to the top again to navigate to other pages.

- If you decide to use frames, be very careful. It is very easy to create a frameset in which a frame is too small and cuts off the content placed within it. Ensure that each frame is adequately sized not only for the default content it starts with, but for every page that might appear in each frame throughout the user's entire visit to your site.

- When possible, make the page size flexible (for example, by leaving one table column or one vertical division to fill the remaining space in the window). If you are specifying a fixed width for the page content, make it no more than 800 pixels wide. That way, even people with low-resolution screens will be able to view it without scrolling.

- Select colors that reflect the content and identity of the site. Reds and yellows build excitement; blues and greens are calming. Body text should be dark letters on a light-colored background.

- Tailor color choices to your target audience. Researcher Natalia Khouw reports, for example, that men prefer blue and orange, whereas women prefer yellow and red. Young people like bright primary colors; people middle-aged and older like subdued colors such as silver, gray-blue, and pale yellow.

- Select a simple, readable font as the default, such as Arial (Helvetica, Sans Serif), at a size that's adequate for your audience.

Designing the Content of Individual Pages

After creating the template that will form the structure of each page, start thinking about the unique content for the individual pages. Here are some tips for creating effective Web pages:

- Use short sentences (20 words or fewer) and short paragraphs (5 sentences or fewer).

- Ensure that there is some vertical space between each paragraph. By default the *<p>* tag leaves a good amount of space, but some people remove or lessen the vertical space by modifying the style.

- Whenever possible, break up information into bulleted or numbered lists for easier skimming. (Isn't it easier to find information in this bulleted list you're now reading than if it were in plain paragraph form?)

- Match the page's length to its purpose. Pages that summarize or provide navigation should be short; pages that provide detailed information on a subject can be as long as needed.

- Keep articles on one page. Do not split up the text of an article onto multiple pages just because a page seems long. Visitors who want to print the article will find it much easier to do so if it is all on one page, and they will appreciate not having to click a link to see the rest of the article.

- Break up long articles by using many descriptive headings. If the article is longer than a few pages, include bookmark hyperlinks at the top of the page that point to the major headings.

- If content goes more than one level deep on your site, use *breadcrumbs* to help users find their way back to where they came from. Breadcrumbs are a trail of hyperlinks that enable the user to back up one or more levels in the structure, like this:

    Home > Jazz > John Coltrane

- Limit the size of the graphics files you use on a page so that the page doesn't take a long time to download on a slow connection. The total file size of all the graphics on a page should ideally not exceed 30 KB. If you need to show larger, higher-resolution graphics, consider using thumbnails.

- Look for ways of reducing unused space. On a page that has a great deal of empty space at the right, for example, consider adding a text box containing information. One way to do this is to use a division with absolute positioning.

Performing Usability Testing

Big businesses spend big money on usability testing for their products and Web sites, but you can test your small business or hobby site much more simply and economically.

Friends and relatives make good usability testers. Sit down next to someone who has never seen your Web site before, and ask him to start exploring and commenting on whatever he notices. Don't explain anything—let him discover it. Pay attention to what catches his interest—and what doesn't. Does he view the pages in the order you expected? How much time does he spend on each page? Are there any pages that he doesn't visit or can't find? Run through this process with as many people as you can round up; the more information the better! Then make changes to your site based on what you learn, and try another round of testing.

B Designing for Accessibility

Accessibility, a subset of usability, refers to a Web site's suitability for use by anyone, regardless of age or disability. Designing for accessibility is not only a nice thing to do, but a smart thing. An estimated 15 percent of the population of the United States has some form of disability, and as the Baby Boomer generation continues to age, that number will only increase. Nobody would intentionally alienate 15 percent of his or her potential audience, but that's exactly what creators of non-accessible Web sites do. A certain level of accessibility might even be required by law if your organization is required to comply with the Americans with Disabilities Act (ADA).

Note Many resources are available online to help Web designers make their sites more accessible. One of the best known is the W3C Web Accessibility Initiative, found at *http://www.w3.org/WAI*. On the WAI site you will find more complete coverage of each of the guidelines presented here, as well as a working draft for a newer version of these guidelines, Web Content Accessibility Guidelines (WCAG) 2.0.

If you have normal sight, vision, and mobility, perhaps you have never thought about the Web surfing challenges faced by people who have difficulty in any of those areas. Here are some of the most common accessibility issues:

- Mobility limitations
  - Users might be limited to keyboard or mouse use only.
  - Users might be using voice recognition software to navigate.
- Visual limitations
  - Users might have difficulty reading on-screen text, especially at its default size.
  - Users might be color-blind or have trouble reading colored text on a colored background.
  - Users might be relying on a program that reads the content of the page aloud.
- Hearing limitations
  - Users might not hear music or narration being played.

To plan for these limitations, W3C has compiled a list of accessibility guidelines for Web designers to follow. The following sections summarize these guidelines; for more complete information about the guidelines, see *http://www.w3.org/TR/WCAG*.

Guideline 1: Provide Equivalent Alternatives to Auditory and Visual Content

Provide content that, when presented to the user, conveys essentially the same function or purpose as auditory or visual content.

You don't have to avoid graphics, audio clips, and video clips altogether; they add interest and excitement to your pages, and the majority of visitors can enjoy them. However, you should not deliver any content exclusively in those forms. Here are some ways to satisfy this guideline:

- Include an *alt=* argument for each picture, describing its content and purpose.
- For complex content where the description would be too long to display in an *alt=* argument, use an accompanying text note.
- Provide a transcript of audio and video clips. It doesn't have to be on the page itself; you could create a hyperlink that connects to a separate page containing the transcript.
- Use client-side image maps with *alt=* arguments for each area. Or, for a server-side image map, provide text hyperlink alternatives.
- In a visually based multimedia presentation, provide an audio track that reads or describes any essential information. Ensure that the audio is synchronized with the video.

Guideline 2: Don't Rely on Color Alone

Ensure that text and graphics are understandable when viewed without color.

Use color freely, but don't use it to convey information without providing an alternative method of conveying the same information. In addition, ensure that foreground and background colors contrast sufficiently so that someone with limited ability to distinguish colors (such as someone who is color-blind) can easily read the information provided.

Guideline 3: Use Markup and Style Sheets, and Do So Properly

Mark up documents by using the proper structural elements. Control presentation with style sheets rather than with presentation elements and attributes.

More Web designers have been moving toward using division-based layouts that separate the page's content from its formatting, as you learned in Chapter 11, "Creating Division-Based Layouts." This approach has many advantages, such as ease of making formatting changes, but one of the best benefits is greater accessibility. Accessibility experts recommend using only style sheet-based layout (that is, a layout with divisions), and not tables or frames. They maintain that tables must be used only for true tabular information, and frames should not be used at all.

Separating the content from the formatting has the side benefit of being able to offer different style sheets for the same content. In "old school" HTML, specific formatting was applied directly to each tag, limiting the way site visitors could modify it in their browsers. In HTML based on cascading style sheets, however, the content and the formatting are independent, so you can provide multiple style sheets and allow site visitors to choose among them by providing buttons that, when clicked, switch to a different version of the page. You might have a regular style sheet applied by default, for example, but also have one with extra-large fonts and high color contrast available for users who can benefit from that.

Here are the guidelines for ensuring that your code is accessible from a structural perspective:

- Use HTML tags and text rather than graphics wherever possible. For example, for a math formula, use text rather than a graphic of it.

- Use document type declarations at the beginning of the HTML file, as you learned to do in Chapter 2, "Setting Up the Document Structure," and ensure that the type you declare is valid.

- Use style sheets rather than formatting tags to control layout and presentation.

- Use relative rather than absolute units of measurement when describing the formatting properties of an item or class. For example, you might use percentages rather than inches or centimeters to describe an item.

- Nest headings, starting with *<h1>* for the top-level headings, *<h2>* for headings within an H1 section, and so on. Do not choose a heading style simply because you like its default formatting; instead, use the next logical heading level and then format it in the style sheet to look like you want.

- Ensure that nested lists are properly marked. For example, if you have an *<ol>* within a *<ul>*, ensure you close the *<ol>* before you close the *<ul>*.

- Format quotations by using the *<q>* or *<blockquote>* tag, not simply by italicizing or indenting them.

Guideline 4: Clarify Natural Language Usage

Use markup that facilitates pronunciation or interpretation of abbreviated or foreign text.

When a visitor is using a screen reading program to read a page, the software that reads the text aloud can have difficulty reading foreign words and abbreviations.

Note *Markup* in this context means *HTML code.*

Sometimes such software can switch to a different mode if you alert it to the change in language by using the *lang=* argument. If there's no existing tag where the language changes, surround the word with a *<span>* tag. You can also identify the primary natural language of the document in the opening *<html>* tag, but if the language is English, most reader software will assume it is even if you don't declare it.

You can use the *<abbr>* or *<acronym>* tag to mark an abbreviation or acronym. Even though Microsoft Internet Explorer does not support those tags directly, the screen reader recognizes them and signals their presence to the user. At the first usage of an abbreviation or acronym, you should spell out the full word or phrase, and use the shortened version only for subsequent occurrences on the same page.

Guideline 5: Create Tables that Transform Gracefully

Ensure that tables have necessary markup to be transformed by accessible browsers and other user agents.

This guideline states that tables should be used only for tabular information and not for layout because tables are difficult for screen reading software to interpret.

When you do use tables, it suggests using some additional tags that you didn't learn in this book to clarify the purposes of various cells. For example, use *<td>* for data cells, but use *<th>* for headers. In addition, for tables with two or more logical levels of row and column headers, use column groups to organize them.

If you do use tables for layout, ensure that the information would still make sense if the table tags were stripped out and the information was presented as plain text. Avoid using table elements strictly for visual formatting; for example, the *<th>* tag makes the text in a table cell centered and bold, but do not use *<th>* simply to achieve that formatting.

Guideline 6: Ensure that Pages Featuring New Technologies Transform Gracefully

Ensure that pages are accessible even when newer technologies are not supported or are turned off.

This guideline states that pages must not rely on new technologies, such as cascading style sheets, XML, JavaScript, Flash, Shockwave, and so on, to deliver their content. It's okay to use these techniques, as long as you provide alternatives, such as the following:

- Ensure that all pages are still readable when the style sheets are not available.
- Make text-only equivalents available for dynamic content, and ensure that the text is updated when the dynamic content changes.
- Ensure that pages still load even when scripts, applets, or other programmatic objects are turned off or not supported. If that's not possible, provide equivalent information on an alternative accessible page.

Guideline 7: Ensure User Control of Time-Sensitive Content Changes

Ensure that moving, blinking, scrolling, or auto-updating objects or pages may be paused or stopped.

This guideline states that whenever there is sound or movement on a page, the visitor should be able to control it. Here are some tips:

- Don't use background sounds that the visitors can't control. For example, don't use the *<bgsound>* tag.
- Provide controls for all audio and video clips, so the visitor can pause, stop, and restart the clip.

- Avoid flickering, scrolling, or blinking elements. For example, do not use the blink or marquee elements (which are both non-standard and deprecated anyway).

- Don't allow pages to automatically refresh themselves unless there is a way for the visitor to stop the page from refreshing.

- If possible, do not use HTML to redirect pages automatically; instead configure the server to perform redirection.

Guideline 8: Ensure Direct Accessibility of Embedded User Interfaces

Ensure that the user interface follows the principles of accessible design: device-independent access to functionality, keyboard operability, self-voicing, etc.

When an embedded object has its own interface, such as a Java applet that plays a game or performs a test, the interface must be accessible, just like the page itself. If this is not possible, provide an alternative, accessible page.

Guideline 9: Design for Device Independence

Use features that enable activation of page elements through a variety of input devices.

Device independence means that visitors can interact with the page by using whatever input device they are most comfortable with: keyboard, mouse, voice, and so on. Someone with a movement-related disability might be limited to only one of those inputs.

Device independence can be an issue with non-text elements on a page, such as embedded user interfaces and image maps. Client-side image maps are better than server-side ones because they are easier to navigate without a mouse.

HTML forms can be made more device-independent by the use of keyboard shortcuts (*accesskey*= argument) and by setting a logical tab order for links, form controls, and objects. For example, you can add a *tabindex*= argument for each form control and set its value to a number representing the order in which the tab key should move a user through the fields.

Guideline 10: Use Interim Solutions

Use interim accessibility solutions so that assistive technologies and older browsers will operate correctly.

User agents and other assistive technologies are being developed to enable users with disabilities to more easily view Web pages that employ the newest features, but until user agents are widely available to all visitors who need them, Web designers must be creative and employ interim accessibility solutions—basically, workarounds—ensuring that the pages are accessible to all.

Here are some tips for avoiding Web design elements that cause problems for many users:

- Don't cause pop-up windows or other windows to appear automatically. For example, avoid using a frame whose target is a new window.

- Don't change the current window without informing the user.

- For all form fields, ensure that the text label describing the field is positioned to the left of the field, so that a screen reader would first read the label, and then move on to the field immediately afterward. Do not position the field labels above the fields (in a previous row of a table, for example), or to the right of the field.

- Include place-holding characters in empty text areas and input form controls. (The most popular one is the non-breaking space: * *.) Some older browsers do not allow users to navigate to empty edit boxes.

- Include non-link, printable characters between adjacent hyperlinks, surrounded by spaces. Some older screen readers read lists of consecutive lines as one link.

Guideline 11: Use W3C Technologies and Guidelines

Use W3C technologies (according to specification), and follow accessibility guidelines. Where it is not possible to use a W3C technology, or doing so results in material that does not transform gracefully, provide an alternative version of the content that is accessible.

The current guidelines recommend the use of standardized HTML coding wherever possible; that's the type of coding you've learned about in this book. Some non-W3C formats, such as PDF and Shockwave, require plug-ins or stand-alone external applications, and these formats sometimes cannot be viewed or navigated easily with screen readers and other assistive technologies.

Guideline 12: Provide Context and Orientation Information

Provide context and orientation information to help users understand complex pages or elements.

When a page has a complex structure, it can be difficult for users to understand it using screen readers or other assistive technologies. Here are some ways to help:

- If you are using a frameset, ensure that each frame has a title. (Use the *title=* argument.)

- For each frame, if it is not obvious what the frame's purpose is and how it relates to the other frames, include a *longdesc=* argument containing that information.

- Divide blocks of information into manageable groups where natural and appropriate. For example, you can create option groups to organize options.

- Associate labels with form controls by using the *label=* argument.

Guideline 13: Provide Clear Navigation Mechanisms

Provide clear and consistent navigation mechanisms—orientation information, navigation bars, a site map, and so on—to increase the likelihood that a person will find what they are looking for at a site.

Throughout the book, I have encouraged you to use clear and consistent navigational aids, but these are especially critical for visitors with disabilities. Here are some tips for making your site easier to navigate:

- Ensure that each hyperlink's target is clearly identifiable. The underlined text in a hyperlink should describe the target page, not simply be an instruction such as "Click here."

- Keep hyperlink text brief—a few words at most.

- Provide metadata to add semantic information to pages and sites. For example, you can use the Resource Description Framework (RDF) to identify a document's author and content type. (For more information about RDF, see *http://www.w3.org/RDF*.)

- Provide a site map or table of contents. Include a description of the available accessibility features.

- Ensure that navigational elements are consistent among pages.

- Use navigation bars.

- Group related items together.
- If you provide a search function, enable different types of searches for different skill levels and preferences (for example, a basic search and an advanced search).
- Place descriptive information at the beginning of headings, paragraphs, lists, and so on.
- Provide a means of skipping over multi-line ASCII art.

Guideline 14: Ensure that Documents are Clear and Simple

Ensure that documents are clear and simple so they can be more easily understood.

This guideline is fairly self-explanatory: keep it simple. Use consistent page layout, recognizable graphics, and easy-to-understand language. All users appreciate this, not just those with disabilities. Use the clearest and simplest language possible, and supplement it with graphics or audio clips only when they help users understand the site better.

C Tags Added and Removed in HTML5

Tags Added in HTML5

Tag	Description	Covered in Chapter
\<article\>	Defines an article	11
\<audio\>	Defines sound content	15
\<canvas\>	Defines graphics	16
\<command\>	Defines a command button	14
\<datagrid\>	Defines data in a tree-list	14
\<datalist\>	Defines a drop-down list	14
\<datatemplate\>	Defines a data template	14
\<details\>	Defines details of an element	
\<dialog\>	Defines a dialog (conversation)	
\<embed\>	Defines external interactive content or plug-in	16
\<eventsource\>	Defines a target for events sent by a server	16
\<figure\>	Defines a group of media content, and their caption	9
\<footer\>	Defines a footer for a section or page	11
\<header\>	Defines a header for a section or page	11
\<mark\>	Defines marked text	
\<meter\>	Defines measurement within a predefined range	
\<nav\>	Defines navigation links	10
\<nest\>	Defines a nestingpoint in a datatemplate	14
\<output\>	Defines some types of output	
\<progress\>	Defines progress of a task of any kind	
\<rule\>	Defines the rules for updating a template	
\<section\>	Defines a section	11
\<source\>	Defines media resources	15
\<time\>	Defines a date/time	
\<video\>	Defines a video	15

Tags Removed in HTML5

Tag	Description
<acronym>	Defines an acronym
<applet>	Defines an applet
<basefont>	Defines the base font
<big>	Defines big text
<center>	Defines centered text
<dir>	Defines a directory list
<frame>	Defines a sub window (a frame)
<frameset>	Defines a set of frames
<isindex>	Defines a single-line input field
<noframes>	Defines a noframe section
<s>	Defines strikethrough text
<strike>	Defines strikethrough text
<tt>	Defines teletype text
<u>	Defines underlined text
<xmp>	Defines preformatted text

Glossary

absolute path Paths that contain a complete address that anyone could use to get to a Web page. (See also *relative path*.)

accessibility A subset of usability that refers to a Web site's suitability for use by anyone, regardless of age or disability. (See also *usability*.)

alignment The horizontal placement of a paragraph, specified by using the text-align attribute.

anchor A marker within an HTML document, roughly analogous to a bookmark in a Microsoft Word document.

argument See *attribute*

attribute Text within a tag that contains information about how the tag should behave. Sometimes called argument.

background image An image that appears behind the text on a Web page. By default, the image is tiled to fill the page, and scrolls with the page.

baseline The imaginary line on which text rests.

block-level element An element that occupies a complete paragraph or more.

Body The section of an HTML document defined by the two-sided *<body>* tag. It contains all the information that appears in the Web browser when the page is viewed.

breadcrumbs A trail of hyperlinks that enable the user to back up one or more levels in the structure of a Web site.

button-creation program A program used to generate buttons for Web pages.

cascading style sheet A document that specifies formatting for particular tags and then can be applied to multiple Web pages.

cell A distinct area of a table, into which you can place text, graphics, or even other tables.

child folder A subfolder of a parent folder.

class A category of content, defined by the Web developer, used to apply consistent formatting among all items in that category. Similar to an ID, but multiple elements can have the same class within a document.

codec Compression/decompression. A helper file that works with your media player program to play a compressed video file.

command button A button that executes a function.

compiled A compiled programming language that runs the human-readable programming through a utility that converts it to an executable file (usually with an .exe or a .com extension), which is then distributed to users.

definition description *<dd>*. A paragraph that defines a definition term.

definition list *<dl>*. A tag that contains the complete list of headings and definition paragraphs.

definition term *<dt>*. A word or phrased to be defined in a definition list.

deprecated A tag that is no longer supported in the most recent version of the HTML standard.

descriptive tag A tag that describes the function of the text, rather than providing directions for formatting. Also called a logical tag.

dithered A color formed by a cross-hatch pattern of two colors blended together.

em A multiplier of the base font size.

entities Special characters in HTML that are created by using codes beginning with ampersand (&), followed by an entity name or entity number, and ending with a semicolon (;).

entity name A name that defines a special character.

entity number A number that defines a special character.

extended name Another way to express color values. Extended names are similar to basic color names, but there are more of them. Not all colors named in the extended set are Web-safe.

Extensible Markup Language (XML) A language closely related to HTML that programmers use to create custom tags.

external style sheet A plain text file with a .css extension that defines styles to be applied to Web pages.

file size The number of bytes a file takes up on the disk.

font family A set of fonts listed in order of preference.

foreground color The default color for a Web page that can be set with the *style="color: color"* argument.

frame A section of a browser window in which a Web page loads.

frameset A container file that describes how many frames the browser window will be divided into and what sizes and shapes they will be.

hanging Bullets and numbers that "hang" off the left edge of the paragraph.

Head The section of an HTML document defined by the two-sided *<head>* tag. The Head section contains the page title and information about the document that is not displayed, such as its meta tags. It can also include lines of code that run scripts.

header A friendly or descriptive title that appears in the title bar of Microsoft Internet Explorer. The text is specified in a <title> tag placed in the *<head>* section.

HTML document See *Web page*.

hyperlink Text or a graphic that you can click to go to a different location on a Web page, open a different Web page, start an e-mail message, download a file, view a movie, listen to an audio clip, activate a Web-based program, and more.

Hypertext Markup Language (HTML) The basic programming language of the World Wide Web.

ID An identifier for a unique element in a document. Similar to a class, except there can be multiple elements assigned to the same class within a document but each ID can be assigned only once per document.

image map An overlay for a graphic that assigns hyperlinks to certain defined areas (hot spots) on the image. The hot spots can be rectangular, circular, or irregularly shaped (called a *poly* hot spot).

indentation An indentation offsets text from the usual position, either to the right or to the left. In HTML, the three types of indentation you can set are first-line indent, padding, and margin.

inline span A shell into which you can place any arguments you need.

interpreted A program that is distributed in human-readable format to users, and the program in which it is opened takes care of running it.

leading The amount of space between each line. Also referred to as line height.

list item <li>. An item within a numbered or bulleted list.

logical tag See *descriptive tag*.

metatag A type of header tag that provides information about the document, such as keywords.

monospace font A font in which each letter occupies the same amount of horizontal space, regardless of its actual size and shape.

navigation bar A set of hyperlinks that connect to the major pages of a Web site.

nested A term referring to embedding within, as when a list is embedded within a list.

one-sided tag A tag that does not have a closing tag and that takes arguments.

ordered list *<ol>*. A numbered list.

page title The text in an HTML document's Head section that appears in the title bar of the Web browser and on the Microsoft Windows taskbar button.

paragraph formatting Formatting that is applicable only to entire paragraphs, and not to individual characters.

parent folder A folder one level above a child folder (or subfolder).

player An external program that plays an audio or video file in a separate window.

plug-in A helper file that allows content that a browser does not natively support to open in a browser window.

proportional font A font in which the characters take up various amounts of space horizontally depending on their sizes.

pseudo-class A class that uses a variable to determine membership.

quirks mode The mode used to process HTML pages when the browser doesn't encounter a DOCTYPE tag.

redirect A redirect sets up an old Web page to automatically display a new Web page.

relative path A path that uses just the file name rather than the complete address. A relative path looks for the destination file in the same folder as the current file's location. (See also *absolute path*.)

resolution The size of a graphic, determined by the number of pixels that comprise it. Resolution is expressed in width and height.

rule An argument, especially when applied within a style tag or section.

samples A series of audio "snapshots" that are taken per second when an audio clip is digitized.

sampling rate The number of samples taken per second.

semantic tag A tag where the name is based on its usage, such as *<aside>* or *<article>*.

spam Junk e-mail.

special characters Characters that are not included on a standard English keyboard.

standards mode The mode used to process HTML pages when the browser encounters a DOCTYPE tag.

style A formatting rule that can be applied to an individual tag, to all instances of a certain tag within a document, or to all instances of a certain tag across a group of documents.

table A grid of rows and columns, the intersections of which form cells.

tags In HTML, tags indicate where the formatting should be applied, how the layout should appear, what pictures should be placed in certain locations, and more.

themes Formatting templates in Word that can be applied to any document.

two-sided tag Tags that enclose text between their opening and closing tags.

unordered list *<ul>*. A bulleted list.

usability A term referring to the experience a user has when they visit a Web site. Qualities included in usability are ease of learning, ease of use, memorability, error handling, and subjective satisfaction.

visited hyperlink A hyperlink to a page that has already been visited.

Web page A plain text file that has been encoded using Hypertext Markup Language (HTML) so that it appears nicely formatted in a Web browser.

Web-safe color A color that exactly matches one of the colors in a standard 8-bit display.

World Wide Web Consortium (W3C) The organization that oversees HTML specifications and is the governing body for most Web standards.

Index

Symbols

A

About the Author

Faithe Wempen, M.A.

 Faithe is an adjunct instructor of Computer Technology at Indiana University/Purdue University at Indianapolis and the author of many books on PC hardware and software. She also develops Web sites for businesses and non-profit organizations, and writes and teaches online computer training courses for corporate clients.

What do you think of this book?

We want to hear from you!

To participate in a brief online survey, please visit:

microsoft.com/learning/booksurvey

Tell us how well this book meets your needs—what works effectively, and what we can do better. Your feedback will help us continually improve our books and learning resources for you.

Thank you in advance for your input!

Stay in touch!

To subscribe to the *Microsoft Press® Book Connection Newsletter*—for news on upcoming books, events, and special offers—please visit:

microsoft.com/learning/books/newsletter